STACKS

I Should Be Dead

I Should Be Dead

My Life Surviving Politics, TV, and Addiction

Bob Beckel

with

John David Mann

hachette
BOOKS

NEW YORK   BOSTON

Copyright © 2015 by Robert Beckel

All rights reserved. In accordance with the U.S. Copyright Act of 1976, the
scanning, uploading, and electronic sharing of any part of this book without
the permission of the publisher constitutes unlawful piracy and theft of the
author's intellectual property. If you would like to use material from the book
(other than for review purposes), prior written permission must be obtained
by contacting the publisher at permissions@hbgusa.com. Thank you for your
support of the author's rights.

Hachette Books
Hachette Book Group
1290 Avenue of the Americas
New York, NY 10104

www.HachetteBookGroup.com

Printed in the United States of America

RRD-C

First Edition: November 2015
10   9   8   7   6   5   4   3   2   1

Hachette Books is a division of Hachette Book Group, Inc.

The Hachette Speakers Bureau provides a wide range of authors for speaking
events. To find out more, go to www.hachettespeakersbureau.com
or call (866) 376-6591.

The publisher is not responsible for websites (or their content)
that are not owned by the publisher.

Library of Congress Cataloging-in-Publication Data has been applied for.

ISBN: 978-0-316-34775-4

To my friend Cal Thomas,
whose persistence made this book possible
and whose friendship helped me get my life back;
and to my children, Alex and MacKenzie,
who taught me to love.

Contents

Author's Note

This book doesn't aim to be a Washington tell-all, but in the course of sharing my story I will say a lot about the players and some of their habits. Over my career I've come to know hundreds of politicians and dozens of TV personalities. Bits and pieces of some of their stories are included here. Some folks may not be too happy with these stories, but they are all true and, to my mind, worth telling. They are not meant to embarrass, and I was a participant in each one. If it's any solace to those mentioned here, I am much tougher on myself in these pages than on anyone else.

I am recounting all these stories to the very best of my recollection, which, with the passage of time and the toll of addiction, is far from perfect. If I misremember a name, date, or location, I ask your forgiveness in advance. In some passages I have used fictitious names and altered personal details (sometimes indicating as much and sometimes not). The sum and substance of everything in these pages is true, and that's ultimately where I hope the greater power of my story resides.

This book is not meant to be an exhaustive autobiography. I chose to include the stories that would best help my readers understand where I came from, how I got to where I am today, and, most important, what it means to be a survivor. My story, regrettably, is not unique. For those of you who have survived childhood abuse and addictions, the illusion of success, and the paralysis of failure—and your number is legion—I hope you will find kinship in these pages, and maybe even some answers. Some of the stories here you may find informative, some funny, and some tragic.

This is also the story of a journey of faith—or more accurately, a halting, stumbling journey *toward* faith. Through my first half-century the only thing I believed in was my own ability to negotiate the rocks and rapids of life. That single-minded focus on myself as sole architect of my fate brought me through a difficult childhood, yet ultimately proved empty and very nearly fatal. It was only through the grace of God, along with the constancy and devotion of true friends, that I escaped that self-engineered path of self-destruction and found my way to an abiding faith in something greater.

Prologue

Sitting outside Studio D at the Fox News building, in the open-air walkway between Forty-Seventh and Forty-Eighth streets in Midtown Manhattan, I am smoking my regular preshow cigar. It's a half-hour before my daily cable show, *The Five*, goes on the air. I smoked a cigar before the very first episode of *The Five* when it premiered on July 11, 2011. It's now three years later, and I have smoked one before each show since, every day, Monday through Friday, no matter the weather. Call it a habit; call it a good luck charm. So far it seems to be working.

Some young people, probably college kids sightseeing in the Big Apple, stop and ask if they can take a group photo with me. Of course, I tell them. I put the cigar down, get to my feet, and take my place in the center of the group so a recruited passerby can snap a few shots.

When you're a public figure people see you as a public utility, like it's perfectly all right to walk up to you on the street and start asking for favors, for a picture or an autograph, or just to converse. Most people in television savor this kind of celebrity. For me, it's still difficult. When I was a drunk and a drug addict I didn't want anyone paying attention to me. I wanted to melt into the wallpaper, be the guy behind the scenes. But now I do it, and with grace and good humor, as best I can.

One day not long ago while walking down the street I heard a voice going, "Bob! BOB!" I turned and saw a complete stranger trotting toward me with his phone in his outstretched hand. "My wife watches you every day," he said. I started to ask him to thank her for me, but he cut me off. "I've got her on the phone right now. Can you talk to her?"

I looked at the guy. "You want me to talk to your wife on the phone?"

He nodded, eagerly. Like this was the most normal request in the world. Of course, why wouldn't I? I took the phone and said into it, "Hi, this is Bob Beckel."

The woman's voice was laughing on the other end. "I don't believe it. No, seriously, who is this. Is this *really* Bob Beckel?" I told her it really was. "I watch your show every day!" she said.

"Yeah, I heard," I said into the phone. "Is this crazy guy who put me on the phone actually your husband?" She said he was. "Well, I'll tell you both at the same time: You could do better. But he couldn't." They both got the biggest kick out of that.

I smile now, thinking about it, as the kids rearrange themselves around me for another pose. I feel the warmth of the New York sun on my face.

We snap the photo and the group of college kids drifts away. The passerby who took the shot grins at me and says, "Bob, I gotta tell you, I completely disagree with everything you say. But my wife and I—you're *our* kind of liberal, and we're about as conservative as they come!"

Nodding, I say, "If I had a nickel for every time . . ." He laughs. The truth is, I do hear that comment a lot, and never get tired of it. *We disagree with you but we love you.* Can't ask for anything better than that.

I retake my seat, reach down to the ashtray on the ground, and get my little cigar going again.

One of our producers, a young lady who couldn't possibly be a day over twenty-three, pops her head out the door. "Ten minutes, Mr. Beckel!"

Ten minutes. A world of time.

A man who works at the office across the way waves at me as he passes.

"Beckel," he calls out, "I have to say, you're looking excellent—for a beat-up old guy. You look like you're enjoying life."

He stops a few paces away, expectant.

This has become a little ritual of ours. We've had this same exchange, or versions of it, countless times before. My guess is he keeps saying it because he likes hearing my answer. Okay with me. It's a story I don't mind telling.

*   *   *

For most of my adult life, politics has been my business. For most of my childhood, survival was my business.

My life in politics has been exciting and rewarding. I was honored to be named the youngest deputy assistant secretary of state in history at the time, and privileged to serve President Jimmy Carter in the White House. I have been involved in close to a hundred political campaigns, including a stint on the national stage managing the presidential campaign of Walter Mondale to the biggest loss in American history. Politics and government led to a second career in television and radio as a political analyst. (Only in America can a guy manage a presidential candidate to a forty-nine-state rout, then go on to be paid very well to dispense political advice on TV and in lecture halls. What a country!)

I am also a recovering alcoholic and drug addict.

Much of my professional success, I attribute to my childhood. I grew up in an abusive, dysfunctional family. We lived just north of the poverty line for as long as I can remember. Both my parents were alcoholics. My father beat on me regularly, both verbally and physically. My mother was too abused and disempowered (and too drunk herself) to protect us. It was a living hell. I hated it. But it also shaped me into who I am.

In my house you didn't learn how to live so much as how to survive. During those early years I developed what are now clinically called "resilient survivor skills." I'm not proud of it. I'm not ashamed of it. It is what it is. And it wasn't a choice, really. Either you developed skills and survived, or you didn't. If you did, there was some hope for a successful future. If not, your soul got stamped on and broken along with your body; you became mired in despair, anger, and perpetual retaliation; your future was bleak, if you had a future at all.

Only God knows why some kids learn survival skills and others don't. It's not a question of intellect; there are plenty of smart kids who end up with wretched, miserable lives. Many die young, some by their own hand. I was among the lucky ones who learned survival skills early. These included, in no particular order: thinking quickly on one's feet; being a fast and smooth talker; hiding from trouble and avoiding conflict; the ability to broker deals and break up fights; and, when the occasion demanded, lying with finesse. I learned how to wear a mask at all times and reveal my true feelings to no one.

In other words, I learned the perfect skills to become a very good politician.

Nor am I alone. Politics is riddled with successful survivors whose early years were spent in some degree of dysfunction. From Bill Clinton to his nemesis, Republican congressman Dan Burton of Indiana, Teddy Kennedy to Newt Gingrich, Richard Nixon to Lyndon Johnson, all are products of dysfunctional—often severely dysfunctional—childhoods.

Virtually all survivors carry a vast load of baggage with them. The more successful they become, the more that baggage seems to resurface. I've yet to meet a political survivor who hasn't experienced the return of childhood monsters as his or her public success grew. Some realize that to hold on to their success, they have to come to grips at last with those monsters. Some remain unwilling to do so and keep on using their survivor skills to avoid the reality of their escalating self-destruction, plunging further into their secret personal hells, losing themselves in alcohol, drugs, or other physical escapes by night while clinging desperately to their masks of respectability by day.

Some have come to realize that living life behind a survival mask is a losing game. Most have sought to save themselves in spite of the public humiliation that often follows. I've seen many of them at AA meetings or in rehab programs. For some, sadly, the last time I saw them was at their funerals.

It still amazes me that not one of those funerals was mine.

*   *   *

"You look like you're enjoying life," my studio neighbor has just said. That's the cue for my response, like the priest saying, *The Lord be with you*, and now it's the congregation's turn to say, *And also with you*.

"I am," I tell the guy. "I'm enjoying the hell out of it." And it's one of the truest things I've ever said. There isn't a lot that bothers me these days. My answering machine (I know, it's voicemail, but old habits die hard) says, *There's no such thing as a bad day*, and I believe that one hundred percent. I look at each day as a gift. A gesture of divine reprieve.

"Hey," I add, "given what I've been through, by all natural and mortal logic, *I should be dead*."

As I said, it's a story I don't mind telling. Though I've never told the whole story, until now.

January 20, 2001

How the hell did I get here?

I wake up with a blinding hangover, the kind that requires opening the eyelids one at a time, and very slowly. As my eyes come into focus the first thing I see is a grizzly bear.

I saw a grizzly once. Up close, near my summer place in Jackson, Wyoming. They're even bigger than you think.

The initial surge of terror passes as my poisoned brain gradually comes to a realization: The slow-moving mass at the foot of my bed is not a grizzly, but a person in a white uniform.

A nurse.

She may well be the largest woman I have ever seen. She doesn't say a word. Seems in no rush to leave, either. She settles herself down into a ridiculously tiny chair by the door of the room and begins to methodically turn the pages of an old issue of *People* magazine.

My eyes turn to the window by my bed.

The weather in Washington is awful. Cold and rainy with a brutal west wind sheeting off the Potomac. The great obelisk of the Washington Monument disappears into low clouds, all but the bottom 100 of her 550 feet of white marble swathed in bales of slate gray.

The Big Pencil, my kids used to call her.

I love that monument. Seeing it—whether from a plane, a train, a car, or on foot—has always told me I was home. I love this city. It's always taken care of me. Here was where I escaped who I'd been. Here, I became *somebody*. Somebody other people liked and admired.

My eyes ache. My head aches. Everything aches.

My soul aches, if there is such a thing.

George W. Bush is an hour away from taking the oath of office as the forty-third president of the United States. This is not a happy thought, at least not for me. On the plus side, I do have my own VIP room overlooking part of the inaugural parade route. I'm sequestered under an assumed name in a guarded room at the George Washington University Hospital psychiatric ward.

Welcome to the nuthouse.

With the foresight that has made our nation's capital so friendly to those in power, hospitals here have rooms set aside in their psych units for VIPs— rooms located at some distance from those for the ordinary nuts. The thinking, I suppose, is that no Washington big shot should be made to feel like a garden-variety fruitcake. It might harm their chances of recovery.

The nurse doesn't say a word. I watch her for close to an hour. The periodic, deliberate movement of her right arm, back and forth, as she turns those damn magazine pages, is as relentless as the turn of the seasons. No other movement, no other sound. Finally I screw up the nerve to ask her why she doesn't go take a walk or something.

"'Cause I'm a suicide nurse," she replies in a don't-fuck-with-me monotone, her eyes never leaving the magazine pages. "All's I need is for your fat ass to jump out that window while I wasn't around and that's the end of my job." You can't fake compassion like that.

Her next move sets me off: She suggests we watch the inaugural on TV. As she reaches for the remote I struggle upright to stop her. "You put that shit on TV and the only dead body here will be *yours*! That jerk and his thugs are the reason I'm in this place—*so back off.*"

It isn't true, of course. George W. Bush isn't the reason I'm here. *I'm* the reason I'm here. But I'm in no mood for honest introspection, not right now.

The nurse backs off.

Settling back against my mound of pillows, I try to reconstruct the events that landed me here. When you're a drunk, recollection is a futile exercise. Short-term memory is elusive at best. Besides, anything a drunk needs to struggle to remember the day after is probably not worth remembering anyway. But I try.

The election, Florida, *Bush* v. *Gore*... my insane plan to persuade a few pro-Bush members of the Electoral College to change their minds... scandal, hate mail, vandalism, death threats against my family...Oh yeah, it's all coming back to me now.

But last night. How exactly did I wind up in here?

The details start floating back from the haze.

When they wheeled me in here last night (discreetly meeting my ambulance at the rear entrance, VIP treatment all the way), I had a blood alcohol level of approximately a hundred thousand. The ambulance guys had found me that way when they scraped my unconscious body off the asphalt in the back parking lot of some lowlife dive in Maryland. And before that? *Think, Beckel. Focus.*

I'm at the bar. I'm drunk, maybe drunker than I've ever been before. I'm propositioning the woman on the barstool next to me. Turns out she's married. Turns out her husband is behind me. I swivel around to look.

The guy is sticking a loaded .45 in my face.

Then he pulls the trigger.

How am I not dead?

CHAPTER ONE

Surviving Childhood

Alcoholism is a progressive disease. It grows, stealthy and relentless, consuming more and more of the host's health and well-being. Like all addictions, it is also most often an inherited disease. The role of heredity has been roundly debated in the addiction community for decades, but the evidence now seems persuasive that for most addicts, addiction is indeed a condition passed down from one generation to the next. Personally, I have all the evidence I need. I come from a long line of addicts stretching back generations on both sides of the family.

Alcoholism is not only progressive, and inherited, but also deadly. Over the years I've watched it claim the members of my family, one by one.

My father, his three brothers, and one sister came from a fairly prosperous Ohio family. His ancestors built the Beckel Hotel, which still stands in downtown Dayton, a dump on the corner of Third and Jefferson. The Wright Brothers assembled their first successful airplane in a garage adjoining the Beckel Hotel. The family's fortunes went down from there. My father and his father were both alcoholics, as was his mother. All five of the Beckel children were Ivy League graduates; very smart, athletic overachievers who in time mastered the art of underachievement through dissipation.

My aunt Barbara was an accomplished poet in New York City. At age thirty-six she checked herself into a flophouse in Hell's Kitchen with a case of gin and drank herself to death.

My uncle Frank was a doctor in North Carolina, and a good one, but a terrible drunk. He developed cirrhosis of the liver from vast consumption of hooch over many years. If you have cirrhosis and don't stop drinking, as I've since been told by doctors who've seen it happen, you'll reach a point of no return and the disease will kill you in a very painful way. Frank belonged to the Hemlock Society, whose members preferred to put themselves out of their misery rather than suffer months or years of pain. When he realized that cirrhosis was going to kill him, he asked his younger brother Bill, probably the least accomplished of the Beckel kids but nonetheless very smart (and a superb golfer), to come do it first. With much reluctance, Bill put Frank out of his misery. After administering the hypodermic, Bill wandered off into the woods of North Carolina and eventually reappeared in Ohio, where he drank himself to death.

Frank also had a twin brother, Sam, who was my favorite uncle.

Sam was a bright light. He graduated from Harvard, spoke seven languages fluently, and could play concert piano by ear. He was also a superb bridge player. Everyone who knew Sam loved him. I say he was my favorite uncle because he moved in with my family when I was eleven years old and took me under his wing. When his wing wasn't flopping from drink. In the summer of '63, when I was fourteen, the state cops came and took Sam away for busting up a local bar. I'll never forget his mournful face, looking at us out the back window as they drove off; ever since that moment, I've had a hard time trusting cops. Despite his drinking problems, Uncle Sam was always kind to me and never yelled or hit me. Later, when I was in the Peace Corps and for years afterward, he would write me very thoughtful letters. I went to visit him twice in Ohio, when he moved back to be near a VA hospital and his favorite bars.

Uncle Sam died a drunk in the streets of Dayton at age fifty-nine.

Sam was a dignified, eloquent man who radiated intelligence. In the mid-1980s I found Sam in a flophouse, living with another man in a filthy one-room apartment. By this time I'd begun my TV career, and Sam took me to his favorite neighborhood bar to proudly introduce his accomplished nephew to his "friends" in the bar. You could not imagine the riffraff that were regulars at that bar. But in deference to Sam I treated them all with respect and spent several hours hearing about Sam's exploits and the long list of things he had done to help other people in the community. None of this came as any surprise to me. I miss him and always will.

I was thirty-eight when I visited Sam and knew by then that I had the disease, too. At that point I was covering it up quite well, although this was not hard among Sam's crowd. In that joint, I probably seemed the epitome of self-possessed sobriety.

At the time I could not imagine myself ever ending up in such a place. In the years that followed, though, I would find myself in places just like that, and worse.

*   *   *

And then there was my father.

Cambridge Graham Beckel, Jr., was born in Dayton on Christmas Day, 1913. The Beckels then moved to Pennsylvania, where he grew up, became a high school history teacher, and enlisted to go off and fight the Nazis in Europe. Returning from World War II he taught high school in New Jersey, then became a professor at Queens College and New York University. In New York he bumped into a woman named Ellen Gilliland, whom he'd known back in Pennsylvania. Ellen, who was exquisitely beautiful, was now working as a model in Greenwich Village. Before long her name was Ellen Beckel and she was pregnant with a daughter they named Margaret, soon followed by a son they named Robert Gilliland Beckel. That would be me.

In 1954 my father wrote a textbook on the United Nations called *Workshops for the World*, and in a radio interview to promote the book he advocated admittance of Red China to the U.N. Under the dark cloud of the McCarthy era that was not the politically correct thing to say. He lost his teaching job. Whether that was the direct result of his controversial comments, nobody's ever said, but I've concluded that it was.

In 1956, now with a wife and three kids—my sister Peggy, little brother Graham ("Buddy"), and me—he left New York City and moved to Connecticut, to a beautiful little New England town called Lyme, today known mainly for the disease that bears its name. Lyme then had a population totaling about 950, a stark change from New York. We moved into a farm that sprawled over 448 acres; the farmhouse itself was a rambling wreck of a place that had served as a tollhouse back in the old Boston Post Road era. At $125 a month it was the only thing we could afford. In New York we'd had dozens of neighbors in the same building. Here there were no neighbors for a mile on either side. I was seven.

My mother dressed us in our church clothes for our first day of school. I remember my heart sinking when we got there and saw that all the other kids wore jeans. The teasing that started that day never stopped.

My father was deeply unhappy with the move. He later said his time at NYU was the most rewarding experience of his career. Life in Lyme was a huge comedown. The only work he could find was a job selling textbooks, and he hated it. Already a drinker, he now began boozing more and more. When he drank he got ugly, and that ugliness manifested most often as shouting, yelling, and sometimes beating. Before long I was wearing bruises to school to go with my jeans.

I don't want to give the impression that my father was a one-dimensional brute. Quite the contrary. If he had been, things might have been easier, because I could simply hate him. The reality was more complicated.

The same violent-tempered and abusive man who would terrorize us at night was a helpful, funny, nurturing father in the morning. He would get up every day to make us breakfast, pack our school lunches, and check our homework. For many years our dad had been a teacher and a very good one. I still have letters from former students, praising his teaching skills and saying what a positive impact he had on their lives. He had a way with words and told very funny stories. Everyone said so.

That was the man I came to think of as Morning Dad.

On the mornings our father was being particularly kind and funny, it would put a spring in our step as we walked to the school bus. We would ride away to school each morning, confused but hopeful that the morning dad who saw us off would be the same one who would come home that night.

It never was. At night that funny morning guy always morphed into a slurring, threatening animal. After work he would stop at his favorite bar and get shit-faced drunk. Exactly how shit-faced could be determined by the sounds of his footsteps when he arrived at home at night. Some nights he dragged himself in, screamed at my mother, and passed out. Then there were the nights he would come home looking for a fight, either with me or with Mom. He used words with her, fists with me. And I would take it, thinking, *Better me than Peggy, or Buddy, or Mom.*

Someday I'm going to be big enough to fight back, I promised myself.

I would spend the next forty-five years fighting back.

*   *   *

My childhood was so dominated by my father's presence that it's difficult for me to remember much about my mother.

I know she missed New York terribly. I recall her reminiscing often about Bedford Street in Greenwich Village and her modeling days. She was a social person who loved to dress up and go out. But those days were behind her now. When we moved out of the city and resettled in Connecticut, she hated it. To her the life of a housewife, having coffee in the mornings with the other moms and keeping house, with little in the way of intellectual challenge, was hell.

She tried very hard to fit into the Ozzie-and-Harriet household ideal of the times. One day a week, she was a Cub Scout leader. When I later went off to boarding school, she hand-sewed my name into my clothes. She cooked; she kept house. But the façade never quite worked. She loved my father very much, but she was also frightened of him. In the late afternoon, no doubt to fortify herself for the storm that would soon blow in the front door, she would start drinking. By the time the old man showed up, he would be roaring drunk—and she'd be well on her way, too. They would start to fight, and she would eventually run off to her room, leaving us without any cover. The old man didn't want to pick on his only daughter, and he wouldn't go after his youngest. You can do the math and guess who ended up as the habitual target for his rage.

My mother not only retreated into her room at night, she also retreated into a shell that increasingly walled her off from the world. It certainly walled her off from me. As I said, I don't have many memories of her. The old man showed up at my ball games sometimes; I don't remember her ever being there. My father, not my mother, would do the parent-teacher meetings. When I went to have my tonsils out, it was my father who took me.

Which goes back to the most confusing and, in a way, the most difficult thing about those years: When my father was Morning Dad, the good dad, he was a *very good* good dad.

*   *   *

Morning Dad was also a man of uncompromising principles and compassion for the downtrodden; it may have been his greatest quality. For as long as I can remember, the civil rights movement was my father's passion. On sober mornings he would teach us about the movement, and especially about Martin Luther King, Jr. And he didn't just talk the talk, he also walked the walk, on the front lines at Birmingham, Montgomery, Stone Mountain, and Skokie. He paid an enormous physical price for his convictions, as they led to his being beaten and jailed numerous times. That kind of thing takes its toll on you, as I would later learn the hard way. He worked for Dr. King's Southern Christian Leadership Conference for several years. When Dr. King moved his family to Chicago in 1966 and marched to protest discrimination there, people threw bottles, rocks, and bricks at them. King later said, "I have seen many demonstrations in the South, but I have never seen anything so hostile and so hateful as I've seen here today." My father was part of that march and took a brick in the head for it.

I was proud of him for his commitment to civil rights. I was also grateful for his involvement—it took him away from home on many weekends and sometimes for weeks at a time, giving my mother, brother, sister, and me a brief respite from the sound and fury of his drinking and anger. For his part, I suspect those civil rights protests also gave him an excuse to get away and drink; I don't know this for a fact, but even if it's true, it doesn't lessen my admiration for his commitment to the cause.

One cold late-autumn night, just a few weeks before my twelfth birth-day, my father and I drove about an hour from our home to Waterbury, Connecticut, where we got out of the car and joined a throng of people standing outside in the cold night. It was November 6, 1960, and John F. Kennedy was supposed to stop by and speak to the crowd. Kennedy had promised John Bailey, then Democratic state chairman of Connecticut and a strong supporter of Kennedy's, that he would campaign in Connecticut at least once before the election. (I didn't know any of this background at the time.) The last campaign stop on the candidate's itinerary was Waterbury.

Kennedy was everything to us. My mother had gone door-to-door for him. Our household was as pro-Kennedy as you could get.

I'll never forget that night. My father, to my surprise and relief, was not all that drunk. We spent hours standing in the rain as the crowd swelled to some fifty thousand people. Finally, at about three in the morning, Kennedy appeared. His voice was hoarse, it was the middle of the night and cold as hell—but still, it was *Kennedy*. The crowd went nuts. Pierre Salinger, JFK's press secretary, later said it was the greatest night of the campaign. It may have been the greatest night of my childhood. I don't remember anything he said, but I remember how I felt.

Two days later I came downstairs in the evening and found my father watching TV. There were pictures of Kennedy and Nixon and all these numbers on the screen that kept changing. Once in a while they'd cut over to individual states. It was not the way it is today, with all the sophisticated graphics. It was more like a simple football-stadium scoreboard, with Walter Cronkite and other newsmen running commentary.

Normally I would never be in the house around the old man on purpose, especially not at night. But this was Election Day.

"Exactly how does this work, Pop?" I asked.

He said, "Well, people are going to their polling places all across the nation, in all fifty states, and every single vote has to be counted before we know who's going to be our new president."

"Wait—in one day?" I said. Somehow it hadn't yet sunk in that this entire nationwide process could all happen in a single twenty-four-hour period.

"Yeah," he said.

I said, "In one day, you know whether you win or you lose?"

He said, "That's right, one day."

I sat down in front of the little black-and-white TV set, captivated by what was happening on its screen. It was cathartic, the way it drew me in, the hypnotic progression of vote tallies, how close they were.

The old man had been drinking, and eventually he got up and crashed off to bed.

I stayed.

If I close my eyes it still comes back to me now, as vivid today as it was then, half a century ago: the shades-of-gray images of the newscasters in their jackets and ties, Cronkite's soothing, grandfatherly voice, the rows of slowly rising numbers, the electric crackle of suspense. The sense that in these mundane images and sounds passing through our darkened living room, history was being shaped before my eyes.

Everything about that scene imprinted itself on my being.

I stayed up all night, watching the returns slowly rolling in. The race was extremely close, and it didn't become clear who would win until the hours of the early morning. When Illinois finally went to Kennedy and put him over the top—he won with a margin of one-tenth of 1 percent of the popular vote—I went running upstairs, woke my father up, and said, "Kennedy won! Kennedy won!"

The old man was lying in bed, already hung over from the night's drinking, and mumbled, "Get the fuck outta here... tell me about it later."

I didn't care. I was elated. Kennedy had won!

After JFK's victory my dad got very excited and immediately turned his attention to the connections he had in the Kennedy operation to push for civil rights legislation. Kennedy, though, proceeded very cautiously. He was mindful of the midterm elections coming in '62; the South was all Democratic and Kennedy didn't want to upset that. This royally pissed off my old man. His drinking got steadily worse.

Meanwhile, mine started.

*   *   *

As with most alcoholics and drug addicts, my addictions did not arrive in full force all at once, like a bolt of dark lightning. They started out as a seemingly innocent pattern of recreational use. As a teenager, I believed that my drinking habits were no different from those of my friends. Looking back on it now, I realize they were quite different. The first clue should have been that despite all the beer I drank—usually a significant amount more than my friends—I never had a hangover. My friends sure did. They would hug the porcelain goddess for hours as I drifted off to a dull sleep.

It was during my high school years, as my drinking increased, that my father's drinking was at its worst. He was constantly screaming at my mother and now hitting her, too, on occasion. As I grew, he and I got into it both verbally and physically more and more often. My brother and sister would hide under my bed until the shouting and fighting stopped.

We had left the farm and moved into a house we couldn't afford on the wishfully named Honey Hill Road, a little gravel country road. My mother had a friend from her modeling days in Greenwich Village who drank herself to death and left her money to my mom. It wasn't much, and the old man blew it all on a down payment for his heavily mortgaged "dream house," which now became a chaotic, brutal, out-of-control madhouse.

In 1963 my father lost his job, I believe (though this was never stated) because of his drinking. He opened his own business in Old Lyme,

Connecticut, called Educational Consultants, where he ran a summer school and consulted with the schools in the area. It didn't last long.

One morning that February, on one of those biting southern New England days that starts out cold and gets colder, my old man and I piled into the car. He was taking me for an interview at Choate Academy, an exclusive boarding school for boys in Wallingford, Connecticut. Why we were even making this trip was beyond me. We could barely afford the gas for the old Studebaker, let alone pay for tuition at one of the most expensive private schools in the country. The fact was, my parents didn't call Choate, they called us.

Why me? Granted I was a good football player, but my high school GPA was terrible. I was always in trouble and had put in hours in the principal's office waiting for one of my parents to get sober enough to come pick me up.

Both my teachers and my parents thought I was far too intelligent to be getting such lousy grades, so they sent me off to Princeton, New Jersey, for a series of state-funded tests. "Very high IQ with verbal skills well above average" was the diagnosis. A direct result, I figured, of learning how to talk my way out of trouble at home. My math was better than average, too, though not by much. The conclusion: I was bored and unchallenged in public schools. The truth was, I just didn't give a shit. All I was trying to do was survive long enough to get away from Connecticut and start over.

It turned out that some of New England's best private schools, those bastions of old money and spoiled children, had gotten together and decided to recruit students from poorer neighborhoods around the region. They were now looking for students who had "potential not yet developed" and couldn't afford private school. Their effort at diversity, I supposed.

So the old man and I were off to diversify Choate.

I hated the whole idea, but my feelings didn't seem to factor into it. I figured my parents wanted bragging rights with their friends. I could hear them now: "Our son is at Choate, and where is yours?" So I'd put on the only sport coat I owned (handed down from my uncle Sam), a pair of patched chinos, and my "good shoes," the ones with gaping holes in the soles and heels worn down to the nails, and gotten myself ready for my interview.

Choate was about an hour from our house. Our appointment wasn't until 11:00 a.m., but my dad wanted to get on the road by 8:30 "just in case it snows, or we get lost." The look on my mother's face should have been a tip-off that there was more to the old man's early start than the chance of snow.

The road to Choate went right through Middletown, a once-booming manufacturing city. Hard against the Connecticut River, Middletown was a place of closed mills and people on the dole, heavily populated with Irish, which meant it was also heavily populated with bars and taverns.

The old man took the Middletown exit and I (stupidly) asked him why. "To get directions to Choate," he said.

"Everyone knows how to get to Choate," I said.

"Well, forget how to get there right now," he shot back. "You got that?"

"I got it," I muttered, knowing the only good news here was that this little diversion meant there was a very good chance our visit to Choate was toast.

My dad parked about a block from Front Street, which ran right along the river. He got out, told me to stay in the car, that he'd be back soon. A cold wind off the Connecticut River sliced through the streets with a fury that somehow seemed right for this broken-down old town. The old man headed straight for Front Street, where every other building seemed to have a bar or tavern sign out front.

I didn't have a coat, and once the car cooled down it felt like being locked in a refrigerated meat truck. After sitting there and freezing my ass off for an hour and a half, I got up the nerve to get out of the car and head over to Front Street myself.

Sure as hell, there he was, sitting on a barstool at the first tavern I found. I looked through the plate-glass front window. He pretended not to see me. The bartender, on the other hand, did. He said a few words to my father and pointed at me. My old man looked at his watch, held up ten fingers, and then, gesturing at me with a clenched fist whose meaning I could not possibly miss, he motioned for me to go back to the car.

Ten minutes went by, then twenty, then another hour. The whole time I sat there shivering in our old Studebaker, the angrier I got. He was the son-ofabitch who wanted me to go to private school, and now he was over there in a bar getting drunk while I sat and froze.

When you come from an abusive home, you learn to stuff your anger. The alternative is a confrontation you are sure to lose. But I couldn't stay in this car another minute without some heat. So I got out and walked back to the bar again, my rage now properly stowed away in the repressed and crowded anger vault deep inside my mind. Now was not the time for anger. It was showtime.

I put on a mask of helplessness and stood outside the bar's front window. I must have looked really desperate, because the bartender took one look at me and started yelling at my father, meanwhile reaching for his glass. Before he could get his hand on the glass, though, the old man grabbed it and smashed it on the bar, lurched to his feet, and came roaring out the door.

"I thought I told you to wait in the car!" he bellowed.

"But, Daddy" (sometimes it helped to call him Daddy), "I was freezing in the car. I couldn't take it anymore." He gave me a look that had ass-kick all over it. I added sheepishly, "I guess we're not going to Choate."

He looked at his watch, cursed, and, stumbling like a sailor just off a long ocean voyage, staggered off in the direction of the car. "We're going to tell your mother that we got lost, and if I'm lucky it'll start to snow. Got that?"

"She'll know you're lying," I said.

"She's not going to think I'm lying, 'cause you're going to tell her. And if you don't stick to the story, I'll kill you." Pretty good incentive to stick to the story.

In fact, it did start to snow. By now the temperature had fallen to below twenty degrees. About two miles from our house he stopped the car, turned to me, and told me to get out and walk.

"Come on, man," I protested, "it's snowing out there! It's freezing. I got no coat, no boots, and no gloves."

He ignored my protests and said, "You go tell your mother that we ran out of gas, and you walked home while I went looking for help. She'll feel so sorry for you, she might even buy it."

With that he closed the door and drove off. I tried to hold back tears, but they came anyway, freezing down the sides of my cheeks.

God, how much I hate him.

God, how much I love him.

By the time I made it home I thought I was dying from exposure. I was so angry and so sad that I really didn't care one way or the other. My mother came to the door, looked at me, and screamed, "What the hell happened?"

You would think that after all I'd been through, I'd tell her the truth. Not me. I stuck to the old man's story. Why? Not for fear of getting beat up; I was used to that. I lied to her because I didn't want to hurt her. Kids from dysfunctional families don't like to see anyone in the family get hurt, especially their mother. There'd been so much hurt already, why heap more shit on the pile?

She heard me out, a look of hurt disbelief on her face the whole time, then told me to go get into a hot bath. It would be decades before the truth of what had just happened dawned on me: She knew exactly what went on out there with my dad, and my not telling her the truth had hurt her far worse than the old man's behavior or our missing out on Choate.

But at the time I didn't know that and sure didn't stop to think about it. Right then, being left by my old man had made me so furious that I'd had to work really hard to keep it all stuffed down inside. As I ran my bath it all came bubbling back up, like a toxic geyser, and I made a promise to myself: I would never, ever, let anyone abandon me like that again.

*   *   *

Although I never made it to Choate, I did get accepted at another private boys' school, Moses Brown Academy, in Providence, Rhode Island. I started there in September 1963. I hated life at Moses Brown. The place was full of kids with too much money and too little concern for other people. I barely had enough clothes and felt constantly ostracized. I was playing some good football, but I didn't do well in my classes.

One day that fall my roommate barged into our room and said, "They shot Kennedy!"

My stomach lurched. I bolted from the room and went tearing down the hall to the hall master's apartment. Each floor in our dorm building had a professor and his family living in an apartment there. I found him sitting in front of his television set, glued to it. He was crying. I sat down next to him and watched. I was crying, too.

A few minutes later we heard a bunch of kids tromping by the open door. One of them said, "Yay, yay, they killed Kennedy!" The professor and I were both up and out of our chairs in an instant. He put his hand on my shoulder and said firmly, "You let me handle this, Bob." He went out into the hall after the kid. I don't know how he dealt with that little snot when he caught up to him, but it's a good thing for the kid that it was the professor coming after him and not me. I would have hurt him, and not just a little bit.

Leaving the dorm building, I walked into downtown Providence in a daze. Providence was heavily Democratic and, more significantly, heavily Catholic. There were cars stopped in the middle of the street, people standing there openly weeping. Churches were packed. I wandered around town for hours, stunned. Everything came to a standstill in Providence that day.

When I finally returned to the dorm I found the professor back at his black-and-white television, and I asked if I could watch with him.

"You can watch all you want," he said. We stayed glued to the TV together throughout the whole weird, tragic aftermath of the assassination. Other students came and went, but he and I were alone there two mornings later when Oswald was shot at point-blank range by Jack Ruby right smack in the basement of the Dallas Police Department.

I turned to the professor and said, "How in the world can a guy who killed the president of the United States be brought out in the open like that and just shot?" It made no sense to me.

He said, "You know, I agree with you. Something here's not right."

In the wake of that horrible weekend I became a devoted student of the Kennedy assassination and its investigation. Another guy who was very strong on that was Dan Rather, with whom I later became friends. Rather was down there in Dallas when the assassination happened, and it was a turning point in his career. He and I spent hours talking about the assassination. Neither of us believed the Warren Commission report, at least not in its entirety, and felt there was a good deal more to the story that has still not come out.

That entire four days—the assassination, Oswald, Ruby, the funeral— felt like one long nightmarish day that went on forever and kept getting sadder and sadder. You couldn't help but be moved by John-John's salute to his father. It was the kid's third birthday. Those black-and-white images were so stark and so painful, and they burned themselves into my heart. To us, it was like what 9/11 must have been like to kids who were early teenagers then. To this day, I haven't gotten over it.

*   *   *

One day in early 1964 my mother told us kids that she had something important to talk to us about. The three of us panicked. We'd all been worried lately. My father had been away on a "business trip" for almost a month. None of us bought the business trip line. Our best guess was that Mom was about to tell us she and the old man were getting a divorce.

They'd been fighting for months before he left. The arguments were vicious and loud and plain scary to us kids. My brother and sister took to hiding in my room with pillows over their heads to muffle the sounds of battle, although it didn't work. Each night we heard the old man threaten to kill our mom. "But first I'm going to teach those kids a lesson." Doing nothing for her was unthinkable. With my brother and sister hiding in my room I would go out and confront him, begging him to stop. For that, I got beaten.

About a month earlier, my father's boss, John Esher, picked him up early one morning. Mom said he'd be gone for a month. "Business trip." Great. The war would stop for now and Mom would be safe. As days turned into weeks, I started thinking maybe the old man was dead. Either he'd died in a drunken car wreck, or else someone had shot him in some low-life bar. I had wanted him dead, and now maybe he was. The guilt crushed down on me like a heavy stone, and I couldn't get out from under it.

Once my mother had us gathered together on the front porch, her message was a complete surprise. Dad hadn't been on a business trip, and they weren't getting a divorce. For the past month he had been in a hospital, learning how to quit drinking. "He's coming home today," she said. "And from now on he'll be a different person." She had even promised to stop drinking herself, as long as my father stayed sober.

After my siblings left the porch, she pulled me aside and said she knew he had been especially hard on me, but that I needed to support him now. "Your father can be a decent man," she said. I could agree with that. That's what made life with him so damn hard and confusing.

So now he was supposedly coming home sober? I didn't give it a week.

My brother and sister were much more hopeful than I was. They wanted their daddy home. They wanted a happy family. I played along. As far as I was concerned, what they wanted was a miracle. Me, I didn't believe in miracles. I didn't believe in much of anything beyond my own chances of surviving this hellhole. Every day I got a little better at it, learning all the survivor tricks. The more I learned, the more convinced I became that I'd make it out of there, eventually. I didn't expect anyone to help me. I wanted to be sure my brother and sister and mom were safe, but beyond that, I wanted to be on my own.

When the car pulled up a few hours later and my father got out, we were shocked. He looked ten years younger. He'd lost weight and was smiling—a real smile, not one of those evil "I'm going to teach you a lesson" grins. He hugged us and seemed genuinely happy to see us. I waited for the pitch. He'd had a month to practice, so no matter what he said, I wasn't buying. But the pitch didn't come.

He stayed sober for a week, and then another. It was the weirdest thing:

We would leave for school in the morning, and when we came home in the afternoon...Morning Dad was still there! It was so strange it was disorienting. What made it worse was that it was so tempting to believe that this was real, that this was the way it was going to be from now on. And I damn well wasn't going to let myself fall for that shit. *No way,* I told myself.

After a month, though, I started feeling the faint rustle of hope stirring inside me. Not only was he sober, he was being a seriously great father. He took a renewed interest in our schoolwork, helped revive the Little League on the Connecticut shore, and got active in politics again. He opened a school in Old Lyme called the River School, renting the basement of our Episcopal church during the week. This was actually a very good idea. They needed a private day school in that area. And he was good at it.

It was like a dream come true. No, not "like"—it *was* a dream come true. Suddenly he was Morning Dad twenty-four hours a day, day after day.

He never apologized for the past. The arguments, the beatings, the nights under pillows, it was as if none of it had ever happened. I figured he thought that by not talking about it, we'd forget. Honestly, I didn't mind that much. At least the trouble had stopped, even if it was only for a while. That was good enough for me.

He kept going to his meetings. Being who he was—smart, verbal, charming—it wasn't long before he was elected chairman of the local AA group.

At six months, my expectations started growing. To a kid, six months is a lifetime. Maybe, just maybe, this time he meant it. This time, maybe, it was for real. It wasn't any Ozzie-and-Harriet life we were living, but compared to the last few years it was damn close.

*   *   *

After JFK's assassination, Lyndon Johnson took up the cause of civil rights with a vengeance. In his first address to a joint session of Congress on November 27, 1963, Johnson told the legislators, "No memorial oration or eulogy could more eloquently honor President Kennedy's memory than the earliest possible passage of the civil rights bill for which he fought so long."

This was music to my father's ears, and by 1964 he was more involved in politics than ever.

That June three civil rights workers who were helping register African-American voters were shot to death by Klan members in Meridian, Mississippi, an event that became known as the "Mississippi burning" incident. National outrage helped passage of the 1964 Civil Rights Act a few weeks later.

My father decided it would be a good idea to organize a caravan of blacks and whites to go down to North Carolina, where his brother Frank was still living at the time, and help register voters there, too. What's more, he thought it would be a great idea if I joined them.

"Why don't you come along with us?" he said to me.

I said, "Pop, I really want to play baseball." I wanted to play collegiate baseball, even if I wasn't nearly good enough.

He said, "No, come—this will be a good civics lesson for you." I was fifteen.

We piled into four or five vans and went down to North Carolina to register voters. As soon as we pulled into a church parking lot, a swarm of angry white locals descended on us, began banging on one of the vans, and rolled it over.

Everyone in our group was terrified, me included—but not my father. He was a big man and not afraid of anything, as far as I could tell. He got out of the van and started going after these guys. My father had tremendous leadership ability, and others in the group soon got over their own fears and followed his lead.

The cops showed up—not to stop the mob who were beating us up, but to stop *us* from fighting back. With their arrival the scuffle only got worse. At one point in the general melee my father broke away from the fighting to come looking for me and make sure I was okay. I was—still terrified, and furious at him for bringing me down there into this insanity in the first place—but okay.

Eventually the police had us rounded up and took us down to the police station. They did not arrest us, but just said, "You guys get out of this state and get out now. We're taking you to the border. Do not come back."

My father said, "We've got every right in the world to come here and register people. It's the law." The cop slapped my dad across the face. My father started back at the cop, but he was restrained by the other cops before he could do anything else.

They escorted us back out. They had picked up the flipped-over van and tipped it back up onto its wheels, but all the windows were broken. Just as we were about to climb back in I turned to my father and said, "Hey, Pop, how about next year we go to the beach?" I was very proud of him for standing up to those cops, but still angry at him for dragging me into it, and too young to really understand what we were doing there. That understanding would come later.

*   *   *

When fall came, I went back to Old Lyme High School. One miserable year at Moses Brown had been enough for me. The holidays came and went, and still my dad stayed sober. By the time his one-year anniversary approached, in early '65, even I was convinced he must be cured. Not only was I no longer humiliated by my father, I was becoming *proud* of him. A completely foreign and unfamiliar sensation. I even brought a few friends from school home.

I started thinking, maybe there *was* a God.

To celebrate his first anniversary being sober, Mom made him a big cake with a single candle on it. The three of us kids each made him a handmade card. I wrote in mine, "I'm so proud of you. You did it. The past is past, and I can't wait for tomorrow—your loving son, Bob." After dinner my father drove off to his AA group to celebrate with his sober friends.

He didn't come home that night.

As we later learned, he went to the AA meeting that evening and gave a heartfelt speech—then left the club and went straight to a bar. When the police eventually found him he was passed out in his car at a rest stop somewhere up on the interstate.

All the relief, all the hope, all the new belief came crashing down around me that night. It would be the last time, for a very long time, that I would ever let my expectations run ahead of me.

It would not be accurate to say that after the old man fell off the wagon, things deteriorated rapidly. It wasn't rapid. It was instantaneous. It was like that North Carolina mob tipping over our vans and smashing all the windows: The dream was flipped upside down, and everything broke. My father had flipped a light switch and plunged our bright lives back into darkness. Overnight, the dream was a nightmare again.

Once he fell, he fell hard. It was as if he hadn't been sober at all, as if his condition had been busily declining for that whole year. He was worse than ever.

This is something most people have a hard time grasping about drunks. Time off for sobriety doesn't make the condition ease up. When you go back, it's worse, not better. For a recovering alcoholic, if you pick up a drink anywhere down the road you're going to be drunker than you were when you stopped drinking.

Many years later, as an adult, I heard about a guy who had been going to

AA meetings for two decades. Sober twenty years, and a sponsor for an awful lot of people. He was considered a real pillar of AA. Then he lost his job and his wife divorced him. For the next week, he didn't show up for meetings. One day he drove down to the liquor store, bought a quart of vodka, drank it down in the parking lot, backed out, and ran over a nine-year-old kid, killing him. The guy was never seen or heard from again.

Alcoholism is a progressive disease. You can be sober for a month, a year, twenty years. It doesn't matter—when you take that first drink, you fall farther than you've ever fallen before.

As I would find out, many times over.

*   *   *

The River School ended up in disaster. The old man's drinking had gotten so bad it now spilled over into the daytime as well. He quickly became an embarrassment to the whole family. After he fell down drunk several times in the playground by the church, the parents decided to pull the plug. After a year of operation, the River School closed.

There are so many bad memories from that time, but one in particular haunts me to this day.

My father had been invited to speak to my tenth-grade history class. This should have been a good idea—when he was sober, he was an accomplished historian with an uncanny ability to make history come alive in a classroom. But it filled me with dread. Sure enough, when he showed up in my classroom that day he was very, very drunk and everyone knew it. He was slurring his speech and having trouble coordinating things like walking and standing. It was so bad that my teacher asked him to step out into the hallway so they could speak out of the students' earshot. He did not return to the class.

More than all the beatings I took, all the direct abuse and physical suffering, this event stung the worst. Sitting there watching this disaster unfold, feeling the other kids' eyes on me, burned worse than any physical punishment he ever inflicted. The scars from that one day lasted for years.

That's a point I want to emphasize: Being physically hit was not the crux of the nightmare of childhood. Cruel words and constant criticism can bite even deeper than fists or whips; so can silence and neglect. Children who are never hit may still suffer the terrible scars of abuse.

I played football. I was used to getting physically pounded. When the old man beat up on me it scared me and I didn't like it—but that was the smaller part of it. Over the years, my old man's words hurt me a good deal more than any physical confrontations. He would call me "dumb," "a loser." "Your grandfather would be so embarrassed if he saw your grades," he would say. Part of me thought, *Fuck you, I'll show you.* Yet some part of me believed he must be right. When I said I felt the other kids' eyes on me that day in class, that wasn't my imagination. My dad's drinking was the source of much bullying directed at me by many of my high school classmates. For years, I'd ignored it. One day, not long after the humiliation of his school visit, I snapped.

One of high school's biggest bullies called my father a dirty drunk and starting hurling insults at my family. I was used to kids insulting my dad, and didn't care that much what they said about me, either—but I was very protective of my family. Slandering them was a major error in judgment on his part.

The guy had four inches and close to fifty pounds on me. A crowd gathered behind the school to watch what they assumed would be a slaughter. I was way outmatched, and terrified. Then a sudden rage came over me. All the abuse my old man had heaped on me and my mom went surging through my fists like lightning bolts. An eerie calm settled in, and the big boy, seeing the change in my eyes, started to back away, suddenly not so confident. As I would learn over many fights in the years to come, when I get out-of-control angry my eyes go from blue to black and my face turns to a mask of rage.

I beat the crap out of that boy. Some of his teammates tried to pull me off, but I was strong and wouldn't stop hitting, my fists smashing into his face again and again. Two of his friends grabbed my arms. Big mistake. I turned my rage on them. I didn't know where the strength was coming from, but I easily threw them both to the ground, gave one of them a vicious kick to the face and locked the other in a chokehold with one arm while making mincemeat of his nose with the other. The poor kid's nose was obviously broken, but I kept hitting it anyway as the blood gushed. I choked that kid to within an inch of his life, until two coaches came running over and hauled me off.

Although the fight was over I was still in a rage and left school grounds with a gang of kids who were constantly in trouble with the law. We dropped in on a local store, E.J. Korvette's, where I shoplifted a ski jacket out of pure spite and self-destructive fury. On my way out of the store, a security cop stopped me. Two cop cars showed up. The cops hauled me out of the store and threw me against the side of one of their cars. I turned around and told the cop he was a dumb redneck with an ugly whore for a wife.

Ever eloquent, even in the midst of the fray.

The cop slammed into me with his nightstick and threw me into the car, bound for the New London jail. It was far from the last time I would be cuffed and bludgeoned by a cop's nightstick.

The old man came to bail me out and I wanted nothing more than to grab a nearby cop's gun and shoot the sonofabitch. On the way home he had the nerve to tell me that he "just couldn't understand" where all that anger came from. Was he kidding me?

I was suspended; both of the guys I'd beaten up ended up in the hospital. The saddest thing about it was, I felt no remorse—at least, not at the time. That would come only years later. Fortunately I dodged any legal charges. From the day I returned to school after the suspension, no one there ever tried to bully me again. My anger had scared everyone. Hell, it had scared me. I tried to let it go, but I couldn't. I became a one-man anti-bully patrol. Whenever I caught someone bullying a kid who couldn't stand up for himself, I'd beat the crap out of the bully. Taking on powerful assholes who preyed on weaker people became an important part of my value structure for years to come. In some perverse way I suppose I could thank my father for that. If the rage he instilled in me was expressed only against bullies and powerful people doing unfair things, maybe it would have been in some way a good thing. But too often the rage I felt for decades would only cause me and others around me great suffering.

*   *   *

Shortly after my suspension the old man left for good. One day that spring, the spring of '65, he and my mother got into a huge shouting match out on the driveway. The argument turned violent. He smacked her. At sixteen, I was old enough now to make good on my promise to myself that someday I would defend her. I grabbed up a good-sized stick of wood from our woodpile and went after him.

He jumped in the shitty old Studebaker and took off. He never came back.

CHAPTER TWO

Fighting for the Cause

I almost didn't make it out of high school. Before that spring shouting match that led to his abrupt departure, my father had arranged for me to double up on some classes and take extra courses, so I could recoup the time I lost from repeating tenth grade after that miserable year at Moses Brown. But I barely crawled past the finish line. My grade point average was 2.001, and it was that high only because I cheated on my French exam. When I applied to colleges the only one that would accept me was a Division II school on Staten Island called Wagner College, and then only because they could see I had some potential as a football player.

My father, whom I had not seen in over a year, showed up at our home with a rental car he'd booked for half a day (I guessed the old Studebaker had finally croaked) to drive me up to Staten Island for the start of my first semester. After leaving the family he had slunk back to Westfield, New Jersey, where he had taught high school for a time after the war. He'd managed to get his old job back, informing and inspiring today's youth by day, doing God knew what by night.

We didn't say much during the car ride.

Most of the freshmen were brought to Wagner by parents who lingered to help their sons and daughters unpack before saying their tearful good-byes. My old man dropped me off at the top of a hill near my dorm, said a quick *So long*, and hightailed it out of there.

On my own at last. Just the way I wanted it.

Watching my father drive away I felt none of the freshman jitters and homesickness most other kids right out of high school seemed to suffer with. In fact, it felt like the shackles had been released from my arms and legs.

It was strange to watch all these parents hugging their kids and getting all weepy. I couldn't understand parents who actually loved their kids enough to cry when they brought them to college. It wasn't that I begrudged them what were no doubt honest emotions. I just couldn't relate. My old man was just as happy to get rid of me as I was to get rid of him. Probably the only thing we'd agreed on in years.

I didn't own many clothes or much of anything else, either, and stood around watching while the other kids unloaded televisions, radios, stereos, and all sorts of crap to fill up their new digs. I didn't feel jealous about this; on the contrary, I quickly turned it to my advantage. One thing a survivor learns in an alcoholic household is to talk fast and make up stories (read: to lie) when necessary. You also learn how to compartmentalize pain and compensate by becoming overly cheerful and friendly.

Right away I met my new roommate and his middle-class American family from New Jersey. Nice guy, nice family. His dad said, "Bob, want me to help you bring some of your stuff in? My son can help."

"Thanks," I said, "but all I really have is this one suitcase and a box with a few things in it."

The mother looked at me with concern in her eyes and asked where I was from.

"With all due respect, ma'am," I replied, "I'm from a place I don't ever want to go back to."

The dad said something breezy like, "Let's let Bob get settled and not load him up with questions." It wasn't hard to read the sympathy in all three faces. It suddenly occurred to me that I should probably just tell the truth and see where it went.

"Look," I said, "you deserve a truthful answer. I come from Connecticut. I was born and raised in an abusive family that was always broke. But don't feel bad for me," I said, lighting up my face with a big smile, "because this is a happy day! I'm finally free from all that."

Their reactions were immediate and heartfelt. The mother wrapped her arms around me and gave me a big hug. My new roommate thumped me on the back, and his dad squeezed my arm.

I realized I didn't always need to hide from my past. If I put it right out on the table, it could actually be an asset. Hell, on the way out of the room my new roommate's dad slipped me sixty bucks and told me to call him if I ever needed anything. He gave me his card and I got another hug from the mom.

*   *   *

The mid-sixties were the perfect time for a survivor to be in college. Rebellion was in the air. Drinking was pervasive, everyone seemed to have some drug or other, and in true sixties spirit, everyone shared them freely—grass, uppers, downers, meth, acid, and Quaaludes (my favorite).

No, I take that back: not *everyone*. There were quite a few students at Wagner who still dressed in the conventional styles of the fifties and early sixties: girls in short skirts and sweaters, boys in khaki pants, button-down shirts, and penny loafers. They had so far resisted getting caught up in the swelling social and political currents of the decade. Yet in them, too, you could still sense a growing detachment from their parents' America. Even for those not quite ready to make the leap, *everyone* on campus was feeling less connected to the culture that had reared them. The counterculture, fueled by drugs, rock and roll, and a growing anti–Vietnam War sentiment, was a faint but very real siren song.

Then there were the students who were decked out in a style entirely new to me. Girls in long, billowing skirts with tie-dyed shirts (and no bras!), wearing all sorts of handmade jewelry, often with the peace sign on prominent display. Boys in bell-bottoms, T-shirts, and American flag headbands. A constant stream of music blared from speakers set into dorm windows, flooding the campus with the sounds of the Stones, the Doors, Hendrix, Cream, the Who, and of course Bob Dylan, the poet laureate of the counterculture.

The two groups were cordial to each other, but I could sense a cultural schism. The conformists still clinging to the conventional norms of their parents' America, versus the growing ranks of rebels ready and eager to toss it all out the window and break completely with postwar America and its traditions.

During my freshman year I sided largely with the conformists. I had grown up in rural Connecticut, where the post–World War II culture and values were still firmly rooted. I was more focused on rejecting my immediate upbringing, and not necessarily cultural attitudes at large. As the year wore on, though, the pull of the counterculture grew stronger. By day conformity held sway: conservative clothes, sports, and fraternity life. By night I was spending more and more time with the nonconformists, where I was exposed to new perspectives—and where my growing attraction to drugs and booze was seen as normal. A one-man generational divide.

What finally tipped me in the direction of the nonconformists was an attraction with even more gravitational pull than drugs and alcohol: the politics of the left.

During college I grew increasingly passionate in my opposition to segregation. Maybe to prove something to my father, but also as an expression of my own growing commitment to the civil rights movement, I started slipping out of school to take trips south to North Carolina with a few of my more anarchistic classmates, to register voters under the new Voting Rights Act. A group of us would head into black neighborhoods and start going door-to-door. Here that expression about being "from the other side of the tracks" was a literal reality. In many of these medium-sized towns in the South you'd find a railroad track running through the town, with one side white and the other side black. After an afternoon spent in black neighborhoods, we would carry our stacks of voter registration forms with us back across the railroad tracks, and like clockwork a gang of thugs would drive up in their cars, screech to a stop in front of us, jump out, and try to grab the forms away from us. (It never worked; we always made duplicates.) Then they would proceed to beat us up. Most of the people I'd come with would sit down, the way Dr. King said to do, hold hands, and sing, "We shall overcome." Not me. I'd be right back in their faces—so I was invariably the first one to get the shit kicked out of me.

This same scenario repeated itself well over a dozen times during those years.

It was eye-opening. You can talk all you want about Alabama and Georgia, but North Carolina probably had more out-and-out racists and Klan members than anywhere else in the nation. (They called it White Citizens' Council, but that was nothing but a cover-up for the Ku Klux Klan.)

After a while I got so pissed off about the fundamental unfairness and bigotry of this whole scene that I started actively going into bars with blacks and demanding to be served, and of course ending up in vicious brawls and beatings. When the police showed up they just joined in the beatings, then threw us in jail.

Looking back, I can sort of appreciate their perspective. Here were a bunch of poorly educated white people who had lived all their lives with blacks and whites separate, who knew no other way of life, and now all of a sudden these white guys come down from the North and try to tell them what to do. Though I hated them for years, I don't hate them now. But it sure was ugly—uglier even than what I'd grown up with. And that was saying a lot.

I also know there is racism in the North, too. I remember the ugliness in South Boston in the 1970s when busing started there, the white mothers coming out and screaming nigger this and nigger that, the attacks and the violence. It was no different than what we saw when they integrated the University of Mississippi; it was the same level of anger and resentment. Busing was a failed policy, but there wasn't really any other way to deal with the situation. How were you going to get these kids to get a fair and equal education? It created a lot of animosity, though. Racism was not limited to the South, it was everywhere. It was just more blatant in the South.

At one point six of us, three whites and three blacks, attempted to integrate a lunch counter in Rocky Mount, North Carolina. The angry, red-faced, gum-smacking waitress not only wouldn't serve us, she wouldn't even acknowledge our presence. I lobbed a salt shaker at her. I know: not exactly what Dr. King had in mind.

Within moments a gang of locals yanked us off our stools, threw us to the ground, and started kicking us and beating us with chairs. A good ole boy passing by, alerted to the brawl, grabbed an ax handle and joined in the fray. I was drunk (though it was only noon) and raged out at him, calling him a stupid pig and telling him his daughter was great in the sack. In retrospect, this was probably not the best way to open up a dialogue about tolerance and coexistence. The next thing I remember was waking up in a clinic—rather than a white hospital, my friends had wisely taken me to a black-run clinic nearby—with a doctor removing splinters and bits of broken-off skull bone from the gash in my head. To this day I bear a large indentation at the base of my skull.

Years later I got even. I ended up managing political campaigns that covered just about every congressional district in the state, and in most of them, I won.

*   *   *

The other great social issue of this generation was the war in Vietnam. The war was raging during my college years, and so, too, was the rage against it on college campuses. It was college students who first led the opposition, but they were soon joined by suburban parents who realized that the war was a mistake—and they didn't want their sons drafted into it. I had never believed the government when they sold Vietnam as a noble anticommunist effort. The bullshit "domino theory" was at first accepted by a gullible public, but as the war dragged on and hundreds more American kids kept dying with each new week, the tide of popular opinion began turning against the war.

This was one of the few positive things my father gave me: an education on Vietnam and his firm belief that the war would never be won. This was not some intellectual pacifist talking. He was a decorated World War II veteran. In his war, the Allies fought great battles and increasingly took enemy ground. He saw nothing like that happening here. He predicted (correctly, as it turned out) that the U.S. would get bogged down in a jungle war with no fixed battles and an enemy committed to driving foreigners from their land. Add to the mix a corrupt South Vietnamese government with a military that would much rather see Americans spill blood than Vietnamese soldiers, and you had a no-win situation.

In the months immediately following the dark days of November 1963, my father and I had both admired LBJ for pushing a strong civil rights agenda. As the war escalated that admiration faded, to put it mildly. When I first arrived at Wagner College in '66 the war under President Johnson was getting steadily worse. In the middle of my second year on campus, it took a turn for the even worse. When the Tet offensive happened in January 1968, Johnson's goose was cooked, and he knew it.

By this time my hatred of the war was equal to my hatred of segregation, and I yearned to become more actively involved. Eugene McCarthy was running against LBJ for the nomination, but I never especially liked McCarthy. I didn't care for the "Get clean for Gene" crowd. They weren't my kind of people.

In March, Bobby Kennedy got into the race. With Bobby in the running, suddenly there was a politician I could believe in, one I actually believed was telling the truth. Two weeks later, on April Fool's Eve, Johnson shocked everyone with the announcement that he was out. Having no incumbent to run against changed everything.

I had to be part of this.

If watching John Kennedy being elected president was the moment I fell in love with politics, working as a volunteer for his brother was my first foray into actually *being* in it. After leaving his post as attorney general Bobby had become a New York senator, so his New York City office was the hub of campaign activities, and in the spring of 1968 I virtually stopped going to any of my classes and spent practically all my time at the Kennedy headquarters.

I fell in love with everything about it—the energy, the mission, the exhausting hours, my campaign friends from wildly different backgrounds coming together to support a man who stood against a war they hated. Even in later years on winning primary nights in campaigns I managed myself, I have never felt more alive than during the Bobby Kennedy days. Campaigns and politics had me completely hooked.

I remember watching a film at that volunteer headquarters of Kennedy's Appalachia trip, where he went to be among the poor. The rest of the world saw snippets of it on the news, but we watched the whole thing. There were people who thought he was a sonofabitch, but the guy I got to know was completely genuine. I met him a handful of times as he came through the headquarters. He always talked to the volunteers and not just the paid people, as a lot of candidates will do. I watched the Appalachian footage, and read his speeches, and listened to him on radio and TV. I was twenty years old, and Bobby for me came to stand for what politics *should* be: a noble calling.

At one of his campus speeches, at a medical school in Indiana, he was talking about programs we needed for the poor and somebody in this audience full of medical students asked, "Who's going to pay for all these programs?" And Bobby said, "You are. And I am." I'll never forget that.

When Kennedy won the critical California primary in June we were all ecstatic.

Then the unthinkable happened. I was at the office in New York hours later when the word came in that he had been shot in California. The next day we learned the shot was fatal. I cried that day.

*   *   *

From the moment we heard the news that Bobby had been killed I doubled down in my involvement with the antiwar movement. I joined the Mobilization Committee to End the War in Vietnam ("the Mobe"), and two months later went to Chicago to join in the protests outside the Democratic convention. As a Mobe marshal, my job was to help keep everyone calm.

That didn't work out too well. I was there in Grant Park when the cops started beating people up and spraying Mace everywhere. It was a horrific scene. Chicago in August 1968 was where I got my first taste of tear gas, and we became very well acquainted. At one point in the melee I was run down by a police horse. You don't realize just how big horses are until you're lying on the ground and looking up at one about to stomp you.

The cops were beating people indiscriminately. I saw one cop bring his baton down on a girl—unarmed, of course. I grabbed the sonofabitch and yanked him off her. The next moment a bunch of other cops were on us and started to whale on me, then dragged me out to Soldier Field, a few miles away, where they hauled everybody else.

I'd been beaten up by cops before, but this was something else. The entire Chicago Police Department that night seemed to have given itself over to vicious lawlessness. My disdain for authority and dedication to serving the underdog reached new heights.

Meanwhile Hubert Humphrey was over at the convention winning the nomination. Humphrey had come late to his opposition to the war, and I think that ultimately cost him against Nixon. I was never much of a Humphrey guy. Toward the end I did a little reluctant volunteer work for his campaign, but that was about it. When Nixon went on to win, it was to my mind the worst thing that could possibly happen. It seemed to me that the assassination of JFK in 1963 was the awful beginning of what now felt like a never-ending wave of national tragedy. There could hardly have been any more bitter way to rub salt in the wound than seeing his 1960 presidential adversary, Tricky Dick, now enter the White House.

When Dr. King was killed in April, and then Bobby in June, I blamed the far right wing of the Republican Party—not for the assassinations themselves, of course, but for fomenting a climate of hatred against those who would challenge the superiority of America in all its arrogance and, in the case of Dr. King, the forces of bigotry and ignorance. The Chicago convention confirmed for me that that climate of hatred had become endemic.

I was now firmly entrenched in the politics and culture of the nonconformists.

And in that culture, drugs and drinking dominated.

I began to drink even more heavily, no longer waiting till the sun went down, and also started routinely using LSD and mushrooms, prescription uppers to wake up and downers to sleep. I didn't think any of this was especially out of the ordinary, and certainly didn't see it as any indication of addiction or relate what I was doing to what my father had done to himself.

My final two years of college were fueled principally by booze, drugs, idealism, and frustration, as I slipped deeper into a life of addiction and disaffection.

*   *   *

As with high school, I barely pulled off graduating, although unlike high school, in this case I was involved in laying siege to the president's office.

In the days that followed the murder of Kent State students at the hands of the Ohio National Guard on May 4, 1970, I joined a mob of radicals who took over the college president's office and held it for a few days.

While we were holed up in there, I made a phone call to my old man.

I hadn't talked to him since the day he dropped me off for my first day at college four years earlier. But he knew his way around demonstrations and civil disobedience. I explained the situation to him and said, "What do you think we ought to do here?"

He said, "I'll get a lawyer to talk to you." Then he added, "Listen, don't you ever get involved in that war. If you've got to go to Canada, I'm with you. Just don't join up."

"I'm with you, Pop," I said. A few minutes after I hung up, a lawyer called. I don't even remember what he said. Somehow or other we eventually left the building, and a few weeks later I left Wagner with my Bachelor of Fine Arts in hand. That was the last conversation my father and I would have for another seven years.

Curiously enough, I was invited back to Wagner College more than two decades later, in the nineties, to give the commencement address and be recipient of an honorary Ph.D. The morning of the ceremony I was treated to coffee in the same president's office.

*   *   *

The draft was a dark cloud that hung over all these events. I was in the first lottery, at the end of 1969, held to determine who would be the next ones to go. My number was 136, which meant I was likely to be inducted into the U.S. military and probably from there shipped off to Vietnam.

It wasn't the idea of war itself I objected to, and I was certainly willing to fight for something I believed in. (Hell, I'd been doing that for years.) I wasn't even especially afraid of dying. But I'd be damned if I'd go get myself killed fighting in some unwinnable war in which I didn't believe in the first place. On this my father and I were in complete agreement.

The Connecticut draft board had ordered me to appear at Whitehall Street in lower Manhattan. I had no intention of being drafted. If I was, I would refuse induction and flee to Canada. Before taking that route, though, I would call on all my survival skills to beat the predraft physical.

A cottage industry had developed around tactics and strategies for failing draft physicals. If you were healthy, as I was at that point, the best course of action was to declare yourself mentally unfit for service. My family had a psychiatrist friend in Manhattan who was strongly antiwar, and he wrote me a letter stating that because of the abuse I suffered as a child and the temper issues associated with that abuse, I was a danger to myself and others. He went on to say that I had experimented heavily with hallucinatory drugs (true) and that the potential for suicide was extremely high (not true, but what the hell).

It was a damn good letter, but by this time so many guys were using mental problems as an excuse to avoid service that I was worried the letter alone might be a long shot. I needed a backup. So I took nine amphetamines on the morning of the physical, an amount that should have killed me and would almost certainly have killed a nonaddict. It was a risk I was willing to take; anything to avoid being drafted. I knew I had overdone it when I began to shake and, despite my repeated attempts, was unable to find the address of the draft board. I approached an old lady on the street, intending to ask her for directions. She took one look at me and ran as fast as her cane could take her. Eventually I found the place on my own.

The first thing I noticed when I walked in was that most of the guys taking physicals that day were black or brown. These poor guys were less likely to have connections in the antiwar underground that provided free help to avoid the draft. I also knew that the government targeted minorities for the draft (though it refuses to admit this even today), especially in the South, which is why the troops sent to Vietnam were disproportionately composed of minorities.

When it got to my turn, the army shrink read the letter, looked at me with disgust, and said, "Bullshit. But nice try." He declared me mentally fit to join the military. I wanted to say, "No one who is mentally fit would show up for military service in this war!" but for once I held my tongue.

When I got to the blood pressure test, the results (as I recall, it read 220 over 160) scared the hell out of the doctor, who immediately declared me unfit for duty. He probably thought this kid was going to have a heart attack right then and there, something he did not want happening on his watch. I was free to go.

As soon as I hit the street I found the nearest bar and put back a smooth dozen shots of Southern Comfort, the drink of choice if you wanted to get drunk fast. The booze countered the speed in my body and I could almost feel my blood pressure dropping.

I had dodged the first bullet, but knowing how desperate the government was for fresh bodies, I figured it was only a matter of time before they would call me up for another physical. I needed to get as far away from my draft board as possible.

A fraternity brother of mine, after failing to get into medical school in the United States, had gone to Guadalajara for his medical training, which was one of the few viable alternatives for those who didn't make it into a U.S. med school. I contacted my friend to tell him I was coming down to Guadalajara so I could learn Spanish, and asked if I could crash at his place. He said, "Come on down."

I climbed into my ten-year-old MGA, still my favorite among all the cars I've ever owned, and made the drive all the way from New York to Guadalajara. I drove almost twenty-four hours a day, nourished primarily by speed and booze. I was stopped by the cops a good three or four times. And here is the amazing thing: Although I was completely plastered every time I was stopped, by this time drunk had become my normal, so each time the cop who stopped me gave me either a ticket for speeding or a warning...and let me go. Not once did anyone give me a sobriety test.

In fact, over all the years of my drinking and driving, I never once got a DWI. They say "God protects drunks and fools." If that was true, I was eligible for a double dose of divine protection.

*   *   *

In Guadalajara I signed up for a thirty-day Spanish class. I flunked. Nobody flunks Spanish in Mexico, but somehow I managed it. That was okay, though, because the dollar was worth a lot of pesos—pesos I could use for drugs, alcohol, and women. My friend's house was about sixty miles from the beach, and I spent a good deal of time there in low-class bars.

One of those dives very nearly got me killed.

I was trying to communicate with a beautiful Spanish woman at the bar. She didn't speak English and I didn't speak Spanish, but I thought my intentions were pretty clear. Just to make sure, though, I resorted to my handy English-to-Spanish dictionary, which I carried with me everywhere. I looked up *Want to go to bed?* and tried it out: *"¿Quieres ir a la cama?"*

This was clearly the wrong approach.

In an instant a big Mexican dude and two of his friends were on me. They grabbed me and pushed me out the back door. The big dude reached behind a woodpile and pulled out a machete.

If you've never seen a machete up close and personal, let me tell you, that is one fierce-looking knife. Try talking yourself out of a problem like *that* when you don't speak the language. My options were obviously limited. I was a good fighter, but there was no way I was going to take on Mr. Machete and his two friends by myself. My normal line of bullshit might've worked, but I couldn't translate it fast enough to do me any good, not even with my little English-to-Spanish book.

So I reached in my pocket and pulled out forty dollars in U.S. currency.

That seemed to do the trick. The machete was tossed back onto the woodpile, and suddenly the three of them were all smiles. Evidently they wanted the money even more than they wanted my gringo ass.

Pointing to the bar and using bad sign language, I conveyed the idea that I'd give them the money inside. Once back inside the bar I handed two of the guys a twenty-dollar bill each, threw in a third for the third guy, and then cleared out of there as fast as I could.

To this day I wonder why they didn't just machete me to death out back and take all the money in my pocket, which was considerably more than sixty bucks.

*   *   *

One day as I was crashing in the garage of my friend's house, his maid knocked on my door. (Everybody could afford housekeepers in those days.) She said there were some people out front who wanted to see me. Since the only people I knew in Mexico were my friend, his friends, a few bartenders, and some hookers, and I couldn't think of a single reason any of them would be coming round to see me during the day, I immediately had a bad feeling about this.

I went to the front door and, sure enough, there were two guys in U.S. military outfits.

"Are you Bob Beckel?" asked one. I considered saying no, but if they had tracked me down in Mexico, they obviously knew this was the guy they were looking for.

"Yes, that's me."

He handed me an official Selective Service letter, stating that I was due for another physical within a week, just across the border in Brownsville, Texas, and that I better be there or face criminal charges.

That last part got my attention. I told them I'd be there.

"You *better* get your hippie ass there," said the other one. This guy was so fat it was highly doubtful that he could have passed a physical himself. I suggested he and I hold a boxing match, the deal being that if I won, I would not have to go for the physical. He only glared at me harder.

"Just be there," said the other guy, and they left.

My draft board must have wanted me in a big way if they were chasing me all the way to Mexico. When the day came I used speed and booze once again, went up to Brownsville, and once again pulled it off.

Clearly, though, it was time for me to get lost, and fast.

Back in the MGA. I drove all the way up to Washington, D.C., and went straight to the offices of the U.S. Peace Corps. Before splitting for Mexico I had applied to the Peace Corps, purely on a whim. I had no intention of actually going. Third World poor wasn't my idea of a fun two years. Still, with the rice paddies of Vietnam looming in my immediate future, the idea didn't seem so bad.

I managed to locate my application file and walked it through the various offices that had to sign off on the application. My well-seasoned charm-on-demand was in great evidence that day. Three days later I received a letter of acceptance. I was heading to the Philippines. I hauled out an atlas and discovered that the Philippines was exactly on the other side of the world from my draft board. Short of going to the moon, I couldn't be farther away. I accepted.

Two months later, I shipped out.

*   *   *

The Philippines was everything I expected. About 70 percent of the country was below the poverty line, while a few rich families controlled the economy. I was assigned to a little village called Villamonte, near the city of Bacolod in Negros Occidental, the western half of Negros Island, where I moved in with a family of ten, with eight kids ranging from two to fourteen years of age, living in a shack on stilts (for the monsoon season, when the streets would turn into small rivers). I slept in the kids' room, where the temperature was ninety degrees at night, the humidity stifling, and the mosquitoes big enough to carry the baby away. We all slept under mosquito netting.

My first morning there I woke up thinking I was having an acid flashback: I was surrounded by hundreds of little lizards clinging to my net. My response, naturally enough, was to start screaming at the top of my lungs. The father came running in and burst into laughter, followed by a train of kids all rolling on the floor and howling with merriment. The father said these were geckos, and they ate the mosquitoes at night. That may be, but from that moment on I've always hated geckos, especially that smug little sonofabitch on the Geico insurance ads that are everywhere you turn these days.

The Peace Corps was no easy ride. They had a slogan, "It's the toughest job you'll ever love," and I found this to be no exaggeration. At the same time, Filipinos are among the kindest people in the world. They were also strong allies of the U.S. and had been ever since we liberated them from the Japanese in World War II. When I was there the memories of the war were still very fresh, and any Japanese who visited the Philippines did so at his peril. The U.S. maintained two huge military bases in the country, Subic Bay Naval Base and Clark Air Force Base. These were the principal supply and support facilities to support the U.S. war in Vietnam. They took their mission very seriously, as I would come to find out.

Strangely, it was while I was there on Negros Occidental, on the other side of the world, that my relationship with my father took a new turn. This unlikely course of events occurred because, to my astonishment, he started writing me weekly letters.

Once he started, he didn't stop. Week after week, he never failed to write, each letter several pages long and all in longhand. Once in a while he would include news clippings or other bits of evidence of life back home. He was a great writer, too; his letters were cogent, funny, and informative, and they kept me up with current political events.

I didn't write back. I still had so much animosity and anger that I just refused to respond. Nevertheless, slowly but surely, I began to warm to the letters, if not to the man. In fact, there was a distinct reason he was suddenly reaching out to me like this: He'd gone through a significant change in his life. But his letters did not explicitly reveal this, and it was something I wouldn't learn about for quite a few years yet. Meanwhile, the steady stream of letters kept coming.

*   *   *

Once in Villamonte I was assigned to a community center in the barrio to provide advice to small businesses, which of course I knew zilch about. My major activity in the Peace Corps was to help out the local economy by spending hard U.S. currency at every "B bar" I could find, this being the local expats' term for bars that fronted as whorehouses. It was at one of these joints that I contracted gonorrhea, which makes you feel like you are pissing through broken glass. I don't recommend it.

After about eight months and four or five more sexually transmitted diseases, the doctors said I was becoming so resistant to the antibiotics they used to treat infections that they would have to ship me home for medical reasons after only one year of my two-year program.

It turned out this wasn't necessary.

One day soon after my dire prognosis, one of the little girls in the family I lived with came running over to the hammock where I was busy recovering from a massive rice wine hangover.

"Uncle Bob, Uncle Bob!" she called out as she ran. "Two! Two!"

Two what? When she reached me, she explained: There were two gringos looking for me. You guessed it. Two air force guys from Clark Air Force Base handed me a letter from my draft board ordering me to report for a draft physical the next day.

I spent the rest of the day and all that night bribing pharmacies in Bacolod for uppers.

The next day an air force car was in front of the house to escort me to the airport, where another air force guy met me and flew with me to Clark, which was the major stopover point for soldiers coming to and from Vietnam. My hair was very long at the time, and when I entered the main hall for physicals I got some mean-ass stares. I whispered to anyone who would listen that I was military intelligence, and what do you know, it worked. At least for a short time. Until a big black air force sergeant stepped to the front of the group with a clipboard.

His first words: "How many are in here for pre-Vietnam checkups?" A chorus of unpleasant growls went up from half the room.

Next: "How many are in here for post-Vietnam checkups?" A different chorus of growls went up, this one with a hard junkie-voiced sound to it. A few of these guys were nodding out right then and there. If Vietnam accomplished anything, it was to transform guys who were previously straight as arrows into heroin addicts.

Then the sergeant lowered his clipboard, glared out at the room, and snarled, "Is there some motherfucker in here for a fucking draft physical?"

Ah, that would be me. Showtime. From my seat at the back of the room, I gave the sarge a half-wave.

"Get your hippie ass up here to the front of the room," he barked.

These soldiers had all seen stories on television about antiwar hippies, and now they had one in the flesh. Oh, boy. As I made my way to the front of the room I was repeatedly pushed and shoved and smacked in the head. One guy actually pissed on me. I saw the blood pressure station and made a beeline for it. An irritated doctor took my pressure; it was nearly 250 over 180.

Pulled it off again! *Damn, I'm good*, I thought.

I asked the doctor how to get out of that house of horrors—and he said, "Not so fast." Instead of pointing me toward the exit, he sent me to see the next honcho in line, Sergeant Johnson, who was even more pissed off than the doctor was.

"Tell you what, you draft-dodging punk," said Sergeant Johnson, "we've decided to hold you overnight and check your blood pressure every hour on the hour."

"That's nice of you, Sarge," I said pleasantly, "and I know you're worried about me—but we have good Peace Corps doctors in Manila who will take good care of me."

"I don't want to take care of you, asshole," he replied. "I'm betting you jacked yourself with speed, and if I'm right it'll wear off by morning."

"But, Sarge, I could die from a heart attack any minute!"

"Go ahead," the sarge growled back at me. "Make my day." It wasn't till more than a decade later that Dirty Harry immortalized that line in *Sudden Impact*. When I first saw that movie, my first thought was to wonder how in hell Eastwood would have ever crossed paths with Sergeant Johnson.

Sure enough, as the speed wore off my blood pressure returned to the normal range. I was completely and fully qualified for military service. Sergeant Johnson just couldn't wait to get the happy news to my draft board.

Once again, though, fate intervened.

*   *   *

The year I was there, 1971, happened to be a time of strong protests and opposition to Ferdinand Marcos's increasingly dictatorial rule. Jovito Salonga was the Liberal Party senator from our area, and he was running for reelection. Salonga was a champion of the sugarcane workers, who were underpaid and had tried to form a union, only to see the union organizers arrested or shot down in the streets by thugs employed by the sugarcane plantation owners.

It would take a few months for my board to draft me, so I decided to help the Salonga campaign—which was against every Peace Corps rule imaginable. (The rules were very specific about volunteers not being involved in local politics.) But what did I have to lose? The draft had me anyway. Might as well do some good before I left. Besides, I liked the guy and what he stood for. And hey, it was a campaign. I couldn't stay away.

I helped Salonga as best I could while doing my best to stay under the radar.

In late August Salonga's Liberal Party held a big rally in Plaza Miranda, a big public square in front of a church in the center of Manila. A short hop by plane from Bacolod. Fascinated with the whole thing, I flew up there to watch.

The rally got under way. It was exciting. The feeling of mission, of fighting for a good cause, was in the air. I loved it.

As I stood there, about fifty yards from the speakers' platform, I heard a huge BANG! followed by a second, equally loud explosion. Suddenly the smell of smoke and sulfur was in the air and a chorus of frantic screaming and pain rose from the crowd. Someone in the audience had thrown a bunch of hand grenades onto the stage. Two of the grenades had gone off, instantly killing nine people and wounding nearly a hundred more. A third grenade bounced off the stage and flew back in my direction, hit the ground and rolled—coming to rest at my feet.

What do you know? I thought. *I'm not going to die in Vietnam after all. I'm going to die right here at Plaza Miranda.*

The third grenade just sat there.

For what reason I will never know, it did not detonate.

For what reason I could not begin to fathom, I wasn't dead.

Among those killed were a photographer for the *Manila Times* and a five-year-old child. Every one of the Liberal Party candidates was wounded. Salonga was left blind in one eye and deaf in one ear, and would have pieces of shrapnel lodged in his body for the rest of his life. The candidate running for mayor of Manila lost his leg and had one arm shattered. It was gruesome.

The next day, back in my barrio, I got a call. I was to come into the Peace Corps director's office. When I arrived at the office I learned that they had photos of me taken by the Marcos intelligence guys at Plaza Miranda. Not only was I there, and clearly involved in the event, but I also happened to be holding a poster.

The poster said, "Fuck Marcos."

This apparently was not in line with how they viewed the no-involvement-in-local-politics rule. I was declared persona non grata and told I had to leave the country.

I replied that the Peace Corps still owed me at least another six months. As unlikely as it sounds, my survival skills (which included the capacity to bullshit effectively) were so well honed that this tactic actually worked. They agreed to pay for me to travel around Southeast Asia checking out potential Peace Corps sites.

I could hardly believe my good fortune. I packed my bags and was on a plane out of there the next day.

When the elections were held that November in the Philippines, every one of Salonga's wounded Liberal Party candidates was swept into office by a groundswell of popular support. Those were the last free elections in that beautiful nation until 1986. The following September Marcos declared martial law, and that was the end of freedom in the Philippines for the next fourteen years.

*   *   *

I hit Hong Kong for the gambling, then Thailand for their world-famous prostitutes, Cambodia to try to find the Buddha Path, Nepal for hashish, Singapore for more gambling at the Raffles hotel—where I took three thousand dollars from a foolish rich Texan who was drunk and thought he could shoot pool, not realizing that he was playing against an accomplished pool hustler—and finally on to one of the most beautiful places in the world, Bali, Indonesia.

In Bali I stayed at Kuda Beach, a popular stop for drifting hippies in the days when a dollar got you a hut and two meals a day. My place was right on the beach looking out at the South China Sea. From my back window, which was a hole in the back wall of the thatched hut, I looked out on the volcano that had formed Bali thousands of years ago and still dominated the island's land mass. Over the centuries, needing space to grow rice, the Balinese had carved terraces out of the side of the volcano, which were now green with rice plants. Too gorgeous for words.

The Balinese are a peaceful and kind people, steeped in tradition. Every day, as the sun set over the South China Sea, dancers in flowing robes would play delicate flutes and stringed instruments for an hour before the sun disappeared over the horizon in a golden fireball.

With thousands of international hippies staying for weeks or months at a time, enterprising Balinese had developed an entirely new industry around them. The rich volcanic soil, they discovered, produced not only bountiful rice harvests but also magic mushrooms, rich with the hallucinogenic chemical mescaline. Every afternoon, about an hour before the dancers appeared, coal fires were ignited to heat the frying pans for cooking omelets laced with mushrooms. Within an hour, as the beautiful Balinese music began, the mushrooms would send one on a magical trip called the Golden Path, named for the sun shining on the ocean as it set.

Of all the drugs I've done in my life, nothing, but *nothing*, has ever equaled the effect of a trip down the Golden Path.

One day, in the midst of a particularly good trip, I thought I heard my name being called. Attributing this to the chemicals coursing through my bloodstream, I paid no attention, until I looked up to see a bellboy from an upscale hotel in Denpensar, Bali's capital, blocking my view of the path.

"You Beckley Bob, sir?"

Close enough. Yes, I said, I was Beckley Bob.

He handed me a Western Union cable, the old kind with strips of ticker tape pasted onto the yellow paper. Since the boy showed no intention of leaving, I tipped him a dollar. One dollar U.S. was big money in Bali in the seventies; with a huge smile and big thank-you, he took off, leaving me to read my message from planet Earth.

The telegram was from the Peace Corps. The opening line was something like, "Where are you?" Apparently I had lost track of time in Bali. My six months was up.

I was ordered to Tokyo for a debriefing on potential Peace Corps sites. This posed a problem, since I hadn't bothered to look for any.

When I got to Tokyo I told the regional Peace Corps office that I had found the perfect site in Bali, and furthermore, that I was willing to re-up for two more years if I could be a volunteer in the place of the Golden Path. It was a very short debriefing. I was soon hustled to the airport for a trip home.

Before leaving I asked if I was being honorably discharged from the Corps.

"Well, let me see," said the assistant regional director to whom I had directed this question. "Thrown out of host company for violating the ban on political activity, a government-sponsored trip to find needy sites that produced only Bali, where you spent 80 percent of your time, failure to report in once from your trip..."

"Guess not," I said, sparing him from going on. "How about dismissal for medical reasons, since I had lost my mind every day in Bali?"

He didn't even manage a reply to that. He was laughing too hard to get a word out.

*   *   *

I arrived back home in the States in early March 1972 to find yet another letter waiting for me. This one was from my old friend the draft board, informing me that, since I was now 1A, I was hereby ordered to appear at Fort Dix, New Jersey, for induction into the army in thirty days.

Once again luck—or whatever it was—was with me. A week later I got a letter from the Selective Service office in Washington, telling me Congress had passed a new law that said, in effect, you could not be drafted if you had been subjected to 1A status and undrafted over two calendar years. I was declared 1A in the Philippines the previous year, but not drafted until this year. My draft notification was voided. I was now undraftable.

To celebrate, I went out drinking. Or to put it more accurately, I went out and *continued* drinking. When the letter came, I'd already been drinking. I was *always* drinking. At this point, in fact, I was drinking so continuously that I was never without some level of alcohol in my system. During the day I would drink just enough to ward off the symptoms of withdrawal, and then I would go all out every night.

Thus I had by now established a modus operandi that would be my "normal" for much of my career. Although always in a continuous haze, I found I could function just fine. The people I interacted with during the workday thought the Bob Beckel they saw was, well, Bob Beckel. Since most had never seen me sober, they assumed this guy who functioned quite well (despite the booze coursing through his system) *was* the normal, sober Bob Beckel. My perpetual personality mask now had its perfect physiological counterpart.

This pattern worked for years—until it didn't. But that piper would not be paid for another three decades yet.

*   *   *

When I came back home to stay at my mother's house in Lyme in the spring of 1972, all I knew was that I wanted to get into politics somehow. It didn't take long.

Our next-door neighbors were a family named the Bennets, and old man Bennet knew a candidate for Congress named Roger Hilsman. Hilsman was a former assistant secretary of state under Kennedy. In fact, he was the back-channel guy who gave the nod to Diệm's assassination in Vietnam, just days before JFK met his fate in Dallas. That was Hilsman's claim to fame in Washington, if you want to call it fame.

Hilsman was running for Congress against Bob Steele, the incumbent Republican. Mr. Bennet called Hilsman and said, "You ought to put this kid Beckel to work."

I went to work for the Hilsman campaign as communications director for something like twenty-five dollars a week. Despite the lofty title, it wasn't a huge role. But the whole thing fascinated me and gave me my real first taste of what it was like to be an actual functioning piece of a political campaign. I had genuine responsibilities and was playing an actual role in making things happen.

As part of my job, they asked me to go down to Washington to advance a fund-raiser for Hilsman among the Washington elite crowd, who all loved Roger and put up the money for his campaign. They had no idea how badly he was going to get beaten.

The event was held at an address way up on Connecticut Avenue and Calvert Street, in one of those wonderful old Washington apartments with fifteen rooms and high ceilings, the kind that hardly exist anymore. It was close to ten o'clock at night before the fund-raiser finally wrapped up and everyone left. I decided to go walking.

I walked down Connecticut all the way to Dupont Circle, past the White House and down to the Mall. I was enthralled the whole way. I kept saying to myself, "I'm coming back here. This is where I'm going to make my future. This is going to be my new home."

I walked up to the Capitol, by the Washington Monument, and over to the Lincoln Memorial, then stood there looking across the Potomac at the Kennedy flame. That closed the deal.

This was where politics was happening.

This was where it all made sense.

This was my new home.

CHAPTER THREE

Capitol Cops and Whores

On my twenty-fourth birthday, November 15, 1972, I moved to Washington, D.C. I had dreamed of moving to America's political Mecca ever since those long hours on Election Day 1960, when I sat spellbound in front of our black-and-white television watching states slowly fall to JFK. In between I had survived the family chaos, gone through college, played football, dodged the draft, and joined the Peace Corps.

I was done with all of it.

The day I arrived in Washington was the day I intended to shut the door on my past. Driving over the Potomac and seeing the city's skyline laid out before me, I thought this must be exactly how the European immigrants felt when they entered New York Harbor and passed the Statue of Liberty: a chance to start their lives over. A place where you could leave the past behind. A place where nobody knew you and where, if you were good enough, you could make a success of yourself.

Which was all easier than you might think in Washington. Here it was not about where you came from or what you used to do that mattered, but what you'd done since you got here. If you could succeed in the Big Show inside the Beltway, people didn't tend to ask you about yesterday. To the extent you needed some background, you could simply make it up.

A survivor's stock in trade.

My first campaign had been a bust. This was the year of George McGovern, who lost every state but one, the first time in U.S. history that had happened. (Though not the last, as I would later find out to my chagrin.) Nixon won reelection with 23-plus percent more popular votes than McGovern, the largest margin of popular votes in U.S. presidential history, then or since. And my own candidate for Connecticut's Second District got whipped by a factor of two to one. It's not easy to lose a race by that wide a margin.

None of that mattered, though—because none of it would ever appear on my résumé. Like my childhood, it all ceased to exist when I crossed the Potomac.

Our defunct campaign's press secretary, Jim Duffy, wanted to come to Washington with me. Duffy was a great guy, but his presence posed two problems. One, Duffy would be evidence of my past life, which would make creating a new life story that much more difficult. Two, as a survivor I wanted no responsibility for anyone but me. That way, whatever happened would be my doing or undoing. Win or lose, I would do it on my own. (Although I had no intention of losing.)

I tried everything I could think of to convince Duff not to come. "Duff, you've never been out of Connecticut. Washington is a big city." No effect. "You know it's 85 percent black, Duff." No effect. "Blacks down there hate Irishmen as much as they hate Jews." Ah. Should have started with that one. Duff looked mildly worried about that many black folks hating his ass. But he's as stubborn as any Irishman. He was going.

There was some good news in this: Duff had a car and ample gas money, assets I lacked. I had all my worldly possessions in a duffel bag and a few hundred bucks in my pocket.

We got a late start that November 15 and didn't hit the D.C. area until dark. We circled the Beltway twice, got lost, and ended up on Benning Road in a tough neighborhood. After a careful study of the area, Duff concluded that I had underestimated the black population by at least 10 percent.

After crossing the Potomac River for the third time we ended up in Rosslyn, Virginia. Today Rosslyn is an upscale business and residential area. In 1972 it was a dingy place with pawnshops, cheap motels, and scruffy bars that stayed open late and reopened early, and scruffy inhabitants to match.

We stopped when we saw a motel sign flashing rooms for ten dollars a night. Good price, and we were beat. We checked in, got a half gallon of very cheap whisky from a joint next door, and went back to the room to celebrate my birthday and our new life. If I leaned way out the window I could just see the tip of the Washington Monument. This was living.

We crashed at about 1:00 a.m.—and were awakened at 1:15 by people in the hall. A little loud, but not too bad. We were both able to get back to sleep again. And were up again at 1:30. More people in the hall. Sleep. Up at two o'clock. People in the hall. This time we cracked the door and caught a glimpse of a white guy in a nice suit and a black girl in pink hot pants and a halter top.

Duff figured the dude must have gotten drunk and picked up what he thought was a good-looking woman, one of those sweethearts who look beautiful through drunken eyes at night and scare the hell out of you in the morning. I could relate. Back to sleep. Up at 2:30. People in the hall. We peeked out the door. Identical types, different people.

"Guys got bad taste in women around here," Duff observed.

This went on all night. By actual-daylight morning we wanted out of this dump. I went down to pay and the guy at the front desk informed me our bill was thirty-five dollars.

"Your sign says ten dollars!" I said.

"Look again," he said. I did. It said ten dollars per *hour*, thirty-five dollars for the night.

This would not be the last time I would sleep at a whorehouse, but it was definitely the last time for Duff. He decided Connecticut looked a lot better from down here, and said he thought it was time for us to go back home.

"Duff, my man, this *is* my home."

"Well I'm sorry," he said, "but I'm splitting."

"Okay, Duff. No hard feelings." We remain friends to this day.

After watching Duff disappear I grabbed my bag and asked someone where I could catch a bus to the Washington Monument. With Duff gone it was time to put on my new mask. It felt great. I got on a bus to go see my new home.

No more whorehouses for me. Not for the moment, anyway.

*   *   *

Some of my antiwar friends had told me that when they went to D.C. for protests, they'd stayed at a cheap place called Hartnett Hall, a few blocks from Dupont Circle, which was the hub of antiwar protest activity in the nation's capital. It wasn't hard to find. A large boardinghouse, Hartnett Hall was a four-story walk-up built during World War II as a military barracks.

They had obviously built this baby fast, but it seemed sturdy enough. The rooms were sparse yet clean. Each floor had its own communal bathroom and a pay phone in the hallway. For forty bucks a week, which included light housekeeping and two meals a day, it was a deal.

Even at that price, the few dollars I brought with me weren't going to last long, so I got down to business in a hurry. I came to Washington to be a political consultant, and for that I needed a good résumé, a sales pitch, and a strong presence. Which meant getting to know my neighbors.

The place was packed with Iranian students who were attending one of the area universities. How they pulled that off I don't know, since their English was nonexistent. They seemed friendly, were very well dressed, and appeared to have lots of money. They didn't seem too happy with the meal plan at Hartnett Hall, though, since virtually all of them cooked on hot-plates in their rooms. The joint smelled like a bazaar I'd visited once in a Muslim neighborhood in New York. To this day I still can't stand the sight of grape leaves and chickpeas, which apparently were essential to every Iranian meal. Fortunately I didn't get invited to dinner much.

However, these guys did have a few things I could use, like nice suits, polished shoes, and silk ties. If I was going to sell myself as a political consul-tant I needed some good clothes.

Survivors can strike up fast (if often meaningless) friendships when nec-essary. I took a friendship run at this big Iranian guy whose clothes seemed like they might fit me. His name was Akbar, or something close to that. As a bonus, he even spoke a little English.

One useful fact I gleaned quickly was that Iranian men apparently cov-eted American women. I invited Akbar to come cruising with me at a local gin mill. Most of the women in this joint were Grateful Dead hippie types and we struck out, but Akbar was nonetheless appreciative. He even picked up the tab.

Our friendship cemented, I asked Akbar if I could borrow some threads. He seemed happy to be asked. He came to my room the next morning with a shiny blue silk suit, pink shirt with pink and blue tie, and matching pocket handkerchief. He was kind enough to throw in a pair of suede shoes and a camel hair overcoat. The clothes did have a little residual body smell to them, so I had them dry-cleaned. They came back smelling like body odor sprayed with air freshener.

While waiting for the clothes I did one last edit on my political résumé. It was definitely impressive: a string of winning campaigns, references from a retired Connecticut senator and a former LBJ political aide, and copies of political ads from previous campaigns. The campaigns and the ads were all real. They weren't *mine*, but they were real. The references were from real people, too, even if they were people I'd never met. I had spent the previous day at the Library of Congress archives cobbling together this completely fictional past life.

When I said I went to D.C. to reinvent myself, I wasn't kidding.

As I reviewed my work, though, I became a little nervous about the extent of the scamming on my spanking new résumé. I looked it over one last time and something caught my eye. It claimed that I had been involved in twenty campaigns. Hmm. I was now twenty-four years old. At my age that would mean I had started consulting on campaigns when I was, what, six?

My survivor mind said this was just the wrong thing to do. "Morally reprehensible," I said to myself. So I cut it in half and made it ten campaigns.

The next day I was up before dawn, revised résumé ready. Big day. I worked the clothes thing hard. Had to be just right. I had trouble getting the tie right, though. I worked up a sweat, which immediately dripped onto Akbar's tie and the damn colors ran. The more I tried to clean it, the more the colors ran. That wouldn't cut it, so I made Akbar's tie into a sort of scarf, put it inside the shirt and let it puff out of the open collar. Not bad.

Armed with the addresses of all House and Senate Democrats, I was on my way over to Capitol Hill before the sun had poked its bleary November eye above the urban horizon. I couldn't afford a taxi and the damn bus routes were too hard to figure out; I would have to hoof it. I walked over to Dupont Circle and picked up Massachusetts Avenue at Eighteenth Street, then eighteen blocks down Mass Avenue all the way to Union Station, then North Capitol Street for three blocks to the Capitol.

Today that route would make for an elegant walking tour, with beautifully restored landmarks dotting the tourist's progress. In November of 1972 it looked like a war zone.

The assassination of Dr. King in April '68 had touched off the most devastating riots in the long and tumultuous history of the nation's capital. An estimated 75 percent of the value of black business equity went up in flames over the next three days. The Fourteenth Street business corridor was gutted.

As the rioting moved toward the White House the military established a perimeter around 1600 Pennsylvania Avenue, with machine guns set on the East and West lawns of the White House and tanks guarding the White House gates.

Now, four years later, as I made my way down from Eighteenth Street toward Fourteenth, the scars were plainly visible. The business district, to the extent that there was one, was now dominated by pawnshops, fast food joints, and liquor stores. The entertainment venues, once home to the finest nightclubs in the city, had been taken over by an array of cheap strip clubs and X-rated movie theaters. As I crossed Fourteenth at Thomas Circle I passed the historic AME Baptist Church, a huge building with marble columns and stairs that sweep down to Fourteenth Street. On this morning those hard stone steps were littered with the sleeping bodies of homeless men and women. Prostitutes sat among them with blank expressions, smoking cigarettes and resting, or at least pausing, after a long night of work.

In the course of my walk I was accosted by a pimp in a tricked-out Caddy, who threatened me because he thought I was a competing pimp, and a few prostitutes, who also thought I was a pimp. I looked down at my clothes and realized why everyone seemed to think I was a pimp: In Akbar's flashy silk-suit outfit, I *looked* like a pimp. I was also working up quite a sweat. I paid a homeless guy five bucks to move so I could sit down and let the perspiration dry. While my back was turned the homeless guy ran off with my coat. I chased him and ran smack into a scene that looked a hell of a lot like a confrontation between drug dealers—lots of leather, lots of chains, lots of guns—which prompted further running.

This wasn't going well.

I needed a drink.

As I passed Seventh Street I saw a bar opening for business, with a line of people outside waiting patiently to get in. It was 8:00 a.m.

It's fair to say most all these folks *needed* to be in a bar at this hour. They were not your social drinkers. They weren't here to take a meeting. They were here to keep a date with a bottle. There were your midlevel federal bureaucrats in cheap suits with plastic pocket protectors in their shirt pockets. There were your blue-collar rednecks coming in from the Maryland or Virginia sticks to work on some new downtown building. There were your street bums who had panhandled enough the night before to start the day with a lovely Chianti. And then there was me.

The place was windowless and reeked of stale beer and smoke. The only light was from neon display ads. The bartender was skilled: He seemed to know exactly what each of these barflies drank. No one looked happy, and no one talked, except to order drinks, as many as they could get down in the shortest period of time. It was one seriously depressing place: perfect for me at the moment.

I threw back two fast shots of cheap bourbon and chased them with a Coke. I was doing a fair amount of drinking by then, but never at eight in the morning. Hell, if you did that, you could end up like one of these losers. But this morning was an exception. I had gotten Akbar's coat stolen, my suit was wrinkled, and I was still sweating. Plenty of reasons for a drink or two.

Looking at this pitiful gathering of humanity made me think of my father. No doubt he went to dumps like this before he went to work, when he had work. Probably came back to drink his lunch, and stopped by for a few shots on his way home. What an asshole. How could anyone live like that? No wonder these people looked like shit. No wonder my old man did, too.

I ordered two more shots.

My money situation was looking more desperate by the day, and I hadn't made my first pitch for business yet. Probably shouldn't try to pitch today. My shirt and tie were still wet from sweat. It was cold out and I had no coat, plus I felt on edge and pissed off. Not the best mood to make a sale.

And then, like winter turning to spring, my attitude began to melt and change. The next two shots took the edge all the way off. I felt a warm glow in my belly and my anger subsiding. Wow, that was fast. I felt my empty optimism tanks slowly refilling. This little dump wasn't so bad after all. I smiled at the people on either side of me. They didn't smile back, but who cared?

The bartender asked if I wanted a refill. I told him I had to go get some work, but thanks anyway. He looked at me with the universal all-knowing bartender look. "New around here?"

"Yeah. Going to the Hill to sell campaign work."

"Now?"

"Yeah, man. Need to get some work fast. Guess what?"

"What?"

"On the way down here this morning a bunch of people thought I was a pimp. Can you believe that?"

"Yeah," he said. "I can believe that."

"Well, I'm no pimp. Who'd want to hang around with a bunch of whores all the time? Not this boy."

"Well, good luck, buddy."

*   *   *

The bar stop gave me a surge of energy and confidence. Why not go to the Hill? Sure, my clothes were wrinkled and my overcoat was gone, but I still had my pitch, and it was very good.

I headed back to Mass Avenue to go take Capitol Hill.

Just before reaching North Capitol Street I looked up at Union Station, the century-old railroad station with its massive marble columns and ornate hand-sculpted bas relief. In front of the station stood a massive marble fountain with carved angels that at one time had sent water cascading down it; the fountain now stood silent. The old building that had once glowed white from the finest imported Italian marble was now almost black from soot and neglect. "The city should knock this eyesore down," I thought, "and replace it with a new station of glass and steel." Today the refurbished Union Station is one of the finest examples of its architectural genre in the country, restored brick and marble and all. Urban planning is clearly not my strength.

Turning onto North Capitol Street, I froze, and an honest-to-God chill came over me. There it stood, in all its grandeur: the magnificent dome of the historic Capitol building. This may sound hopelessly naïve now in these more cynical days, but for a twenty-four-year-old kid who had dreamed of politics his whole life, this was magic. Behind those walls some of the most powerful people in the free world gathered together to do the business of governing. The senators and representatives who worked in that building served there at the will of the people who elected them. My goal was to help some of them keep their jobs, and others to lose them. It sounds like the height of arrogance as I write this now, but with the confidence of youth? Anything was possible.

The history of the place was firmly established in my mind. I had read everything about Washington I could get my hands on. The Capitol was built in 1793, its cornerstone laid by President George Washington, and rebuilt a few decades later after the British burned it, before we kicked their asses for the second time. The members of Congress, the body operating under a succession of various names as the country went through its birth pangs, had met in Philadelphia, New York, and other locations, until holding its first joint session in this very building on November 17, 1800—172 years earlier, almost to the day.

Lost to me in the midst of these historic wanderings was the crowd of people that streamed by me, coming by the hundreds off commuter trains from Union Station. I didn't notice them until someone bumped into me. Time to get moving. It was like merging with a busy interstate, but I managed to join the herd heading in the direction of the Capitol.

I couldn't believe all these people worked there. Not knowing who was important and who wasn't, I said good morning to everyone I could make eye contact with, which was not all that many.

We're not in Connecticut anymore, BoBo.

I walked to the West Front of the building. The massive columns and balconies of the West Front looked west down the great expanse of the National Mall: the Lincoln Memorial, with its high ceiling covering a huge sculpture of Abe in his massive chair, its walls engraved with the great man's words. It gave me comfort to know that Abe was still guarding the Republic. Extending out from the steps of the Lincoln Memorial was the Reflecting Pool where 250,000 civil rights marchers had gathered in 1962 to hear Dr. King declare for all of history that he had a dream. Then I felt my pulse quicken.

There it was.

In the middle of the Mall's great old-old-lined lawns stood the majestic obelisk of the Washington Monument, for my money the most imposing site in all of Washington, gateway to the Capitol City. A beacon of white marble, a lighthouse that would guide me home dozens of times over the years ahead.

If home is where the heart is, on that day in 1972 I was home for the first time.

*   *   *

To my left, across Independence Avenue from the Capitol, stood the three buildings that housed the offices of all 435 members of the U.S. House of Representatives. The most senior members of the House had their offices in the Cannon Building, the largest and most spacious of the three. I decided to start there. Might as well try my hand with the big boys first.

In 1972 I didn't have a clue about the politics of campaign consulting. For example, I didn't know I was starting in the wrong place. By definition, the most senior members of the House had been in office the longest, which meant they'd all kept winning their races every two years. If by some chance they had a tough reelection ahead of them, most of them already had long-term relationships with political consultants. The place I should have started was the Longworth Building, which housed the newest members. The Rayburn Building, which was the newest of the three structures, held a mixture of old-timers and new guys. But what did I know?

Also, this was late November 1972. I was about to learn a lesson on political timing.

I followed the crowd descending on the Independence Avenue entrance to the Cannon Building. Several U.S. Capitol Police guarded each entrance to all three buildings. I noticed that the cops at the door smiled as the Union Station crowd walked through the doors. I also noticed that they all seemed to have some kind of ID hung around their necks.

The cops watched me approach the entrance with some interest. As I stepped up to the entrance they stared at me with the kind of suspicious, police-type looks that I always find unsettling. They were not smiling now. It dawned on me that this was an entrance for House employees. Not wanting to start my visit by going in the wrong door, I took an abrupt left to go find the visitors' entrance.

Evidently my about-face was a little too abrupt. As I started up Independence Avenue, I heard the crackle of walkie-talkies. Glancing back I saw that the cops at the entrance I had just avoided were now talking excitedly into their microphones. Geez, maybe the president was visiting the Hill! That would be exciting on my first day here. Sure, it was the hated Richard Nixon, but I'd still have liked to see a presidential motorcade. (I could never have imagined on that fall day that in a few short years I would be *riding* in a presidential motorcade.)

I turned at the next corner onto the south side of Cannon and saw a large bank of glass doors off a semicircular drive. Lots of cops here, too. It had the look of a visitors' entrance, so I walked up the driveway toward the doors. Just before I reached them, someone grabbed my arm. Thinking it was some jerk looking for trouble, I turned around abruptly and found myself staring into the eyes of a cop. Looking down, I noticed his hand was firmly attached to my wrist.

"Can I help you, sir?" he said, but not in one of those nice voices cops use with lost tourists. This was more like the tone they use when you just got pulled over for speeding. No hellos, just a gruff "license and registration" with maybe a "please" added.

"Ah, no thanks, officer. I'm just going in there to hit up as many offices as I can, looking for work."

He seemed to miss the last three words of that sentence. "Step over here, sir." His massive hand squeezing my wrist a little harder. His voice definitely not in lost-tourist mode now. More like keep-your-hands-where-I-can-see-them mode.

As we moved away, more cops started showing up. A police car with lights flashing roared up the drive. I heard another cop say that the captain was coming. All this because I wanted to hand out some paper? What was going on here? I was starting to get edgy. And the buzz was wearing off from those drinks I'd had, which wasn't helping the situation any.

Now I was being surrounded by cops. These were the same guys who took away my favorite uncle Sam. The same guys who whaled on me and cuffed me in high school. Who threatened and terrorized my father and me in North Carolina. Who I watched beat defenseless women with nightsticks in Chicago and who blasted us with tear gas.

No, this was not my favorite crowd.

The police captain waded in through the ever-expanding knot of blue. There are over four thousand cops on the Capitol Hill Police Force, more police officers than in a medium-sized city, and all this to guard about ten buildings covering a few hundred acres. There was very little crime on the Hill. When there was an incident it became a big deal, no matter how small it really was.

"What's going on?" asked the captain.

The cop holding my wrist said, "Sir, this guy was going into the Independence entrance, saw our officers, and ran off."

"That's bullshit," I objected. "I didn't 'run off.' I thought it was an employee entrance and went looking for a visitors' entrance, that's all."

The cop continued with his monologue, now adding that I had come around to this entrance carrying a paper bag and muttering something about "hitting some offices."

"That's ridiculous!" I said. "I have a list of offices where I wanted to try to sell some business. I've got it right here in my suit coat."

I reached for the list with my free hand and heard a voice go, "*Freeze right there!*" That was the captain. "We'll get what's in your pocket."

He reached inside my pocket and pulled out the list. The offices I wanted to visit were underlined in red. Bad choice of colors, I guess.

"Sir," he barked at me, "what's in the paper bag?"

"My résumés," I replied.

"In a paper bag?"

"Can't afford a briefcase," I said, a bit indignantly.

The captain asked if he could look in the bag. Fine, anything to get going. He poked around in there and, sure enough, there were a hundred copies of my résumé with a business card clipped to each one: "Bob Beckel, Consultant to Campaigns," with the telephone number of the pay phone in Hartnett Hall.

"So, you're looking for a job?" said El Capitan.

"I'm looking for some campaign work," I replied. "I want to hit—er, visit these offices today, if possible." Then I added, with some edge to my voice, "Something wrong with that, sir?"

"Got any ID?"

I reached for my wallet and heard it again: "*Freeze!* I'll get that." El Cap reached for my wallet and as he opened it, out fell a FUCK NIXON button. Oops.

"Forgot I had that," I said a bit nervously.

"Free country," said the captain with a slight grin. Ah, I got it: El Cap wasn't too fond of Nixon either! Maybe a possible breakthrough here. "Okay," he added, "you can go, but I'm sending two officers with you."

"Oh, that's nice of you, but no thanks," I said.

"No, it's our pleasure, Mr. Beckel. Swanson, Moore, go with this gentleman."

"It may take a while," I said, but he wasn't buying any attempt to shrug off his goons.

"No problem," he said. "We've got plenty of time."

Off I went to the first office on my list with my security detail on either side of me. We strolled in, the receptionist took one look at us and immediately looked alarmed.

"Hi, name's Bob Beckel," I said quickly. "I'm in the campaign business. Like to talk to the congressman. He around?"

She favored me with an "Are you out of your mind?" look and said, "He's busy, but I'll be sure he gets it," as I handed her a résumé and business card.

"Okay," I said pleasantly, "but he should call today. I may fill up my campaign schedule by the end of the day."

She went back to whatever she was doing without a word.

I hit up another four or five offices and got the same result. Then I walked into what would turn out to be my last office of the day. The receptionist here was clearly gay. I've always liked gay folks, but the cops obviously did not, and the receptionist returned the favor. I got the immediate sense from this guy that he had been harassed by his share of cops. Which was already a point in his favor, and possibly mine.

I introduced myself.

"Name's Bob Beckel. I'm in the campaign business. Like to talk to the congressman. He around?"

He looked at me and said, "And what are the Lone Ranger and Tonto doing here with you?"

An opening. I caught the seductive whiff of potential solidarity here.

"Captain made them come with me." I shrugged. "I guess he didn't like the way I looked."

"Know the feeling," he said, then he turned to one of them and said, "You two officers, back up please. I want to talk to Bob privately." Good for him!

Once the two cops had grudgingly stepped back a ways so we could talk without them listening in, my new friend, whose name was Gary, said, "Bob, let me give you some advice. The campaign season ended three weeks ago. No one will be hiring consultants for the '74 campaign for at least a year."

"You're kidding, right?" I said.

"Wish I was, but that's the deal."

"Wow. Thanks for telling me. That'll sure save me some time." As I turned to leave, he leaned over toward me again and whispered, "One more thing, Bob—you look like a pimp in that suit."

"Yeah, so I've heard," I replied. "But thanks for the advice."

I felt incredibly dumb. Of course nobody was hiring! Election Day was a few weeks behind me. Our Connecticut campaign was over, obviously everyone else's would be, too. How had I not thought of that?

I told my police escort I was done for the day. They looked heartbroken. I'm sure they thought I was going to pull something, and they would get the first and likely the only real police action of their lives.

When we walked out of the building the captain was still there. Slow news day for the Capitol Hill Police Force. "What happened?" he said. "That was short."

"Captain," I replied, "all I can say is, I learned a lot today."

As I walked off he called after me, "Where you going?"

"For a few drinks." I smiled at him. "Want to join me?"

He returned the smile and said, "Wish I could. Good luck." Not such a bad guy.

I headed back the way I'd come, bound for my dingy little bar for some confidence enhancement. After today I needed it more than ever.

By the time I reached my little hole-in-the-wall bar it was late afternoon, and the place was packed with some of the same crowd that had been there in the morning. From the looks of a few of them, they'd also been there for lunch. This time I didn't get many stares. In fact, I got a few nods of hello. "They may be drunks," I thought, "but they seem like nice people." It didn't occur to me that they were probably just recognizing and acknowledging a member of the brotherhood.

The bartender remembered me and asked how the day went. I told him my sad story about the cops, the fact that campaign work was a year away, and that for the most part the day sucked.

Leaving the Hill after that first fruitless visit, I was ready to throw in both the towel and Akbar's suit, follow Duff's lead, and go back to Connecticut. Who was I kidding? Be a big shot in this town? *In your dreams, Bob, in your dreams.* My father was right. I was nothing but a dreamer.

The bartender asked what I was going to do now. With my head hanging over my drink, I said my plan at this point was to get out of Dodge and go back home. As I said this, the thought occurred to me that I had barely enough money for a bus ticket home, let alone more drinks. Well, maybe enough for a bus ticket and two drinks. No more than two, though, or I'd be thumbing my way to Connecticut.

"Here," he said as he poured a second drink. "This one's on the house." I nodded my thanks. He looked at me again, and said, "You know, you don't look like the type of guy who gives up easy."

Ouch. That one hurt.

With my on-the-house drink gone I ordered a third, then a fourth. I'd come here for confidence enhancement, but instead I was just brooding worse than ever. So this guy thought I was a quitter? I called him over, leaned across the bar until I was within six inches of his big Mick face, and told him that I may have been a liar, a scumbag, and even a pimp, but I was no quitter.

"Look, man," I said. "I grew up in a hellhole. My old man abused me and my mother was too drunk to care. I had to get by every day using my head and sometimes my hands. So please don't call me a quitter," I said.

He was as unruffled as any weathered bartender. "I didn't call you a quitter, son," he replied. "I said you don't *look* like the type to quit. Big difference."

He had a point. That was what he'd said, all right—but I'd read it as him calling me a quitter. Why was I taking what was sort of a compliment and turning it into a negative? (And why was I telling him my life story?) I supposed I wasn't used to compliments. I told him I was sorry, and meant it.

He put one more drink down on the bar in front of me. This time I told him, "Thanks, but I'm out of money."

He nodded toward a construction worker down the bar and said, "It's on the hardhat."

I looked down the bar and caught the hardhat's eye, then raised my glass and said, "Thanks." The guy came over and asked if he could join me. My first thought was, *Oh, great, he's gay and about to come on to me.* Sure didn't look gay, but hell, you never knew.

He said his name was George and he'd heard me talking to the bartender. "I came here looking for construction work twenty years ago, but nobody was building back then."

"So why are you still here?" I asked.

"I was all set to leave. Then I prayed, and the Lord told me to stay. Within a week I got work."

Oh, great, not a cruising gay, a Bible thumper—just what I didn't need.

"Well, I don't know anything about God. One thing is for sure, He's not gonna find me any campaign work, not right now," I said, each word dripping with ill-disguised contempt.

"You never know what the Lord's got in mind," said George. "Ever work construction?" I said sure I had, which was bullshit. He asked if I had a union card. I told him I had a Teamsters card from when I worked moving vans in college. That one was actually true.

"Why don't you stop by my site tomorrow? We're building the city subway under Dupont Circle," he said. That was not far from Hartnett Hall, so I said sure. He gave me a card and an address, told me to be there at seven the next morning. I told George I'd be there—but I wanted him to know that if I did get a construction job, I'd leave it the moment a campaign opened up. He said that was no problem.

After George left, I asked the bartender if this guy was for real.

He nodded and said, "George is leaving his job in a month."

Now I was pissed. "Why did he want me to come to work with him if he's about to leave! I had a feeling this was all bullshit."

The barkeep grinned at me and said, "He's leaving his job because he's just been elected to some high-up post in the local carpenters union. And you are one lucky sonofabitch."

The next morning I showed up at the address George had given me, and sure enough, he was there to meet me.

"You look like a strong kid," said George. "I can give you a job as a carpenter's helper. It's ball-breaking work, but the pay's good and you get time and a half after forty hours."

"What's the pay?" I asked.

"Fourteen dollars an hour plus benefits." In the seventies, that was big bucks.

"Thanks, George, I'll take it. Man, was I lucky to run across you in the bar."

"What makes you think it was luck, Bob?"

I asked him what else it could possibly be.

He asked if I'd ever considered that it might be God's work.

"Sorry, George, I don't buy into the God stuff. Anything that comes my way is because of hard work or plain dumb luck. No offense."

"Not offended at all. Someday you may see there's no such thing as coincidences," he said.

"I doubt it, but who knows," I said, trying not to sound smug.

*   *   *

George was right about the work; it was tough. Washington, Maryland, and Virginia were building a regional subway system called the Washington Metro. It was a huge undertaking; when it was completed it would be the nation's second-busiest rapid transit system, after New York City's. Trying to construct a subway underneath an existing city that never planned for one was an enormous and massively expensive endeavor.

Our section was the toughest. We were building tracks right underneath Dupont Circle on the Connecticut Avenue route. This meant putting the tracks several hundred feet underground. When it was completed, the Dupont Circle stop would employ what was then the longest escalator in the world.

My job was to carry ten-foot-long two-by-six-inch boards down ladders to carpenters who were building molds for the concrete walls. It was tiring, physically demanding, cold and dangerous work. Already two guys had fallen and one was paralyzed for life. Suddenly the fourteen bucks an hour didn't seem that big. But it kept me in shape, and I loved the guys I worked with. These were blue-collar workers who made their living with their hands and muscles. I gained an enormous appreciation for them and their union. Contrary to right-wing hype about union workers being lazy, I never saw a harder-working group in my life. They took pride in what they were doing and counted on the union to negotiate a fair wage, health benefits, sick pay, and decent working conditions.

The hard physical labor through those cold winter months was good for me. It kept my head clear and my body strong. At the same time, it also opened up an interesting perspective on the social life of the nation's capital. I became a friend and advocate of the city's population of prostitutes.

*   *   *

Not far from the Dupont Circle Metro project stood an old three-story, brick-and-granite mansion, built back in the late nineteenth century by a wealthy merchant. In its day this mansion was among the largest in Washington. Over the intervening decades it went through a colorful parade of transformations, including a series of different restaurants and nightclubs, some of them less reputable than others. By 1972 it was home to one of the less reputable sort, a cheap place owned by a restaurateur named Joey. At the time, there were a lot of sketchy establishments in that part of town. I'll just call this one "Joey's Place."

Joey didn't much like the restaurant business, but it was good cover for his two other businesses: gambling and prostitution. The restaurant took up the old mansion's second floor. The first floor, which was partially below ground, became a gambling joint, while the third floor was converted into a bordello. The restaurant never received especially good reviews, but the other two businesses were considered among the best in town.

Joey went out of his way to cultivate a police clientele, particularly with members of the city's vice squad. The cops got free food and drinks and each Friday an envelope from Joey, which contained a cash contribution for the Police Widows and Orphans Fund. How many widows and orphans actually received any of this money is anyone's guess, but the contributions clearly paid off for Joey. Despite a city-wide crackdown on gambling and prostitution in the early seventies, Joey's two main businesses were allowed to operate without police interference.

For the guys on our construction crew, the Joey's Place bar became a popular after-work stop. Most of these guys were married, and they would spend an hour drinking and then head home to their old ladies. For a bachelor like me, Joey's Place was a paradise, and soon I was going up there for breakfast, lunch, and dinner. I had a designated seat at the bar, I played cards with the cops in the basement, and I became friends with some of the best call girls in town. I spent so much time there that Joey eventually rented me a room on the third floor, though far enough away from the girls that I wouldn't scare the johns. Which was important, because most of the girls' clients were important people who had a distinct interest in no one knowing their private business. It was impossible for me not to notice some of these guys, since a number of them were high-profile politicians.

My third-floor room notwithstanding, it soon became clear that I needed an actual place of residence that afforded me a little more privacy than Hartnett Hall and was close to my new social hub. It's a little awkward to invite your date home when you live at a whorehouse. So after a few weeks, I gave up my room at Hartnett Hall and found myself a little apartment near Joey's Place.

I use the word "dates" advisedly. I didn't have a girlfriend. Like most survivors, I generally avoided any relationship that hinted at commitment—other than to booze. I'd had a relationship with a girl during my college years that did not end well, and I wasn't interested in repeating the experience.

However, I did grow quite close to the girls who worked the third floor at Joey's Place. I was never a customer, although on occasion I was given free advice on the finer points of sex. Mostly they treated me like a kid brother. Late at night, between tricks, the girls would sometimes wander into my room for a smoke and to talk about life. For the most part, they were good people.

Having become friends with many of them, there were times when I felt drawn to protect them. I regarded them as human beings and was not the least bit judgmental about their profession. I didn't like it when people at the bar made fun of them, and I never hesitated to let my feelings be known. Several brawls followed my defense of hookers. In a strange way it felt gallant to defend the ladies' reputations. Whether it was my classmates picking on weaker kids, or self-important patrons treating these prostitutes like their inferiors, I never had much patience for people who looked down on others. In the years ahead I would find myself constantly defending people who were looked upon with disdain by Washington society.

The sex business fascinated me. It was adventuresome and seedy at the same time. Although I did not patronize the third floor at Joey's Place as a customer, over the years in Washington I did have occasion to frequent many other sex services. I liked the edge to it, and I also liked the fact that it was just business: When you were finished, it was over. No emotions, no hurt feelings, no desire to get attached. Just like politics. It all came down to one day or one hour, and when it was over you moved on. As a survivor, I could come to the defense of the girls' virtue on the one hand, but have no hesitation in using their services on the other. This may seem like total hypocrisy, but I didn't see it that way at the time. Survivors have sympathy for anyone who is being attacked, verbally or physically. They also don't trust relationships. Being with prostitutes was one sure way of staying unattached.

And I felt no guilt being around the business. The girls made good money, they were young, and they were all convinced they would be out of the business and on to a better life within a few years' time. In that, they were dead wrong, but back then what did I know?

In later years my attitude toward the sex industry changed. I now know the sex business well enough to know that prostitution is not a victimless crime. The number of women in the business who are physically abused by customers is large and growing. The percentage of prostitutes with drug habits is huge, and the number of unwanted pregnancies and abandoned children is staggering. In recent years I've engaged in a great deal of nonprofit work for prostitution causes and have become deeply involved in countering the horrific problem of human trafficking.

Having said that, it would be disingenuous not to acknowledge that I *do* carry with me the hypocrisy of having patronized massage parlors and call girls myself in the past, so I'm not exactly clean hands in all this. Maybe that's part of it—that I feel a need to atone for using those services as much as I did.

*   *   *

A few weeks into the job I was backing out of a supply area carrying a long two-by-four. I ran into a couple who were walking on a restricted area of a sidewalk. He was dressed in a three-piece suit with a Nixon pin on his lapel. She looked like someone straight out of the Junior League.

Even though they shouldn't have been there, I immediately apologized and asked if they were all right.

The guy said, "Watch where you're going, you dumb-ass."

"Hey, I said I was sorry," I retorted, my voice rising with each word, "—and watch who you call a dumb-ass." The guy took one look at me and decided it was probably in his best interests to let it go and move on. Good judgment on his part. Except that as he was walking away, he made one dumb mistake—and a dangerous one, as it turned out: He tried to get in the last word.

"Trailer-park trash," I heard him mutter to his lady friend.

I was on him in three strides.

Before the other guys could stop me I smashed his face with a forearm. I heard the cartilage in his nose crack. The guy went down fast and was almost out, but I jumped on him anyway and whaled away with my fists. Suddenly this guy was every asshole who'd ever made fun of me as a kid. He was my old man, and now I was big enough to fight back. He was my mother, with her slurred words and unkempt hair. He was the state police who took my favorite uncle away. I was completely out of control, venom pouring out of me like magma from a volcano.

By the time three other workers got me off him and pinned to the ground, the guy was a mess, the girl was screaming, and a growing crowd of bystanders was looking at me like I was an uncaged animal. Then I heard the sirens. Two cop cars screeched to a stop next to the sidewalk. They looked at the bloodied guy lying there unconscious and asked us who did it. My buddies quickly let go of my arms, but it didn't take the cops long to figure out that I was the one—because the moment my friends let go of me I jumped back on the guy and started whaling on him again.

I felt an explosion on the side of my head. Then another on my back. I tried to get up, but the world went dark.

I woke up an unknown length of time later in a hospital emergency room. As I cracked open my eyes, the first person I saw was George talking to a bunch of cops, including a sergeant who looked none too happy about it all. The first words out of my mouth were, "Where's the asshole who called me a dumb-ass?"

George hustled over to my side and told me to shut up. In a hushed voice, he told me the guy was in surgery and in bad shape.

The sergeant came over to me and said, "Listen, I know the other guy started this thing, but why did you have to beat him so bad? That man may die," he said.

Die? He had to be kidding.

"And if he does," the sergeant continued, "we're arresting you for manslaughter." His words hit me like a slap across the face. This was serious.

The room started spinning. I reached out for George. He called a nurse, who called for restraints. "No, please don't restrain me," I pleaded. "I beg you, don't—" Too late. I felt the straps go around my arms, legs, and belly.

I couldn't move or breathe. I was terrified. I kept struggling to break free from the hospital straps, and I was making progress, too, until I felt a needle explode in my arm. In a matter of seconds I was out cold.

That night I dreamed I was killing my father.
I was putting his head down in the tub. The tub was full of water.
He fought it, but I was a grown man now and too strong for him.
I felt the life seep out of him, felt him go limp. I wasn't sad about what I was doing. I felt happy. I was free.
I turned to walk away. I heard water sloshing.
I turned around.
My father was lurching forward, coming at me—

I came to in a panic, feeling groggy and disoriented. I recognized George. We could hear the sergeant in the hall talking to someone else. His eyes on the cop, George came over to my bed, leaned down close to me, and spoke in a hoarse whisper.

"The boys at the site found the pen knife the guy used to try to stab you," he whispered.

"What pen knife?" I asked, too loud.

"*Shh!* Just remember," he whispered again, more softly but at the same time more emphatically. "He had a pen knife. He was aiming it at your eyes. You panicked and hit him. You got it?" he said.

Oh yeah, I got it.

The sergeant came into my emergency cubicle and glanced at George suspiciously before turning his attention to me. "Doctor says the guy's gonna make it. He's one lucky sonofabitch," he said. "And so are you. Now what's with this pen knife?"

"The guy had it in his hand when I turned around after I bumped him," I said. "I told him I was sorry. Next thing I know he's pointing the pen knife at my eye and coming at me. Ask the guys at the site."

"We already did," said the cop, glancing again directly at George as he spoke. "They all have the same story. Exactly the same story, word for word. The girl can't remember anything. She's in shock. We spoke to people in the crowd. No one saw the fight start."

He turned back to me. "So I guess it's self-defense. But listen, that degree of force wasn't called for. You better get control of that temper of yours, son, or you're going to kill someone or someone's going to kill you. Got it?" he said.

"Got it," I said, as a wave of relief swept through me from my toes up through my spine and clear to my scalp. The cop must be right. I must have been one lucky sonofabitch. Here was the thing, though: I thought I'd started a whole new life. But no matter what it said on my résumé (and more important, what it didn't say), I was still carrying my old life around inside my head. I needed to up my game, keep that childhood rage in check, get that mask on tighter. For a survivor that should be no problem.

I hadn't killed the guy. I wasn't going to prison. Now all I had to do was keep my head down and stay out of trouble.

CHAPTER FOUR

Campaign Years

Over the long months of lugging cold lumber by day and frolicking by night I never for a moment lost sight of the reason I'd come to Washington in the first place. I kept up with politics each day by reading the *Washington Post* and the *New York Times*, and I never missed what was then the only political talk show on television, *Martin Agronsky: Evening Edition*, which aired on our local PBS station. (A few years later the show went national as *Agronsky & Co.*) My gay friend, Gary, who had been so good to me that first day on the Hill, kept me current on Hill business and gossip. Every now and then he took me to lunch and introduced me to various players.

As much fun as I was having, though, I still hadn't made any progress on my political career. My Metro construction job came to an end in the middle of '73. I kicked around at a few other menial jobs to pay the bills. I kept my spirits up by remembering that the political season wasn't far off. When it came, I was determined to be a part of it.

One day that fall I finally got my chance when the phone rang in my little apartment. "Bob?" said the voice on the other end. "It's Doug."

When I first arrived in Washington in November 1972, Doug Bennet, Jr., was the only person I knew there. Son of the guy who'd gotten me the job with the Hilsman campaign that spring, Doug had served as a speechwriter for Hubert Humphrey and was then chief of staff to Abe Ribicoff, the senator from Connecticut. Although Doug and I had grown up in the same town, he was several years older and our paths hadn't crossed so far. Soon after I arrived in town I went to see him, hoping he could help me find something to do for a living there.

I liked Doug the moment I met him. He didn't have the arrogance typical of so many top staffers on the Hill. He did his best to find me something, but there wasn't much around at that point. We stayed in touch, had lunch together occasionally, and he'd talk about maybe taking a run at the congressional seat that Hilsman had tried for, if it ever opened up.

In the fall of '73 Bob Steele, the incumbent U.S. House member from that district, announced that he was running for governor. House members in Connecticut typically didn't leave their seats without an assist from the undertaker, so when the Second District opened up, a lot of people showed interest. One of them was Doug.

When Doug called to tell me he was probably going to run, I assumed the call was to let me know that one of my few Washington contacts was leaving. Then came the words I'd been waiting to hear for a year. For that matter, ever since I was twelve.

"So," said Doug, "how about coming with me to do the campaign?"

"I'm packed!" I said in a near scream. "Let's do it!" Finally I was getting a shot, and I was more than ready. We threw together everything we had and drove to Connecticut. Good-bye to D.C. for now.

We ran the campaign out of Doug's house. He was the candidate, I was the campaign manager, and that was about it. You could call it a shoestring campaign. It certainly was that; maybe more like a few threads of a shoestring.

Connecticut went by a caucus system, so instead of holding a primary we would go to a convention to pick the district's nominee. Which meant we were dealing with delegates from each of the sixty-four towns represented in our district, from Andover to Woodstock—and Bennet had to go around to talk with each of those sixty-four delegates individually. As campaign manager, I had to set up all these schedules myself and found myself with a huge range of responsibilities to learn and manage on my own. It was an incredible learning curve.

A big problem we faced was that Chris Dodd had also decided to enter the race. The Dodd family roots ran deep in the Second District and the Dodd name carried a lot of weight. Tom Dodd, Chris's father, had been the senator from Connecticut for more than a decade, until he got into trouble for a campaign fund scandal.

As if that weren't enough, we also had Jack Bailey to deal with. Jack's father, John Bailey, was another major figure in Connecticut politics, chairman of the Connecticut Democratic Party and then chairman of the National Democratic Campaign Committee. Bailey (yes, the same Bailey who had wangled that promise from John Kennedy for a late 1960 campaign stop in Connecticut) was a strong-arm guy and had a lock on everything. And now his son Jack decided to get in the race, too. With three candidates in the running, Doug and I didn't really have a chance. But we became very close, and I learned a lot about the whole process.

The final result was pretty close, but the Dodd name was just too powerful.

The Bennet campaign was technically my second campaign, but it was the first one in which I played a serious role. Doug was one of the smartest and most decent men I'd met in politics. He was one of that rare breed in Washington who was totally loyal and honest. And people in Washington loved him, which would soon prove an invaluable connection.

*   *   *

After Doug lost that spring I was closing down the campaign office when I was surprised by a visit from Anne Canby, who was heading up a campaign consultancy project for a powerful Washington group called the National Committee for an Effective Congress (NCEC). NCEC was a bipartisan liberal group that supported progressive Democrats and Republicans with five-thousand-dollar contributions. (Yes, Virginia, there were at one time a large number of progressive Republicans in this great country of ours.) Founded by Eleanor Roosevelt in 1948, it was one of the oldest political action committees in the nation.

In the course of the nomination fight NCEC had endorsed Bennet. In 1974 NCEC decided to give both cash contributions and in-kind contributions of political consultants to the candidates they endorsed. Back then there were not the thousands of political consultants there are today, and because of that the few there were tended to be big names in the business. Having one of them giving advice to a campaign for free was a very big deal.

NCEC had sent Bob Squier, a Democratic media consultant, and Peter Hart, a highly respected pollster, to give advice to our campaign. Squier was considered the best media consultant in the country at the time and was a legend by the time he met an untimely death from colon cancer in 2000. Hart is still a legend today, with hundreds of successful campaigns under his belt. Peter is today the leading Democratic pollster for the *Wall Street Journal* and NBC News, among other positions.

To a new political consultant like me, working alongside the likes of Squier and Hart was a dream come true. These guys were already heroes to me. Although they stayed only a few days, since NCEC was giving consulting help to dozens of campaigns across the country, I soaked up every bit of campaign advice they gave us.

At first I assumed Anne must be coming by to offer condolences for our losing the race, which seemed like an unusual gesture. Once we sat down to talk I learned the actual reason for her visit. To my absolute astonishment she was there to ask if I wanted to become one of NCEC's consultant corps. Evidently I had come highly recommended by Squier and Hart and a group of wealthy contributors to both the Bennet campaign and NCEC.

I was so shocked I literally could not speak.

Since I was sitting mute in my chair, Anne kept talking. NCEC's consulting group was working with so many campaigns, she explained, that they'd become overextended. If I was interested in the position, she wanted to warn me that I would have to cover campaigns in several states, and would be on the road for a good six months.

Did I need a few days to think it over?

That last was when I found my voice again. In fact, I nearly laughed out loud. A few *days*? Hell, I didn't need a few *seconds*. I jumped out of my chair, hugged her, and told her I was ready to leave the next morning. Talk about drawing to an inside straight! I couldn't remember ever having been this happy.

*   *   *

In the spring of 1974 I hit the road for the first time as a professional political campaign consultant. Over the course of the following year I covered ten states and twenty-one campaigns for NCEC as the new kid on the team. The barroom brawls were far from over. (After all, somewhere out there was a .45 with my name on it, waiting for Inauguration Day 2001.) But in this campaign work I'd found a place where I could duke it out with my wits and my survival skills, rather than my brawn and fists. This was politics, the noble and the down and dirty, and I loved it from the start.

Many of these campaigns were long shots, and some were *long* long shots. But the tide of history was on my side: This was the year the crescendo of Watergate reached its climax. President Nixon was forced to resign that August, the first president in our nation's history to do so, replaced by his sitting vice president, Gerald Ford, who had taken office when Nixon's first vice president, Spiro Agnew, resigned to plead *nolo contendere* to criminal charges for taking construction kickbacks as governor of Maryland. Talk about a government—and a political party—plagued by scandal at the top.

Yet even the president's resignation didn't stem the tide of public outcry. After Nixon stepped down the calls for him to be indicted for his many Watergate crimes grew only more strident every week. Then, on September 8, one month after stepping into the Oval Office and just two months before the 1974 elections, Vice President Ford shocked the nation by granting Nixon a full pardon, meaning he could never be tried for anything related to Watergate.

Jerry Ford was a low-key, thoughtful, decent man and was well liked by Democrats as well as Republicans. Nevertheless voters, especially Democrats and independents, were outraged with him for pardoning Nixon, and with the Republican Party in general for the Watergate scandal and everything it represented, and that November they went to the polls in huge numbers to express that outrage. The result was a landslide for Democrats running for Congress. A total of forty-nine freshmen were elected to the House that year. Known as "the Watergate babies," this new generation of Democratic congressmen included such now-familiar names as Henry Waxman, Pat Leahy, and Tom Harkin. The Democrats now controlled both the House and Senate by good margins.

What a fantastic time to be in politics!

Among my campaigns, I had Max Baucus in Montana, a Democrat running in a tough state. Max won, was reelected two years later, then went on to run for the Senate, where he served for six terms. (I did Max's Senate race in '78 as well.) Today he is U.S. ambassador to China.

I had Toby Moffett in Connecticut, who won the Sixth District seat that year and held it till '82, when he ran for the Senate but lost to Lowell Weicker.

Then there was Tom Downey, who was running for New York's Second District on Long Island, which was a *very* long shot because Long Island is strongly Republican. We won that race and Downey, at age twenty-five, became the youngest member of Congress that year. Tom went on to serve nine terms.

In the South, I had Steve Neal in North Carolina. Steve was running in a tough district, Winston-Salem, in the north central part of the state. We won that one in a surprise upset against the incumbent, a popular former Pittsburgh Pirate pitcher. Steve served ten terms in Congress. (Take *that*, North Carolina!)

I also had Leon Panetta. Leon started out in his political career as a Republican who served in the Nixon administration, but quit in 1970 on philosophical grounds and switched the following year to the Democratic Party. In 1976 he decided to run for Congress in California's Sixteenth District. We won that race, too, and he served ten terms before going on to become director of OMB, White House chief of staff, CIA director, and secretary of defense—an unbelievably prestigious career. Leon is a very funny guy and I loved working with him; we've remained good friends ever since.

One district I was given that was an especially gratifying race was the Seventh Congressional District of Pennsylvania, which had been Republican-dominated continuously since the Civil War, with Democrats interrupting that winning streak only twice, for a two-year term during the Gilded Age and another two-year term during the Great Depression. At this point, the district had not elected a Democrat in thirty-six years.

The Democratic candidate was a low-profile Methodist minister named Bob Edgar, who had never before run for any office in his life. Bob was particularly incensed by the spectacle of Watergate, and when no establishment Democrat stepped forward to claim the nomination, Bob threw his hat in the ring. Voter registration in the district was three-to-one in favor of Republicans, and the GOP had plenty of money. Bob had zero name recognition and no money. With nothing much going for him other than a passionate group of anti-Nixon volunteers, Edgar was given virtually no chance of winning.

In our first phone call I said, "Bob, can you gather up whatever volunteer base you have, so I can meet them?" When I got to the meeting the place was overflowing with people, a combination of antiwar groups, anti-Nixon groups, and his own parishioners, a mixed bag to say the least. But they formed a powerful volunteer force, and there's nothing quite as strong as a mass of people united by a deeply held conviction and a passion to overturn the status quo.

The result? On Election Day, Bob Edgar took the U.S. House seat by a wide majority of votes—and a previously unknown Democratic consultant named Bob Beckel became the talk of the political establishment.

Since NCEC had given me only House races, and those seats were mostly the long shots that hadn't been considered very likely to win, I had hit the jackpot. Of the twenty-one House seats I consulted to, nineteen won their elections.

Here I want to make sure I clarify something: When I say "I won" these races, it was the candidates and the consulting group that won them; I was simply one of this group. Although I'll admit, I did have a lot of the really long shots. Also it just so happened that the most experienced consultants in the group, Squier and Hart and the others, didn't particularly want to emphasize their own involvement; they were doing this work for NCEC essentially pro bono, and they didn't want their big-money-paying corporate clients to think they were running around working somewhere for free. So I probably got far more credit for the successes of the NCEC group than I deserved.

I was happy to take it.

After the incredibly successful campaign season of '74 I received a lot of calls to help with campaigns for the '76 elections, and these I did on my own, and not as part of NCEC. I did nine races during the '76 campaign season, many of them for candidates I had worked for in '74. Out of my nine races, I lost only one.

There was no denying it: I was on a roll. The '76 campaign record more or less sealed my reputation and created what would be my career for the next decade.

Over the years I have covered nearly a hundred campaigns. Some I've won, some I've lost. Some I was prouder of than others. I've come to think of them in three broad categories: the good, the bad, and the downright ugly. Later on in this narrative we'll come to the ugly; for now, let's pause to walk through an example of the good and one of the bad.

You'll be able to guess which is which.

*   *   *

Nineteen seventy-five was an off-year election, a time when most political consultants don't normally get much work. I didn't expect to get much campaign business that year, if any. Until I received a call from the county judge of Jefferson County, Kentucky, one of the few states that hold off-year elections.

Jefferson County, the state's largest, was dominated by Louisville, the state's largest city. The man calling me introduced himself as Todd Hollenbach, Sr. (not to be confused with his son, Todd, also a Kentucky politician), and said he was calling to ask me to come to Kentucky to interview about a consulting job in his run for lieutenant governor. He said he'd heard about my accomplishments the previous year.

After checking in with some sources in Kentucky, I learned that Hollenbach was an excellent campaigner and the likely front runner for the lieutenant governor's seat. Even better, Kentucky was one of the very few states in the nation that elect governors for only one four-year term. Historically, the lieutenant governor would automatically become the prohibitive favorite for the governorship the next time around, which made the lieutenant governor's seat a prize especially well worth winning.

What I did not learn in my research was what a willful guy Todd was.

I flew to Kentucky to meet with Todd in his office in Louisville. The first thing that struck me was what a remarkably handsome figure he presented. He had a full head of sandy blond hair and the most amazing blue eyes I'd ever seen. He had an engaging grin, a firm handshake, and when he spoke he looked you straight in the eye. I immediately liked the man. How could you not?

In Kentucky county judges (today they are called county executives) were very powerful politically. They controlled large budgets, provided police and fire services to all but the largest cities in the county, and, in Hollenbach's case, had hundreds of employees. Most important, they controlled federal grants to any jurisdiction in the county.

In the year before our meeting Todd had been on a roll. He successfully dealt with devastating floods in the county and also with an enormous methane fire that threatened the health of county residents as well as several neighborhoods near the garbage dumps where the methane fire had originated. Hollenbach received favorable press, both locally and statewide, for his performance throughout these crises.

This was also a time when the federal government had released millions of dollars to jurisdictions around the country for new water and sewer lines. Jefferson County received very large grants—and the purse strings were controlled by Todd Hollenbach. Which of course meant that he controlled the awarding of contracts to build this new infrastructure.

The longer we talked, the more impressed with him I became. I understood now why he was the strong front runner for the Democratic nomination for lieutenant governor. The current governor was Julian Carroll, who had been lieutenant governor under Governor Wendell Ford—until Ford vacated the governor's office halfway through his term to become a United States senator. This elevated Carroll to the top job and left the lieutenant governor's office vacant. Which meant whomever the Democrats nominated for lieutenant governor would have no incumbent to face. In Kentucky in the seventies, the Democratic nominee was heavily favored to win a general election, so the Democratic nomination was tantamount to being elected.

One of the first things I do with candidates who want to work with me is take them out to walk on the street, just to say hi to voters. It helps me judge whether they look phony or they look real. I asked Todd if we could go out onto the streets of Louisville, just to see how he interacted with the voters. He said, "Fine," and we went out for about an hour. This guy was one of the best street politicians I'd ever seen. He was a natural. *Everybody* liked this guy, and he gave every person he talked with the impression that they were the only ones in the world to him in that moment, much like Bill Clinton.

When we got back I told him I was impressed and would like to make a bid for the job. "That won't be necessary," he replied. "The job is yours if you want it."

Yes, I said, I definitely wanted it, but before we finalized anything I had to ask him something.

"Todd," I said, "I've got to ask you the obvious question I ask every candidate I work with: Is there anything I need to know?" In other words, were there any skeletons in his closet? "I've done some background work on you, and I understand that you come from a very wealthy family, you've done a magnificent job dealing with these methane fires here, and you've got a good reputation around the state.

"Except," I added, "there seems to be somewhat of a woman problem."

Todd nodded and said that, yeah, they'd tried to use that against him when he ran for county judge, and that he'd tell me now the same thing he told them then. "Bob," he said, "the only way I'm gonna lose this thing is if they find me with a dead woman, or a live boy." Quite a sense of humor, His Honor had.

"What about other women?" I repeated. He acknowledged that, yes, there'd been some, but they were not going to say anything. I'd heard that before. How sure was he? Very, he said. And he'd be careful.

"Well, you've got to be," I said, "because here in Louisville is one thing, but when you get out in the rest of Kentucky you're out in the Bible Belt here, so you've got to be *really* careful."

He reassured me again, and I said okay, though it still worried me a bit.

That was when he hit me with the blockbuster.

As we shook hands he looked me square in the eye and said, "Bob, there's been a change of plans. I've decided to run for governor."

You could have knocked me over with a pint of cheap Kentucky bourbon.

This made no sense to me. With no incumbent lieutenant governor to run against, Todd had a solid path to that seat. And since Kentucky's governorship was limited to a single four-year term, once Hollenbach was lieutenant governor his boss's seat would automatically open up in the following election. So why make this much riskier bid now?

I said, "Nobody in my memory has ever challenged a sitting Kentucky governor." This, of course, was mainly because Kentucky governors had only one term. In this case, though, since Carroll was currently finishing out Wendell Ford's term, he would now be running for his own full four-year term, so Todd was technically correct: He could challenge Carroll for the governor's seat. But could he win?

No matter: His mind was made up. He wanted to be governor, and he didn't want to wait years to do it. So I moved down to Kentucky and we started setting up our campaign.

Our most immediate problem was that nobody wanted to give Hollenbach money. Or to say that more accurately, it wasn't that they didn't want to give him money, but they didn't want to be on record as giving him money—because the governor went through the list of contributors very carefully, and nobody wanted to be on the other side of the governor.

A friend of Todd's gave us four rooms in a cheap motel he owned to use as our headquarters.

Family money was enough to get us kick-started. But right away we had serious cash needs.

One day I went into Hollenbach's office and he handed me an envelope. I looked inside and saw that there was about two thousand in hundred-dollar bills inside.

Just the year before, the federal government had approved billions of dollars in infrastructure repairs around the country, and Jefferson County got a huge amount of money for projects like new oil, gas, and water pipes. Hollenbach had been the one to distribute those jobs to the contractors, so he had a lot of guys who owed him in a big way. My guess was, the judge had paid a visit to some of his contractor friends.

I used the cash to pay the staff.

Meanwhile, I was getting an education in Kentucky politics. One of the first things I did was travel to Lexington to pay a courtesy call on former Kentucky governor Happy Chandler, who had also served as commissioner of baseball and was now retired and in his seventies. I loved baseball; I loved politics; Chandler was a living legend of both worlds. And I'd heard he was a serious drinker. Obviously, a guy I had to meet.

I got to his southern plantation-style mansion in Lexington at about ten in the morning, and there he was, sitting out on his big front porch, already well into a bottle of Maker's Mark.

He said, "You drink, son?"

I said, "Yeah, a little."

So he and I sat down together and proceeded to get loaded together.

In the course of our conversation I asked him, "Governor, why is it the state legislature in Kentucky only meets for sixty days every two years?"

He said, "Son, if it were up to me, they'd meet for two days every sixty years."

A little later on I asked, "Governor, tell me this. Why is only one term allowed for governor in this state?"

He said, "Son, if you can't make fifteen or twenty million bucks in four years as governor of this state, you don't deserve to be governor."

Chandler was an incredibly colorful character and we hit it off famously. I didn't ask him for anything; I wasn't there for an endorsement (which I wouldn't have gotten anyway) or anything else. But I did get something from him: a serious education in how politics works in Kentucky. As I was getting up (finally) to leave, he said, "Bob, you know, Carroll's just going to smother your guy. You have no idea how much power the governor's got. I know. I used it."

I believed him.

One day I went with Todd out to eastern Kentucky, to coal mine territory, and Todd decided to go down one of those long mine shafts, where you have to lie down on your back on a railroad car as you're shuttled down into the shaft.

"There's no way I'm going down that thing," I said. "I guarantee you that."

He told me to wait up there for him while he went down. He climbed onto the railroad car and disappeared from view. As I stood around waiting, there was an old, rangy miner leaning against a tree who kept staring at me. Here I was, in my three-piece suit. Not exactly fitting in out there in coal mine country. I decided the best defense was a good offense. I went up to him and said, "Sir, you want to tell me what the things are that disturb folks here? What are the issues that concern you up here in the mountains?"

He looked at me and said, "What'd you say, honey?"

"What are the issues?" I repeated. "Is it education? Is it roads?"

He said, "Honey, where you from?"

"Well," I said, "I'm from Washington, D.C."

He said, "Well that figures. Lemme explain something to you, all you need to know about politics up here in the mountains."

I said, "Yes, sir."

He said, "Up here, if you can't drink it, drive it, fight it, or fuck it, it don't exist."

This eloquent disquisition was one of the best lessons on Kentucky politics I got the whole time I was there.

*   *   *

As the May primary got closer, we started really suffering for money. I had an idea: We would put on a huge oldies-but-goodies concert in a big auditorium in Louisville. We'd get Fats Domino and a whole list of old Motown guys. The auditorium held about thirty thousand people. I figured at ten or fifteen dollars a head, that's a lot of tickets to sell, but we could take it in cash, and that would take care of all our worries about campaign funding.

When I told Hollenbach my thoughts, he said, "Brilliant idea."

We were able to sell maybe five thousand tickets to our supporters, but the rest had to come from the general public. We got busy advertising for the concert. But something strange happened: Even with as good a lineup as we had, and it was excellent, ticket sales were slow.

It didn't take long to figure out why. A good part of the ticket sales you expect for an event like this comes from businesses, who buy them in lots and then give them out to their employees. Some of Carroll's supporters had made it very clear they didn't want any Kentucky businesses buying tickets to our concert. And they weren't shy about it. When they wanted to intimidate you, they intimidated you. The night of the concert, the state police set up roadblocks a mile away. I must have been stopped by the Kentucky state police at least fifteen times while I was down there. I had the tires on my car slashed. These boys play rough, particularly when it's the governorship at stake.

Happy Chandler was absolutely right: A Kentucky governor is very powerful, one of the most powerful governorships in the country. And Carroll used all the power at his disposal to make Todd's life as a candidate unbearable.

We ended up selling enough tickets to fill the auditorium about halfway. Not what we'd hoped for. I went back to Todd and said, "Judge, we're going to have to hit those contractors again." We made another round and pulled together enough cash to last us through to the end of the campaign.

Since we had to conserve what little money we had and couldn't pay for major advertising, we decided to put Todd in a small mobile-home-type van and send him off with a few aides to travel around the state to do meet-and-greets and mingle with people, because he was so good at that. Before long I started getting reports from one of the aides that every night he would go over to check on the judge, and that van would be rocking, back and forth, back and forth, back and forth.

"Bob," he said nervously, "we didn't want to go in there . . . but we had the sense that Todd had some company."

I'll bet he did. My guess is Todd screwed his way all across Kentucky. A monumental undertaking on his part, but he could have pulled it off. He was one of those guys who was a total magnet to women. He didn't even have to ask, it was just all there; the only question was, "Who do you want to pick?"

Something did start to leak about the womanizing, and we had some bad press. But in the end it didn't matter. We didn't have a chance. We shouldn't have been in that race to start with. Hollenbach was such a good candidate that he could have won the lieutenant governor's seat easily, and then four years later made his run for governor, and he would have gotten in almost automatically. But he was just too impatient.

The final tally at the end of the May primary was pretty miserable. Carroll took 264,136 votes, Hollenbach 113,590. In other words, we got beaten by a margin of better than two to one.

It was a terrible campaign all the way around. It was the wrong seat to run for, the money situation was terrible, the opposition's tactics were downright brutal, and we got crushed. Nothing about it worked out well.

Soon after the campaign was over, Todd and Mrs. Hollenbach got divorced.

*   *   *

That was one of the bad campaigns. Now let me take a short detour ahead to the 1980s to tell you about one of the good ones: Ike Andrews's last congressional run in 1982.

Ike Andrews had represented North Carolina's First Congressional District, which includes most of the area known as the Triangle—Raleigh, Durham, and Chapel Hill—for a decade. Ike's politics tended toward moderate, but it was tough to pin a political label on him. He was very conservative on military issues—he was a veteran and proud of it—but when it came to government's responsibility for helping the poor and downtrodden, he was a Roosevelt liberal.

Ike was not an ambitious man, unlike so many of his House colleagues. He never wanted to be governor or senator. In the House, he didn't make waves. He never sought out the Washington press corps' attention, and never got it, which was fine with Ike.

Ike was quick on his feet, never looked for confrontation, and was a great people pleaser. He was also quick to say yes to damn near any request. The problem was that he sometimes couldn't deliver, which got him in trouble a few times. People would get mad...but never for long. Ike had a survivor's unique ability to induce people to forgive him. Ike loved his job and his constituents loved him. When it came to constituent service, no one did it better. He loved to write handwritten notes. Birthdays, anniversaries, athletic awards, graduations, marriages, births, deaths, dead pets, you name it: Ike would have his pen handy. Since I'd been hired to do the media for Ike's campaign, I traveled across his district to get a feel for the place, and when I did I was amazed to see how many of those letters had been framed and proudly hung on living room walls.

Ike Andrews had just one problem: He was an alcoholic.

Not all alcoholics are alike. Some are binge drinkers who don't drink for four or five days at a time and then go on a binge that may last for weeks. Some alcoholics drink only at night; they are usually the hardest to convince that they have a problem. There are those who drink morning till night; they usually don't have to be told they have a drinking problem.

Morning-to-night drinkers tend to be maintenance drinkers. They need a certain blood alcohol level to function. They are the hardest type of alcoholic for the nonalcoholic to detect. Because they maintain a blood alcohol level at all times, they tend not to change their behavior patterns. Most of these drunks pose no real problem for their campaigns or, if elected, for their service. In fact, there are several active alcoholics of this type sitting in Congress right now.

Binge drinkers, on the other hand, almost always undergo a personality transplant when they drink. Sober, they can be the sweetest, kindest people you can imagine. On a binge they became the devil incarnate. Not surprisingly, they can be deadly to a campaign. Smart campaign managers can usually predict when a binge is coming and pull their candidate off the road to avoid disaster. If they miss the signs, all hell breaks loose.

I've had my fair share of alcoholic candidates. Being an active alcoholic is never a good thing in politics, but give me a morning-to-night drinker over a binge drinker any day.

Ike was a binge drinker. From what I'd been told, a bad one.

When Ike hired me he had been sober for just over a year. He attended Alcoholics Anonymous meetings and, like many recovering alcoholics in their first year of sobriety, he was relieved, happy, and proud of his recovery. In AA they call this experience a "pink cloud." It's a great feeling. (My father went through his pink cloud in 1964, and several years after Ike's campaign I would experience my own that would last nearly two years.) The problem is, pink clouds eventually go away, and then the alcoholic is faced with the reality of living without his booze crutch.

Ike had come from a long line of drunks. Most alcoholics do. A child of an alcoholic learns many ways to survive. One is to avoid dwelling in the moment and focus on the next move. That's why Ike Andrews was such a good politician: He would stay a step ahead of his opponent. However, as they stress in AA, recovering alcoholics need to live recovery a day at a time, which flies in the face of that constant three-steps-ahead approach to life. Ike couldn't have it both ways, and because of that he was a disaster waiting to happen.

Ike's opponent that year, Bill Cobey, was typical of the new breed of right-wing Republicans in the South. They worshipped Ronald Reagan and were supported by Reverend Pat Robertson's Christian Coalition, a formidable grassroots fundamentalist church–based organization. The Christian Coalition was particularly strong in the southern Bible Belt that included part of Ike's district.

Like many southern small cities, Raleigh was growing rapidly. Tobacco farms were giving way to sprawling suburbs, filled with young transplants from the North. The politics of these new voters were heavily conservative. In the years ahead they would help turn most of the Old Confederacy states, once overwhelmingly Democratic, into a solid Republican base. In the early eighties, though, this transformation was still in its infancy, and North Carolina's First Congressional District was still leaning Democratic.

Our first polls had Ike up by twenty-five points, with his opponent virtually unknown. An incumbent with no obvious negatives, an opponent that could be ignored, and a substantial bank account that comes with being an incumbent member of Congress? This was a political consultant's dream.

The strategy in a race like this is fairly simple: Ignore the campaign and play hardworking congressman as long as possible. Avoid debating your opponent until the end of the race, and never, ever mention his name. Increase your press efforts by highlighting accomplishments for the district, and about eight weeks before the election saturate the paid media.

That's the script we followed in Ike's campaign. We concentrated on Ike's positive results for the district and said absolutely nothing about Cobey. Positive TV and radio spots are not hard to do, and I had put most of them in the can before Labor Day. I figured Ike would win by 10 to 15 percent, a big win by any definition.

Our opponent was predictable. He immediately attacked Ike as a big-spending, liberal Washington Democrat who was out of touch with his district. This worked with some conservative voters new to the district, but had little effect on the majority. Attacking a popular incumbent can be dangerous. Voters can get prickly when an unknown attacks a well-regarded politician. By attacking an incumbent whom most voters had supported in past elections, a challenger is saying, in effect, that the voters have made a mistake. Without some clear evidence of that mistake, the voters can turn on the challenger hard.

We polled again in October 1982, about four weeks before the election. Ike was up by a solid 15 percent. "Great," I said.

"I'm in trouble!" said Ike.

This is a peculiar problem with incumbents: They tend to have an irrationally strong belief that *everyone* in their district loves them, except for maybe a few extremists on the other side. Ike had been used to winning by margins larger than 15 percent. We explained to him that the census of 1980 and the redrawing of congressional boundaries that resulted were bound to make his district more competitive. He heard it but probably didn't believe it—another problem associated with incumbents: an inability to accept reality.

Ike grew quite nervous and decided we needed some new commercials.

After sobering up Ike had become a champion of North Carolina's new campaign against drunk drivers. Huge billboards were put up on major roads throughout the state that asked motorists to "Turn in a Drunk" (TID) by calling an 800 number. Ike had gotten federal money for the project and it seemed to work. People would see a car weaving and stop to call the police on the 800 number with a car description and tag number. Most of the drivers turned in were stopped and arrested for drunk driving.

Now Ike wanted an ad that highlighted his involvement in the TID program. We planned out a spot that showed Ike pointing at a TID billboard and taking credit for getting federal dollars for the program. We shot the spot and put it in rotation with the other positive spots on a Friday, eleven days before Election Day. When I got back to D.C. I was exhausted. I had done eleven races that year and I was beat.

At two o'clock the next morning my phone woke me out of a dead sleep. It was Ike's lawyer, Bill Kragen, on the line. He asked if I was sitting down, to which I responded, "No, Bill I'm actually *lying* down. It's two in the morning, and I'm trying to get some sleep."

The next words I heard were a campaign consultant's worst nightmare.

Bill said, "Ike's been arrested."

Arrested? For what?

"For DWI."

It turned out that Ike, who always drove himself the four hours from Washington to his district, was so worried about this race in which he had absolutely nothing to worry about that he had stopped at a liquor store in Virginia and bought two bottles of rum. By the time he hit the North Carolina border he was wasted.

And of course, someone saw him weaving—and called the TID line.

Ike was arrested about two miles from his home. That wasn't all. Police records revealed that, before his year of sobriety, Ike had been arrested four times before for drunk driving.

I snapped awake. The damn billboard ad! I had to get it off the air—a nearly impossible task over a weekend, when programming at TV stations is taken over by computers. I called and tried to ask nicely, then forcefully, then in a full-throated scream. No luck. Couldn't be done. The spot would run until Monday.

When I saw Ike later that day I damn near cried. He was a broken man. Like many survivors, Ike had a great deal of pride in his having overcome enormous obstacles on the road to a successful career. He was a World War II war hero who won a Purple Heart and Bronze Star on the fields of Europe and had a distinguished career in politics. Now he felt utterly humiliated, and for a politician, that is about as bad as it gets.

I had to convince him to cut a new spot apologizing for his actions. He agreed to meet me in a studio early that afternoon. I had written what I thought was a good thirty-second script. Ike, still shaky from his binge, could hardly talk, let alone read a teleprompter. We tried a dozen times, but Ike just couldn't pull it off. Finally I went over to him and said, "Ike, I don't care what you say, forget my words and go with your gut. What would you tell voters if they walked in here right now? Because if you can't do that, you lose."

I'll never forget the look that came into old Ike's eyes.

When political candidates suffer a huge setback like this, they react in one of two ways. Some react by blaming other people and crawling in a hole. They usually lose. Others somehow find the strength to fight back, and approach the fight with ice in their veins. This is especially true for survivors, who learned as children how to be resilient in the face of trouble. Ike's whole demeanor suddenly changed from that of a stooped, frail man into that of a warrior standing tall with fire in his eyes.

He looked back into the camera, no script, and gave the best thirty-second statement I had ever heard from a politician in trouble. He held nothing back. He said he was an alcoholic who by his actions had disgraced his family and his constituents. He explained that alcoholism was a disease he would always have, even if he wasn't drinking. He asked for forgiveness.

When he finished, I was speechless. His blonde-haired, blue-eyed, eight-year-old granddaughter came running up to him, reached up, and hugged him. She clambered up onto his lap—and an idea popped into my head. I asked her mother, Ike's daughter, if I could have the girl say something to the camera while she was sitting on Ike's lap. Ike immediately said no, but his daughter overruled him.

We turned the camera back on. I asked the little girl if she would tell people about her granddad. Without any other prompting than that, she looked straight into the camera and said:

"This is my Poppy Ike. He's the best granddad ever. He never misses my birthdays, and I love him. I know he made a mistake, but when I make mistakes Poppy always forgives me. Won't you all forgive my granddad? He's a good person."

There was not a dry eye in the joint. I immediately told the editor to put it in the lineup to run side by side with Ike's own ad. My cameraman grinned at me and said, "Beckel, you are shameless."

Eleven days later, Ike Andrews won another term as the gentleman from North Carolina's First Congressional District, by 950 votes out of 170,000 cast—a margin of about one-half of 1 percent.

Two years later Ike ran against Cobey again; this time Cobey won, and Ike hung up his spurs at last. But in 1982, Ike got to have his day and serve his people for one more term.

*　　*　　*

Nineteen seventy-four had been a midterm election year, with only members of the House and one-third of the Senate up for election. The 1976 campaign was dominated by the presidential race.

The Republican nominee was most likely to be the incumbent, President Gerald Ford. Although that wasn't necessarily a foregone conclusion. Ford had never run for office outside his own congressional district, and because his pardon of Nixon was perceived as making him vulnerable, he was sure to get stiff competition for the nomination from other Republicans. Former California governor Ronald Reagan gave Ford a serious run for his money, and even by the start of the Republican convention it was still a close contest. Reagan would have been a formidable opponent (as we would find out a few election cycles later), with none of the baggage or vulnerability that crippled Ford. Who knows how the general election would have turned out if Reagan had edged Ford out? But that didn't happen: Ford took the nomination, putting the Democratic candidate up against a fatally weakened incumbent.

The Democratic nomination featured a jam-packed slate of fifteen candidates, including:

- Birch Bayh, U.S. senator from Indiana
- Lloyd Bentsen, U.S. senator from Texas
- Jerry Brown, governor of California
- Robert Byrd, U.S. senator from West Virginia
- Jimmy Carter, former governor of Georgia
- Frank Church, U.S. senator from Idaho
- Walter Fauntroy, U.S. delegate from Washington, D.C.
- Fred R. Harris, former U.S. senator from Oklahoma
- Henry M. Jackson, U.S. senator from Washington
- Ellen McCormack, housewife
- Terry Sanford, former governor of North Carolina
- Milton Shapp, governor of Pennsylvania
- Sargent Shriver, former U.S. ambassador to France, from Maryland
- Morris Udall, U.S. representative from Arizona
- George Wallace, governor of Alabama

Talk about a grab-bag of candidates.

Once again, history was on my side: Out of that whole crowd, the one guy I ended up helping turned out to be the horse that won the race.

Back in '75, while I was running the Hollenbach campaign in Kentucky, I got a call from Hamilton Jordan, who had been Jimmy Carter's chief of staff in Georgia and was now his campaign manager. I had met Carter in '74, because he was then head of the Democratic Congressional Campaign Committee, and our paths had crossed a few more times since.

When Carter decided to run for president, everybody thought it was a crazy idea. His name recognition was so low that when he went on the TV game show *What's My Line?* in 1973, none of the panelists could guess his occupation, even after a few rounds of hints and guesses. (He was governor of Georgia at the time.)

Jordan told me they were assembling Carter's campaign and they needed some help putting together their fund-raising structure and organization. During that year, even as I worked on the Hollenbach campaign, I helped them do that part-time while I was doing Hollenbach, and I continued help-ing the Carter people through the end of '75.

Once the '76 races got under way I had plenty of my own campaigns to run, and I did not get involved much with the Carter campaign. I did give them some help with the caucus in Iowa, where he stunned all observers by coming in first among the five candidates there, with more than 27 percent. (Actually, "Uncommitted" came in first, then Carter.) That was a huge upset, and his campaign took off from there.

At the time I did not have the slightest inkling that this rather incidental connection would play a pivotal role in shaping the rest of my career.

*   *   *

Two weeks after Jimmy Carter won the presidential election, I went to North Carolina's Outer Banks with a bunch of my campaign friends for what had by now become my annual campaign vacation. We rented a cottage on the ocean. It was time to party and to celebrate.

It was, in other words, time to get drunk and stoned.

There are few places as rustic and beautiful as the barrier reefs of North Carolina. Most of the Outer Banks is designated as National Park land, which meant hundreds of miles of unspoiled beaches. I've never been a sum-mer beach person. Too crowded and claustrophobic. In the fall the beaches are empty, melancholy, and safe. A survivor's paradise.

Coming to the Outer Banks was becoming a biannual ritual for me, spring and fall. I had learned how to surf fish a few years before and loved it. It's not all that tough. You buy a big rod, lots of bait, a pair of wading boots that go waist high, a rod holder to stick in the sand, a beach chair, a cooler full of beer, an ounce of good pot, and you're all set.

In both spring and fall the bluefish run along the Atlantic Coast. Back in the seventies and eighties they ran in huge numbers. Hit it right, and you'd catch a fish on every cast. You grab your rod, cast that big boy out as far as possible with plenty of weight attached to the leader, take up any slack, put the rod in the holder, and sit down to drink, smoke, and wait. That's surf fish-ing. If you're lucky you'll have time to get a nice buzz on before the blues hit. Sometimes the inconsiderate bastards strike right away. You've just put the rod in a holder, have a beer in one hand and a joint in the other, and *boom!*

Blues are powerful fish and can pull your rod right out to sea, so when they hit you have to pull them in hard or lose your gear.

As the week went by I began thinking about the road in front of me. I was about to turn twenty-eight. It was only four years since I had showed up in Washington with nothing but ambition and a doctored résumé, but my career had surged light-years ahead. Sitting on the Outer Banks with my surf rod safe in its holder lent itself to a good deal of what's-next thinking. A survivor's mind never focuses on the past or on the immediate moment. You're too busy. There's just too much thinking that needs to go into the next chapter. Years later I would learn that living in the present moment was the key to staying sober. But in that gloriously triumphant November of '76, staying sober was the furthest thing from my mind. Besides, how I actually felt at any given moment in those days was irrelevant, because I never let my mind dwell on the present. I would decide how the present moment felt the next day. That way I could decide that yesterday was great, even if in reality it had sucked. Controlling your own history: a key to surviving and a key tool for politicians.

By now my reputation was well established. In the next campaign cycle, I could pick and choose the campaigns I wanted. No more lousy candidates running in awful places. And no more campaigns that struggled to pay the bills. In the campaign business, being able to pick and choose was about as good as it got, and that's exactly where I was.

Yet for some reason I didn't feel all that happy.

Maybe I was just strung out from all the campaigns over the past four years. For a brief moment it occurred to me that maybe it was time to try another line of work. But that was nuts. I'd worked so hard to get where I was, and had made it a hell of a lot sooner than I'd ever dreamed. Now was the time to enjoy it. I had money in the bank, a new house, no commitments, and the Democrats were in power. I was money, baby!

So why wasn't I content? Why did I still feel that hole in my stomach?

That damn hole. No matter how good life got, the hole was there. No matter where I went, there it was. The only known cure was booze. But I couldn't drink all the time. This got me to thinking: Hey, it was near cocktail hour. The hole could be filled.

We partied late that night. On the list of things to celebrate was my annual changeover from vodka to Scotch. In those days I drank vodka from April to November, when the weather was warmer, Scotch in the late fall and winter when I needed red liquor to brace against the cold. The morning after the changeover was always a little rough. My body had to get adjusted to the heavier malt. So I was a bit hung over the next morning. But nothing serious.

This changeover morning was no different from all the others. I decided to pass on fishing and stay in bed. In my bed that morning was the lovely Ms. Angie. Tall, red-haired, and sexy as hell. Like me, she liked her sex on the edge and (again, like me) never had any regrets the next day. I liked that. As I was contemplating Ms. Angie's attractive form from the bed, my friend Jim Cando started banging on the door, telling me I had a call.

"I'll call back," I yelled.

"Better take it," he yelled back. "The guy says he's calling from the Carter transition office."

"What the hell is *that* about?" I wondered out loud. I dragged myself to the phone. "Hello," I said in a sleepy voice.

"Bob, Doug Bennet here. How would you like to be a deputy assistant secretary of state?"

I recognized that voice. Sonofabitch, it *was* Doug Bennet. After losing the House race Doug had become staff director for the new Senate Budget Committee. I'd heard he was Secretary of State Vance's choice to be assistant secretary of state for congressional relations. A big-time job.

"Deputy assistant secretary of what state, Doug?" I said.

He laughed. "Of the United States of America."

Wait—*what?* Now I was sitting up in bed, jamming the phone against my ear. Maybe the increased pressure would clarify the words.

"Doug, are you serious? Deputy assistant *secretary of state*? I don't know squat about foreign policy. I'm a politician, not a diplomat!"

"That's just why I need you," he said. "Have you followed the Panama Canal treaty debate?"

I hadn't, not much, at least not lately—but I'd sure followed it during the primary season earlier that year, when it had the potential to affect the outcome of the entire race.

"The Canal Treaty was what kept Reagan in the race right up to the convention," I said, grateful to be able to say anything about a foreign policy issue. "It almost cost Ford the nomination."

"That's what I thought," said Doug. "It was the hottest issue of the whole Republican campaign, wasn't it?"

"It's still hot," I replied. Doug asked for a little background, and I gave it to him.

Before becoming Richard Nixon's running mate in 1972, Ford had been the minority leader in the U.S. House. Ford was a moderate Republican from Michigan. His selection had been controversial among the GOP's conservative wing. Sensing vulnerability in the unelected president, former California governor and conservative darling Ronald Reagan decided to challenge Ford for the Republican nomination in 1976.

The GOP establishment rallied around Ford out of fear that Reagan was too conservative and therefore unelectable. Reagan was getting his clock cleaned by Ford in the early Republican primaries and was close to dropping out of the race. Then Reagan decided he needed to make a last stand in the North Carolina primary. Before a Reagan speech at a conservative rally in the Tar Heel State, one of his advisors, Lyn Nofziger, suggested Reagan attack Ford for pushing ahead with negotiations to turn control of the Panama Canal over to Panama.

Started by the French and completed by the United States, the Canal was a crucial commerce and military artery between the Atlantic and the Pacific. U.S. control of the Canal and a large U.S. military force stationed there to protect the waterway had been a sore point in Latin America for years. Negotiations on a new treaty had been started during the Johnson administration. Nixon and then Ford had inherited the ongoing negotiations.

The Canal Treaty then barely registered as an issue with the average U.S. voter, but among committed conservatives it was boiling hot. Reagan used the North Carolina speech to launch a vicious attack on Ford by suggesting that the president was negotiating the surrender of U.S. territory. "We built it, we paid for it, it's ours—and we're going to keep it," became Reagan's mantra. The crowd went wild that night, and a new issue was born. Reagan went on to beat Ford in North Carolina and in a string of primaries that followed. Reagan came within a hundred delegate votes of defeating Ford at the GOP convention in Detroit that summer.

Reagan's spectacular comeback was attributed by many to his opposition to the treaty negotiations. Conservatives were determined to keep the issue alive.

Ford went on to lose the general election to Carter—but the Panama Canal issue had gained political traction. Now it had become Carter's problem. He could have put the negotiations on a back burner, but that wasn't

Jimmy Carter's style. Despite the political land mines, Carter ordered the negotiations be completed.

After finishing my tutorial I said, "Doug, the Panama Canal is going to be a real problem for Carter."

"Why's that?" Bennet asked.

"Because the Canal is as much a domestic political issue as a foreign policy issue."

"Well put," said Doug. "Which is exactly why we need a politician to get the treaty through the Senate—and you're perfect for the job, my boy."

I asked if I could think about it. Doug gave me forty-eight hours. Those were two of the longest days of my life.

*   *   *

After the conversation with Doug I went back to bed, my head spinning. Sweet Angie asked what was up. I said, "Carter's people want me to be a deputy assistant secretary of state."

"You're still drunk," she said. "Go back to sleep."

"No, I'm serious."

"You're not thinking of doing it, are you?" she said, a note of concern in her voice.

"I don't know," I said, a little defensive now. "Maybe. No, probably not—but it's damn nice to be asked."

That was what I couldn't understand. Why would these guys want me? Sure, I was getting a name for myself in the campaign business. My survival skills were perfect for the political business. I talked a good game, kept my candidates out of trouble, and had a good sense of what voters wanted to hear. But that was political campaigns. This was something much bigger. Probably too big.

I got a lot of advice from my political crew, especially Jim Cando, my cameraman from the NCEC days, who remains one of my best friends to this day. Jim was a drinker but not into drugs like most of the rest of us, and he was the guy I respected most in the group.

Jim said he didn't want me to do it, for two reasons.

"First reason's selfish," he said. "You're hot in the campaign business right now, and that means business for me." That was true for a lot of the others, too, only they wouldn't come out and say so. Cando's candor—one of the reasons I've always loved the guy. But it was Jim's second reason that gave me the most concern.

"What about the background check? You know, for security clearances?" I knew what he was getting at. Any high-level political appointee was subject to a thorough background check by the FBI. The process was detailed. Every year of your life could and would be investigated and gone over in detail. Former addresses would be verified, past college and high school friends would be contacted. Every place you had ever lived, every job you'd ever held, every country you'd ever visited, everything was checked out.

What did I have to worry about? Plenty! There was my drunken father and all his skeletons. Steroid use. Being expelled from the Peace Corps for political activity. Using drugs to jack up my blood pressure to avoid the draft, and my rap sheet from the antiwar movement. Drugs in college, drunken brawls, whorehouses, and illegal gambling. If they ever opened up my closet it would sound like the Boston Pops on the Fourth of July.

There was just no way. With that kind of background investigation, everything I had worked for could blow up in my face. There wasn't a mask good enough to get by the FBI. And besides, who was I kidding? I couldn't handle a big job like that. It wouldn't take long for them to figure out I wasn't up to the job. No matter how good my survival skills were, I couldn't bullshit my way through the job of deputy assistant secretary of state—as in, the United States of America.

I took a walk on the beach with Cando and told him what I'd been thinking. I was surprised when he got up in my face.

"Getting that clearance isn't gonna be easy," he said. "I agree with that. But the rest is bullshit."

"What do you mean? You don't think, even if I got by the background check, they wouldn't get wise to the con? Get real, man." Now I was a bit pissed. This was one of my closest friends. How come he couldn't see it?

Jim Cando is only five foot eight, but it's all muscle, and when he's mad he looks like an eight-foot grizzly. (They really *are* terrifying up close.)

"What the hell you mean, a con?" he growled. "What con? You're smart, you stupid shit. You understand Washington, you're the best strategist I know, and you're great with people. Where's the con in that? You get down on yourself, Beckel, and I don't get why. Give yourself a break. You could be a deputy state whatever, in your sleep."

"Thanks, Cando. That means a lot. You're right—I get down on myself too much."

That's more or less what I said—but I was thinking something different. I was thinking how sad it was that I had even conned a good friend like Cando. If he only knew how I grew up. If he only knew the number of times I'd lied to get ahead. If he only knew about the masks I wore continuously and the hole in my gut.

And then it hit me. Cando *did* know all those things.

"So you going to go for it?" Cando was saying.

"Don't know, Jim. I've got till tomorrow. I need to think about it some more. But thanks for what you said. Nobody close to me ever said nice things like that to me. People who don't know who I am say those things, but what the fuck do they know?"

Then Cando said something that I would remember for the rest of my life:

"I'm not sure *you* know who you are, Bob. Those people who don't know you may know you better than you do."

Shit, I needed a drink.

Sweet sleep did not pay me a visit that night. I couldn't even drink myself to sleep, usually a foolproof tactic. Where did Cando get off asking me if I knew who I was? Of course I knew who I was. I was what I was, and what I was, was *not* up to being a deputy assistant secretary of state for the entire frigging country!

I decided to turn the job down. I would call Bennet first thing in the morning and tell him thanks, but no thanks.

It would take me more than a quarter-century to begin to understand what happened when I called Doug the next morning. For years, I puzzled over it and could not figure it out. I'm still not sure I understand it fully. All I can tell you is that I had practiced my lines carefully, and my answer was clearly, unambiguously, emphatically, no. A nice no, but a definite no.

Doug picked up the phone on the first ring. Which startled me a little.

"Doug," I said, "I can't thank you enough for asking... and I accept."

CHAPTER FIVE

In the White House

It takes sixty-seven votes, a required two-thirds majority out of one hundred seats, to ratify a treaty in the U.S. Senate. In today's political climate you'd be lucky to get sixty-seven votes in support of Mother's Day. In the late 1970s the political climate was not as polarized as it is today, but still, getting sixty-seven votes was no walk in the park, especially for an issue as unpopular and bitterly divisive as the Panama Canal Treaty. Democrats controlled the Senate sixty to forty, but sixty is not sixty-seven—and we were far from assured of all sixty of the Democrats' votes. A number of those Democratic senators faced tough reelection campaigns in the next election cycle. Ronald Reagan's 1976 nomination campaign had poisoned public attitudes toward the treaty, and most national polls at the time showed most voters opposed to ratification.

After years of running political campaigns I was suddenly in a whole new position: I wasn't trying to get someone *into* office, I was working for someone *in* that office. But whether from the outside looking in or the inside looking out, politics is politics. As far as I was concerned, my new job was still all about running campaigns.

And we had a very tough campaign in front of us.

There were three senior officials who were key to the treaty project: my boss, Deputy Secretary of State Warren Christopher, and the two men who'd negotiated the treaty, Sol Linowitz and Ellsworth Bunker. Sol was a wealthy lawyer who had also served as chief counsel and then chairman of Xerox before being tapped by LBJ to negotiate the treaties. He also happened to be exactly my father's age. Ellsworth, who was even older, had served as ambassador to Vietnam under Johnson.

Almost the moment I started working there someone grabbed me and said, "Bob, we want you to go in and meet Ellsworth Bunker and Sol Linowitz, the treaty negotiators. You're going to take them to the Hill to get them in front of Congress..."

Oh, shit, I thought. I'd suddenly remembered that years earlier, before I joined the Peace Corps, I was part of a huge antiwar protest in Washington when Bunker was in Washington for some meetings. We got word that Bunker was leaving the State Department to drive over to the White House. When his car came out a bunch of us lay down on the road so they couldn't pass. As his car approached and pulled to a stop, I flipped Bunker the bird.

Fast-forward six or seven years: I was now going in to meet this man face to face.

I headed over to the office where we were meeting—Warren Christopher's office, I think it was. Bunker was by this time a very old gentleman, in his eighties. The first thing I noticed on entering the office was that he still had the same lead-lined briefcase he'd carried with him in Vietnam, which had bullet holes all over it from the Tet offensive, when they broke into his office and shot at him. Ellsworth had ducked under a table and our security forces killed the guys who were breaking in. This was a guy who'd been awarded the Medal of Freedom not once but twice, by JFK and then again by Johnson. And the leather on his briefcase was still chewed up from the Vietcong's bullets.

This was not a guy you would want to bullshit. I figured, go for broke.

As we shook hands I said, "Mister Ambassador, I've got to confess something to you, since you and I are going to be working together. When you came back from Vietnam, I don't know if you remember this, but there were a lot of protests going on. I lay down in front of your car with a bunch of other people."

He peered at me and said, "Bob, were you the guy that flipped me the bird?" It was his way of saying, *It's okay—don't worry about it.*

Ellsworth and I became very close friends, as did Sol and I. Talk about two guys who had been around a long time and seen everything. We'd go to Capitol Hill together and I would listen to Ellsworth's stories about Vietnam, which completely fascinated me. All three of them—Ellsworth, Sol, and Christopher—became mentors to me. Whenever I had a life question, I would call them and see what they thought—especially Bunker—and they would always give me sound advice.

They're all gone now; Bunker died in 1984, Linowitz in 2005, and Christopher in 2011. And each time, just before they died I got a phone call, just to talk. I guess when you know you're dying, you go through a list of people you want to talk to.

I'll never forget those three conversations.

*   *   *

Since my role at the State Department was strictly to work on ratification of the Panama Canal Treaty, I spent a lot of time in Senate offices and on the telephone with the White House Congressional Relations Office, headed by Frank Moore, a Georgian friend of President Carter's and one of the gentlest and finest men I've ever met.

One day not long after arriving at State I got a call from Frank telling me I needed to report to the White House the next day to brief the president on the current vote count for the treaty.

I had met Jimmy Carter several times on the campaign trail, but had not seen him since he was elected president, which meant I had at this point never been inside the Oval Office. It had always been one of my dreams to visit the Oval Office, the most storied and powerful political room in the world—not as a visitor but to meet with the president of the United States as a White House political advisor. For the next four years I would most likely be stuck at the State Department, in the Harry S. Truman building over on C Street, four or five blocks away from the White House, so this meeting was as close as I was going to get to my dream job. I was damn sure going to be ready.

I spent the entire day and most of the night on the phone and going over my notes on visits I'd had with senators and their staff. By the time I left for the White House I knew all there was to know about where the U.S. Senate, senator by senator, stood on the Panama Canal Treaty. Hell, if I had studied this hard in college I might have become a doctor or lawyer. A terrifying thought.

My appointment with the president was scheduled for fifteen minutes, though I'd been told that we could go over that time if necessary. Frank

Moore knew I was nervous. "Be to the point, with no small talk," he'd told me, "and you'll be fine."

The next day I arrived at the White House, passed through security, and was ushered into the Oval Office. I've never experienced anything quite like walking into that room. It was in fact oval, with recessed lighting, antique furniture lining the walls offset by modern comfortable couches and arm-chairs, all dominated by the president's massive oak desk, the desk once used by President Kennedy. Portraits of former presidents hung on the walls, jux-taposed with pictures of the current president's family on a credenza behind his desk.

It was incredibly intimidating, and it was obvious that I was in awe and very nervous.

Sitting at that historically charged desk, President Carter seemed to know exactly what I was feeling. He broke into the famous Carter smile and said, "Welcome, Bob—I had the same feelings you do now when I walked into this room for the first time. Don't think of this room as a museum, but rather as a place to work. Have a seat, and let's get down to business."

I thanked him and, strangely, felt comfortable right away. Carter has an amazing gift for making people feel instantly welcomed and appreciated.

Scheduled for fifteen minutes, our meeting stretched out like a cat sun-ning itself in the September sun. As was his style, Carter asked detailed ques-tions, listened intently, and wrote copious notes. After a good hour I wrapped up, and the president thanked me for an excellent briefing. The next words out of his mouth not only shocked me, they literally changed my life.

"Why don't you come to the White House and work for me?"

Just as I was about to say I was honored that he would even make such a suggestion, Frank Moore (who'd been there the whole time) spoke up and said, "Mr. President, we don't have any available White House staff slots available."

Carter smiled that Carter smile and said, "I'm the president. Can't I cre-ate a slot?"

Frank said the only way to do that would be to convince Secretary of State Cyrus Vance to give up my current State Department slot.

On every president's desk there sits a phone that connects him to every cabinet secretary's desk. The president immediately picked up the line that went directly to Vance's desk. Now I was screwed for sure. There are over a hundred deputy assistant secretaries of state, and at this point I hadn't even met Secretary Vance. He wouldn't know me from Adam.

The president's first words were, "Cy, I just got an excellent briefing on Panama from your guy Beckel, and I need you to transfer him over here."

The jig was up. My White House dream was shattered. *I* knew I was a phony, Secretary Vance must know I was a phony (since he'd never heard of me), and now the president of the United States would know I was a phony. I was right when I told Jim Cando I had no business taking this job. I'd tried to tell Doug Bennet no. How did I get myself into this mess?

Then the president said, "I know this will be a big loss for you, and I'll make it up to you. Thanks, Cy."

Hanging up the phone, he turned to me with a big smile. "He hated to lose you, Bob, but he'll reluctantly do so. Welcome aboard! Clean out your desk over at State and report here tomorrow morning at seven, and not a moment later."

I thanked him and promised I would do my very best to justify his decision.

I learned a political lesson that day. Not from Carter, but from Secretary of State Vance: When anyone in Washington asks for a favor, no matter how little the favor means to you, act pained and get as much as you can in exchange—even if the person asking is the president of the United States.

*   *   *

At the White House my new official job title was deputy assistant to the president for defense, intelligence, and foreign policy. What that really meant was that I was there to help negotiate ratification of the Panama treaties. In other words, I was campaigning again, only this time for a treaty rather than for a candidate, and to a very select constituency: the one hundred members of the U.S. Senate.

By this time I had dozens of campaigns under my belt, several of which had been against very long odds. My number-one rule for campaigns was that you did everything necessary to win, used every resource available to you, and stayed within the law...when you could. So I was shocked to hear the president say, at the beginning of our first treaty meeting after I arrived at the White House, that he wanted to exchange *no political favors for votes on the treaty*. He believed the Panama Canal Treaty should rise or fall on its merits.

That was the equivalent of sending us to a gunfight with our hands tied behind our backs. Was he serious? No, he couldn't be.

After the meeting I followed Frank Moore and White House Chief of Staff Hamilton Jordan back to Ham's office, where I immediately asked Ham if the president really meant what he said about no political favors for treaty votes. I fully expected him to say, "Officially, yes—but no, not really." I figured Carter had made the statement for public consumption, but had in private let Frank and Ham know that he was prepared to deal.

To my utter shock, Ham said, "Oh yes, he's deadly serious." In fact, he continued, Carter had opposed bargaining for votes all the way back to his days in the Georgia State Senate.

"Are you kidding me?" I said. (I'm not sure why, but I used that expression often in those days. Maybe I thought I was kidding everyone and was naturally suspicious that they were doing the same with me.)

Jordan said he could understand my frustration, but that he went back with Carter to his days as Georgia's governor and that when it came to dealing for votes on anything, Carter was immovable. By invoking this pious— and in my mind naïve—political rule, the president was taking a long shot and turning it into a virtual impossibility.

"Just do your best," said Ham.

My best. Okay. That's exactly what I was prepared to do: my best. Which was thoroughly pragmatic and completely unscrupulous.

If the president was going to be inflexible and by doing so doom the treaty effort, I reasoned, then there was only one choice open to me: I needed to run a rogue campaign from within the White House, without the president or the rest of the White House ever knowing about it.

So here I was, on the first day of my dream job, and already I was putting myself at a very high risk of losing my job. On the other hand, my first job assignment was to pass the treaty. And the president himself had made that impossible. So what was better, I asked myself: risking my job to get the treaty passed, or playing it safe, keeping my job, and probably losing the treaty? If it failed, I probably wouldn't take too big a hit. But then, if it passed, my star would shine.

I liked the risk/shine option.

Perhaps you've seen the 2012 Spielberg film *Lincoln*, which chronicles the wartime president's efforts to pass the constitutional amendment

banning slavery. The wonderful James Spader plays a completely unscrupulous lobbyist, W. N. Bilbo, who will happily do absolutely anything, ethical
or not, moral or not, legal or not, to get his boss's nearly impossible legislation passed through an unwilling Senate. Now, I'm not comparing Carter to
Lincoln, and the Panama Canal Treaty certainly wasn't the Emancipation
Proclamation—but at that moment, I became W. N. Bilbo.

There were eight to ten senators whose votes on the treaty were still very
much undecided, and we needed at least six of those votes for ratification. I
picked the six senators from the list who I thought would be most open to
political deals in exchange for a yes vote on the treaty. I then contacted my
best "oppo man" (i.e., opposition researcher), a fellow I had used before in
several campaigns. Let's call him Ron.

Ron was one of those guys who is without conscience. He didn't care who
won or lost, just how much he was paid. And he was very good at what he
did. Ron could find information on any U.S. citizen that was almost always
accurate, and more often than not potentially very embarrassing.

Ron was not cheap. To investigate six senators would cost approximately
fifty thousand dollars. I knew of only one place I could get my hands on that
kind of cash: through a guy I knew who was connected to people who stood
to gain a good deal from the treaty's being ratified.

I called my friend and told him that we simply couldn't depend on selling the senators on the treaty's virtues, but would have to deal for their votes.
I also told him that the president would not under any circumstances agree
to cutting any political deals for treaty votes.

My friend thought this was quite naïve. I reminded him that Jimmy
Carter was a man who ran for president in the aftermath of the Watergate
scandal, with a commitment to always tell the American people the truth.
And that I completely understood his position. Which was true, sort of.

I also told him there were ways to get around the president's orders—but
it would have to be done without White House involvement. I explained the
opposition research idea to him, and he asked me how much it would cost.
About fifty grand, I told him.

He said I should meet him in two days at the Washington Mall near the
Lincoln Memorial.

On the appointed day I arrived at the Mall with time to spare and sat on the bench waiting for my friend to arrive. As I sat there, the enormity of what we were doing hit me like a wall of Washington humidity in the dog days of August. I was putting my dream job at the White House on the line—not to mention that, if what I thought was about to happen actually happened, I was about to break several federal laws. I could lose not only my job but my liberty here. Sitting under the stone gaze of our sixteenth president, I wondered what old Abe would think about this transaction.

My friend showed up about fifteen minutes later, carrying an expensive briefcase. He sat down next to me and got right to the point.

"Bob, if this ever gets out, we're in real serious trouble. And let me emphasize, *serious.*"

I nodded, picked up the briefcase, and walked away, making sure not to make eye contact with Honest Abe.

Back at my apartment I opened the briefcase, and there it was: fifty thousand dollars in hundred-dollar bills.

I called Ron and told him I had the money; it was time to go to work.

*   *   *

The first thing Ron came back to me with was information on a senator whose state was a major producer of copper. The biggest buyer of copper was the Defense Department, but at the time the DoD had stopped buying because it already had tons of excess sitting in stockpile. As those copper supplies had piled up, thousands of miners in this senator's state had lost their jobs. Ron also said he suspected that this same senator was contemplating hiring—with money from his campaign funds—a former general who was well connected in the Pentagon. This would have been a high-risk strategy.

The following day I set up an appointment for Warren Christopher and myself to go see the senator together. When we got to the senator's office we found him in his bathroom shaving, getting ready for a black-tie event. Chris (as his friends call him) took a seat on the toilet while I sat on the heater, and Chris began making policy arguments in favor of the treaty.

The senator cut him off. "There's only one word I want to talk about, and that word is *copper.*"

Chris looked at him nonplussed and said, "What does copper have to do with voting for the Panama Canal Treaty?"

I jumped in immediately and suggested to Chris that he might want to go on ahead to the next appointment we had set up. I would stay and talk to the senator.

"Fine," said Chris, "but be careful, Bob." Christopher, a highly respected Los Angeles lawyer, believed (like Carter) that political trading for votes on the Panama Canal Treaty was a bad idea. In his view, a treaty finally turning the Canal over to Panama was long overdue and was strong enough to survive on its merits. As much as I had tried, I could never convince Chris that on highly political issues like the Panama Canal Treaty, votes rarely turned on merits.

After Chris left I followed the senator into his office and told him that I had the notion he might be contemplating hiring a former general, using campaign funds, to lobby the Defense Department. "I don't want you to confirm or deny that," I said, "but in any case, I don't think it would be a very good idea."

The senator had the good sense not to push me on where the hell I had come up with this notion.

"Look, Senator," I said, "if you want to persuade Defense to buy more copper, why don't you let me try to convince Harold Brown [the secretary of defense] to consider increasing their stockpile of copper?"

He told me to go ahead. I asked if I could use his phone.

Before leaving the White House that afternoon to go to the Senate, I had told my assistant to answer my private phone and no matter what I said, to just go along with it.

Dialing my own number, I got my assistant on the line, waited through a few seconds of silence (normally it would take a few moments to get someone this important on the line), and then asked if Secretary Brown was available to take a call from Bob Beckel, with the White House legislative affairs office.

"Yes, ma'am, I'll wait," I said to the puzzled but obedient silence on the other end.

After letting a minute or so go by, I straightened up as if someone had come on the phone and said, "Mr. Secretary, how are you?" (Pause.) "I'm fine, thank you. Mr. Secretary, I understand that the Department of Defense is no longer buying copper because you have all you need. As you know, I've got responsibility for the Panama Canal Treaty, and I'm running a fine line here, considering the president's views on trading political favors for votes, but I thought in this case it would pass the president's test."

I went on to suggest that if the Defense Department were to buy copper now, it would be at fire sale prices, and that perhaps for once the Defense Department could be seen as shopping for bargains instead of buying eight-hundred-dollar hammers.

"I think it's a good story, Mr. Secretary," I added, "and if we do it we could leak the 'frugal Defense Department' line to a few defense reporters in town. So, would you be willing to send some people out to the state to look quietly at some bargain-basement copper purchase opportunities?" (A pause as I listened to more of my assistant's silence on the other end.) "Yes, sir, I can't tell you how important it is."

I then made one of the riskiest moves of my political career.

Turning to the senator, I said, "Secretary Brown is willing to look into a significant purchase of copper. Would you like to speak to him to confirm it?"

Knowing that I knew about his secret lobbyist plan, the senator waved his hand as if to say, *I don't want to be in the middle of this.* I turned back to the phone and loudly thanked "Mr. Secretary," telling him the senator was very happy and that I'd get back to him with more details the next day.

Then I hung up—and so did my assistant, wondering (I'm sure) what the hell *that* had been all about.

Two days later I leaked a story to a reporter friend of mine in the senator's state, saying that the Defense Department was contemplating buying surplus copper at low prices, and that the reporter could quote a White House source. I explained to him that if he tried to obtain confirmation from Defense he wouldn't get it, since the standard practice of the Defense Department was to have no comment on the department's potential purchases.

The reporter, who had been on the political beat for several years and was no dummy, immediately asked if I was trying to get the senator's vote for the Panama Canal Treaty by doing this. I said flatly that there was no quid pro quo, but that I knew the senator had been working very hard pushing the Defense Department to purchase copper, and if it happened he deserved a lot of credit. I also covered my own ass by explaining to him that the president had expressly said this was the kind of deal that he was not willing to do for votes. That's what I said on background, but to maintain some credibility with the reporter I then said, "The answer to your question, off the record, is of course I want to use copper as leverage with the senator on Panama."

The reporter ran a story the next day, saying exactly what I had hoped he would say. Because he had a White House source it lent a good deal of credibility to the story.

Now I went back to the Senate to see the senator and ask him bluntly if Secretary Brown's comments and the news story had convinced him to take a fresh look at the treaty.

"Bob," he said, "I'm much more inclined to support the treaty—but I want to make it clear that any copper bought by the government would not affect my vote."

I assured him that that would be exactly what I would say and I appreciated his willingness to work with me.

The senator eventually supported the treaty. As far as I know, he may still be waiting for the Defense Department to come shopping for more copper.

*   *   *

Some political advisors can have a great deal of power with the senators who listen to their advice. The key, from my perspective, was to find out who the powerful advisors were and what was the best way to get close to them. I asked oppo Ron to go through the list of undecided senators on the treaty and find out which advisors had clout, and what were those people's interests and—especially—their vulnerabilities. It took Ron about a week of digging to hit gold.

One senator on our undecideds list had an advisor who was very close to the senator. He was one person to whom the senator would definitely turn for advice on casting his vote on legislation that was controversial and politically charged, a description the Panama Canal Treaty fit in spades. We'll call this advisor Charles.

From what Ron had discovered, the senator relied on Charles for advice on many matters, but particularly on controversial issues that would have political consequences with his state's voters. Ron also learned that Charles was happily married, with four kids, but also had a fondness for good Scotch whisky and beautiful women. Charles's enormous appetite for booze he apparently fed daily. On the beautiful women front, Charles was obsessed but kept himself on a look-don't-touch basis. As far as Ron could learn, he was faithful to his wife.

It looked like Charles and I had a lot in common. By this time my love affair with alcohol was deeply entrenched. As far as beautiful women were concerned, I was definitely a fan (although unlike Charles I was not constrained by allegiance to a marriage).

I called and invited Charles to the White House for a drink, an invitation few politically-minded players would turn down.

I decided not to talk about Panama in our first meeting, but that we would just get to know each other. I broke out my best Scotch and asked him how he liked it. He told me straight up, no ice. My kind of guy. We had three drinks in my office and then went over to the Round Robin bar at the Willard hotel, one of Washington's oldest institutions, and drank well into the evening. As we got drunker we decided to play an old bar game: rating the women we saw at the bar on a scale of one to ten. I will say this: Charles's taste in women was much finer than mine.

We had a good time that night, and I suggested we get together once a week to down Scotch and rate women. On our third night out, Charles asked me if I knew where he could get a discreet woman for sex. I said I did, and why not go the next day?

The following day we met at the Willard and proceeded to get very drunk. Experience told me that when a guy makes his first trip to a whorehouse, his nervous system needs to be soaked in lots of booze or he'll back out. I told Charles that one of Washington's best whorehouses was a place I frequented, located just past Georgetown University on MacArthur Boulevard, on the way out of town. I suggested we head over there after a few more drinks.

The place was called Mama's Health Spa. I assured Charles this would be a safe place to engage in carnal pursuits. I called Mama and told her I was bringing over a very important person and needed her to get her best girls, and I would pay for everything. We took my car, because Charles didn't want his anywhere near Mama's.

We arrived, parked, and went up the back staircase, and when we got inside it was clear how much Mama valued my patronage. She introduced us to two beautiful Korean girls, neither of whom I recognized, which was strange, since I thought I had been with every girl in the place. Both girls took Charles back to the VIP room, which was slightly bigger than the other rooms but with a double-sized massage table and a treadmill. After all, this *was* a health spa.

When he came out two hours later Charles had a big grin on his face.

As soon as we got in my car to drive back to his, Charles's attitude began changing. He grew more and more worried about his wife finding out about his cheating. This is not uncommon after a first fling. I knew that Charles's sudden change of mood was a direct result of the booze wearing off. It got so bad that he began to cry. I assured him that it would not get out, because there were only four people who knew about his tryst, and that included two girls who probably weren't in the country legally; Mama, who is always discreet with a lucrative business to protect; and myself, and I had absolutely no reason to discuss the afternoon with anybody.

Charles wanted to get together the next afternoon.

"Of course," I said, "let's meet back at the Willard."

When we both arrived at the Willard the next day I could see Charles was still very nervous. I did everything I could to calm him down, knowing full well he was about to get the shock of his life. And then: Into the bar walked the very same girls he had been with the day before, on the arm of a guy named Ron. Funny, I knew a guy named Ron.

Poor Charles went into a state of shock. I told him to stay there and let me handle it. I walked over to the three, exchanged a knowing glance with Ron, and quietly told the girls to go back to Mama's.

I went back to sit with Charles and told him this guy was one of Mama's best clients, and she'd let the two girls go out with him for a few hours that day. Charles didn't buy the story. He was terrified. I suggested we stop talking about this, and instead, talk about Panama. As distracted as he was by his terror over the girls, that got his attention. He was listening. Charles was no fool.

"Charles," I said, "we need your senator's vote. I want you to stop obsessing about those girls and focus on this vote, which is just two weeks away."

As we were leaving I assured him that the events at Mama's were not going to get out, and that I would take personal responsibility to ensure they did not by convincing Mama to send the two girls to one of her other spas, preferably one in Los Angeles. I also told him that this was *not* a quid pro quo for the senator's vote. Of course not.

He said he would look at it carefully and talk to the senator the next day.

I said while he did that, I'd go back to Mama and get her to commit to moving the girls, and suggested I'd make it worth Mama's bottom line.

Charles asked if he could throw in some money, but I warned him that this plan was borderline illegal, and he wanted to stay far away from it. I promised Charles I'd get it done that day.

Now it was Charles's turn to play the pressure game. He said he wanted the girls out of town before the vote, and he was sure I understood.

I reminded him, and not subtly, that we both had an interest in the girls' moving—and I was sure *he* understood.

Two old pols finally putting their cards on the table. God, I loved this game.

A week later he told me the senator was *inclined* to vote for the treaty, but was still reluctant, and by the way, were the two girls getting settled in their new city? Tougher guy than I had given him credit for. Good for him.

I've never felt good about how I pushed Charles and took advantage of his weaknesses. But this was a political campaign, and in those days I was prepared to do whatever it took to win it.

*   *   *

There was one more vote that looked like it would take some finessing. There was one senator, we'll call him John, whose vote was impossible to predict because he had a history of being unpredictable and not consistently voting the party line. To make matters worse, John had decided to poll his constituents in his state and then let the outcome of the poll determine how he would vote. That was dangerous for us, of course, because this was not a popular issue, which we knew from our own poll.

By a stroke of pure, unadulterated luck, the Washington pollster who was tasked with designing and running that poll happened to be a friend of mine, and he came to me for advice on how to word the polling script the people on the phone would be reading from. Incredible, I know, but true; Washington is a small town. It wasn't difficult (and, since I received no compensation for this advice, not downright illegal either) to jury-rig the questions so that instead of saying, "Do you favor and support the Panama Canal Treaty?" the poll offered two arguments. The first was, "The Panama Canal belongs to the United States, and we should keep it." The second argument was, "The Panama Canal is in an area that is highly susceptible to sabotage, and there is a very strong belief that if the Panama Canal Treaty is not ratified the Canal will be blown up or shut down. If you knew that to be the case, would you favor or oppose the treaty?"

The poll came back favorable, which of course we knew it would. A lot of agricultural product from John's state went through the Panama Canal. John never was the sharpest knife in the drawer, and he said, "Okay, I'm going to be for it."

With the copper senator, Charles's senator, and the polling senator, things were starting to look a little better for us. But we were about to be thrown a curveball that not even the most seasoned political operator could have seen coming.

*   *   *

When I walked into the Cabinet Room the first thing I saw was that the president was clearly not happy. This was a man noted for his famous smile. On this cold early-spring morning his facial features bore not the slightest hint of a smile. His jaw was set and locked, his blue eyes fixed like lasers as he stared at the people around the large conference table. He was dressed in blue jeans with a blue work shirt, his preferred dress on weekends when no events were planned. He hadn't planned to be here, and he was angry.

President Carter didn't like surprises and he had just gotten a very big one. That was the reason for this hastily convened meeting in the Cabinet Room, a few steps from the Oval Office. Attending were Warren Christopher; Secretary of Defense Harold Brown; Stansfield Turner, the director of Central Intelligence; Phil Jordan, a top lawyer at Justice; and Madeleine Albright from the National Security Council staff. From the White House staff there was Ham Jordan, Frank Moore, and me.

Sitting directly across from the president were the chairman and ranking member of the Senate Select Committee on Intelligence, Democrat Daniel Inouye of Hawaii and Republican Barry Goldwater from Arizona. The ever-efficient White House operators had managed to track down this entire group on extremely short notice just a few hours earlier. Like the president, neither Inouye nor Goldwater was smiling.

The subject of the meeting was drug trafficking. More specifically, drug trafficking by Moises Torrijos, formerly Panama's ambassador to Spain and brother of Panamanian strongman and head of state, Omar Torrijos. Sometime the previous week, a top secret CIA cable had leaked. The cable revealed that a federal grand jury had previously handed down a sealed indictment against Moises Torrijos for facilitating shipments of cocaine to the U.S.

The indictment had been issued before Carter took office. No one at this meeting had been aware of it. But the leaked cable contained information that was potentially even more damning than the indictment itself. It revealed a bizarre tale of subterfuge and potential treason.

Moises Torrijos had resigned as Panamanian ambassador to Spain a year earlier and was returning to Panama by ship. The ship was scheduled to dock in the Panama Canal Zone, then a United States Territory. U.S. officials, armed with the sealed indictment, were waiting to arrest Torrijos when he stepped off the boat. A few hours before landing Torrijos had been tipped off about the pending arrest. His ship was diverted to Panamanian waters and docked in Panamanian territory where the U.S. couldn't touch him.

And that wasn't all. Where the cable was discovered was even more bizarre: It was found in the lunchroom of a factory in . . . wait for it . . . *North Carolina*. Which happened to be the state whose senior senator, Republican Jesse Helms, was leading the opposition to the Panama Canal Treaty in the Senate. All of which seemed like one giant hell of a coincidence.

The drug revelation and the bad light it threw on the administration in Panama could not have come at a worse time. The treaty required a two-thirds vote in the Senate for ratification. We needed sixty-seven votes for passage, and we were getting close. Momentum in the past two weeks had gotten us to sixty votes. Helms and the opposition were stuck at thirty votes. Of the ten senators who were undecided, eight were leaning in our direction. The drug story was a bombshell that had the potential to tip them back to neutral or against.

The president looked around the table, and then directly at the two senators. He told them that he was unaware of the indictment or the intelligence leak to Torrijos. He quickly added that he and his administration *should* have known, and he took responsibility for what had happened. He apologized to Inouye and Goldwater. I sensed that they believed him completely. Whatever his faults, Jimmy Carter did not lie.

Goldwater spoke first. He told the president that he opposed the treaty, but he opposed leaking intelligence even more. He said that if the Panama Canal Treaty went down, he did not want it to fail because of selective leaks, and he promised to state that publicly when the story reached the press. Goldwater ended by telling Carter he stood ready to do whatever he could to get to the truth. He also intended to talk privately with Jesse Helms.

Inouye reiterated his support for the treaty. He was furious about the intelligence leaks and intended to use the Intelligence Committee not only to investigate Panama drug trafficking but also to find out who leaked the intelligence. Inouye did say that if drug trafficking went beyond Moises Torrijos and implicated Omar Torrijos, he would have to oppose ratification.

I had gotten to know both senators in my role as White House liaison to the Intelligence Committee. I immediately liked Inouye, but Goldwater had been a real surprise. He was the opposite of everything I believed about him in the aftermath of his landslide loss to Lyndon Johnson in the 1964 presidential campaign.

During that campaign, Goldwater had been portrayed as a right-wing extremist who wanted to go to war against the Soviets. Such a war would almost certainly have involved atomic weapons. Goldwater's running mate was General Curtis LeMay, who, if anything, was to the right of Goldwater. The Johnson campaign made a now-famous television ad portraying a little girl picking the petals off a daisy, counting them off, one by one. When the petals are all gone, suddenly we hear a loud announcer's voice in a countdown from ten to one—and when it reaches zero an atomic explosion fills the screen.

The ad ran just once. That was all it took.

But the Barry Goldwater I met after coming over to the White House was nothing like the Goldwater portrayed in the 1964 campaign. He was smart, razor-sharp, courteous, and above all a patriot. For Goldwater, partisanship had no place in the affairs of state, especially when it concerned national security. Jimmy Carter was our commander in chief and deserved full support on security matters. He got it from Barry Goldwater.

Don't misunderstand. Goldwater opposed Carter on virtually every domestic issue and most foreign policy issues as well. But unlike so many politicians in Washington, Goldwater put his cards on the table. If he disagreed he would say so, and not play any games. If he was with you and said so his word was always good. In Washington Goldwater's word was "bankable." High praise, and well deserved.

The senators asked Carter if there were any other documents relating to either Moises Torrijos or his brother and drug traffic. Carter said he didn't know, but would find out quickly. He promised any information that could be found in the government would be in the hands of the Intelligence

Committee by eight o'clock Monday morning. When Jimmy Carter gave his word it, too, was bankable.

Inouye and Goldwater both assured the president that any information that was turned over to the committee would be secure. They also promised that the full Senate would review only that information pertinent to the treaty debate. Goldwater promised to act quickly so that the treaty could be voted on as scheduled.

After they left the president's eyes circled the table. I had never heard the president raise his voice until that day. He wanted to know why no one in the administration knew anything about the intelligence on Torrijos or the sealed indictment. A few brave souls who tried to respond were met by the famous Carter stare. Those eyes shone like diamonds when he smiled. When he didn't smile they could cut you in half.

Carter looked around the table and said he expected everyone to work through the weekend to gather any related information. Then he looked at me and Phil Jordan. He said he wanted everything found to be turned over to the two of us no later than midnight Sunday. Phil and I would be responsible for getting the information to the Intelligence Committee by eight o'clock Monday morning. Before anyone could say, "Yes, Mr. President," he was gone.

A collective silence descended on the Cabinet Room. The people around this table had spent endless hours on the ratification of the Panama Canal Treaty. These were the true believers. They understood better than most the profound effect failure to win ratification would have in all of Central and South America.

Ratification of the Panama Canal Treaty was essential if the U.S. hoped to restore strained relations in the region. Those relationships had been badly damaged by a series of U.S. missteps during the Cold War with the Soviet Union. For years the U.S. was all *get* and no *give* in the Americas. Large U.S. corporations exploited the region's natural resources. The CIA, in its proxy war with the Soviets, had backed military juntas hated by the people they ruled. The U.S. ignored human rights violations and stayed silent while dictators' opponents disappeared. The CIA even helped facilitate the murder of Chile's legitimately elected president, Salvador Allende, in 1975.

The stakes for passage of the Panama Canal Treaty were enormous. The information about Moises Torrijos had the very real potential of sending the treaty down to defeat. Yet I did not share the gloom that was so pervasive that morning, and this did not go unnoticed.

"You don't seem all that upset, Bob," said Ham Jordan. "You know something the rest of us don't?"

I probably should have shut up, but I didn't.

"What I know, Ham, is that we have all let our expectations get out of hand. This was always a long shot. Did anyone here really think that the treaty opponents were just gonna sit back and lose? I'm not happy about any of this, but I'm not surprised, either. Just when you think something good is going to happen, it falls apart."

"That's what I'd call negative thinking, Bob," said Ham, obviously frustrated.

"Comes from experience, Ham," I replied.

I'd watched my father stay sober for an entire year, even gotten to the point where I believed he would actually stay that way. When he went out on his one-year anniversary and brought it all crashing down around himself, and us, I learned the survivor's number-one lesson: Don't trust good news. Don't trust those who bring it.

In fact, don't trust anyone or anything.

What I didn't mention to Ham Jordan (then, or ever) was that in the service of getting the votes we needed on Panama, I'd engineered some fairly dirty tricks. Why shouldn't we expect the same thing to happen to us?

*   *   *

Phil Jordan and I spent the rest of the weekend going to Justice, to the CIA, to everyplace we could go, loading up Phil's car with a growing stack of top secret information. By Sunday night we figured we'd gotten it all, and then we looked at each other and said, "Where the hell should we put this stuff?" We weren't going to keep it at either of our houses, for heaven's sake; this stuff was highly classified. We ended up leaving it at the FBI field headquarters. The next morning we picked it up and taxied it all over safely to the committee on Monday morning.

But somewhere along the way, there was a leak.

The next day the Associated Press put out a story saying that Bob Beckel and Phil Jordan had taken a stack of highly sensitive drug information, destroyed parts of it, and only then delivered it to the Senate. We had no idea where this story came from. There was no truth to it whatsoever. But if it went out, it would be catastrophic.

Jody Powell, Carter's press secretary, called the AP reporters and the head of the AP Bureau into the White House. Jordan and I were both there. They had sent the story out embargoed, meaning it was already out there to all the AP subscribers but hadn't yet actually run anywhere.

Powell was furious. It was one of the more magnificent performances by a press secretary I've ever seen. He stomped around his office, threw cigarettes into the fireplace, and grilled those poor reporters to a crisp about where they got the information. As he did, it became clear to everyone in the room that the story didn't hold together and had clearly been trumped up. The head of AP said, "We're wrong and we're going to pull it back." It was the first time in my memory that a story like that was withdrawn.

Some of it actually did get into a few papers in a couple of places where they did not wait for the embargo, but it never got much circulation. If it had taken hold, that would have been the end.

Somebody had set us up. We never did find out who, though we certainly had our suspicions.

The Senate Intelligence Committee processed the information we handed over. Then the Senate held its first closed-door meeting in at least a hundred years, at which the Senate majority leader, who was then Bob Byrd, insisted that all one hundred senators be physically present in the chamber— no staff, no anybody else—to hear the report on the Panama drug issue.

To us this was critical, because we still had these undecided senators, and if this committee came out describing this information differently than we had described it to them it would be disastrous. But the committee reported that, yes, in fact, there was a sealed indictment against Moises Torrijos, and in fact his boat was warned off the Panama Canal Zone, but it happened before the Carter administration's time and the information was sent to the boat from places unknown.

The burning question was, just how *did* the boat get that information?

Clearly somebody in the intelligence community had gotten to the boat's captain and told him not to dock. The best guess was it was probably the CIA—back then we had people on the payroll everywhere in Latin America, and General Torrijos had been on the CIA payroll for a long time—but nobody could ever prove it.

Considering the timing of the leak, and the way the cable turned up in North Carolina, there was no question in anyone's mind that it was a Jesse Helms–orchestrated event. Whoever had leaked the information to the boat in the first place had no doubt also gotten the cable to Helms and said, "Hey, this might be a good story." Helms was disliked in the Senate, even among the Republican caucus, and this ploy was so blatant that a lot of senators said, "This is bullshit."

Another reason we all thought it was the CIA was that it was such a classic CIA move. On the one hand, they prevented an asset from being arrested, so he could continue running around free and giving them information. On the other hand, it also gave them a piece of information that might kill the Panama Canal Treaty—and since most of those guys over at Central Intelligence are decidedly right-wing in their views, they didn't want the treaty to go through, either. So that's how the thing ended up in Helms's state. Exactly how it got to the lunchroom, who knows.

In the closed-door session (as I later learned) Byrd looked pointedly at Helms and said, "Jesse, I don't know how this cable got into your state, but you've been the strongest opponent of this treaty. And the rest of us have got to ask the question of ourselves, why did it end up in a lunchroom in your state? I can only conclude that a national security issue was given to you in an illegal way, and you used it in an effort to defeat the treaty."

Helms of course stood up and said, "Absolutely not. I wouldn't do something like that. I have no idea how it got there." And most of the other senators just went, "Yeah, sure Jesse, fine."

Debate on the treaty now proceeded on the Senate floor. Every other issue was tabled. Bob Byrd took personal charge of the whole treaty proceedings. It was decided that the Senate deliberations would all be broadcast on radio (this was before C-Span), which of course meant it was broadcast into Panama. Some of the things being said by conservative senators were just awful. Omar Torrijos kept calling Ham Jordan at the White House saying, "You've got to shut this thing down! I've got people in the streets here. They're calling us a bunch of bean-heads and all kinds of stuff." But we couldn't shut it down. We had to weather it.

At this point we were only one or two votes off. The whole Torrijos affair had slowed things down, but it didn't kill us. One strong factor going for us, from a public relations standpoint, was that the business community was largely in favor of the treaty. There really was a case to be made that without the treaty, there very likely would be sabotage on the Canal, and that would be disastrous to the business community.

And we had one more unlikely factor in our favor: We had John Wayne on our side.

Wayne was a big supporter of the Canal Treaty because he had a house in Panama and he was a friend of Omar Torrijos's, and we got him to sign a letter to all of the senators saying he favored the treaty, which was extremely helpful. He was also a well-known conservative. Talk about the perfect PR guy. This was near the end of his life (he died two years later), but in 1977 John Wayne rode again, on our behalf.

*   *   *

The day of the vote finally came. We *thought* we had the sixty-seven votes we needed by a margin of one or two votes—but we weren't sure. There were still a couple of senators who just wouldn't say which way they were voting.

Before roll call began, Byrd made every senator come and sit at his desk. This was the first time this had happened in a very long time. Normally the president of the Senate will start calling out the names, and it takes him an hour to get through them all, because it takes that long for everybody to pop in and cast their vote so they can get back to lunch or whatever else they were doing. But Byrd had them all there together, sitting in their seats, before they started the roll call—so nobody was able to duck around and watch what other senators were doing.

Under the Constitution the vice president is the president of the Senate, so he has an office right up on the floor of the House, which was where we operated out of when we were on the Hill. Sitting there in Vice President Mondale's office, listening over the speakers to the vote going down, senator by senator, was one nerve-racking session. There was a lot riding on this, both for the country and also for ourselves.

When the final vote was tallied it was sixty-eight for the treaty—fifty-two Democrats and sixteen Republicans—and thirty-two opposed. We had won, with a one-vote margin. The sixty-eighth vote came from a senator who was fairly safe in his seat; Byrd had convinced him to wait and be the sixty-eighth, so that on the campaign trail the following year, nobody whose seat was at risk could be accused of having been the one who put us over the top on the Canal Treaty. Smart politics on Byrd's part.

All three senators I had approached with my nefarious schemes to get votes—the copper senator, the unpredictable senator with the poll, and Charles's senator—did in fact vote for the treaty. The other votes we needed we got mostly by persuasion, and not by getting their advisors drunk and into a whorehouse.

The truly sad part about the whole business was that because the vote was so deeply unpopular with the public, a number of very good senators, both Democrats and Republicans, went down as a result of their votes on Panama. Frank Church from Idaho, George McGovern from South Dakota, Bob Morgan from North Carolina, and a lot of other good people who had the courage to vote for the treaty were attacked for it the following year. The Panama vote was *the* major issue in those races, and they lost their seats.

Howard Baker, the Republican Senate minority leader, suffered greatly as a result of his vote, which was probably the biggest reason his run for president in 1980 failed. Although Baker had been considered a favorite for Reagan to choose as a running mate, he was passed over in favor of George H. W. Bush. In 1984, Baker didn't even try for reelection.

The Panama Canal Treaty vote turned out to be a very important step in my career. For Congress and the country as a whole, it was a costly ratification.

*   *   *

As Panama wound down, I became involved in two other pieces of foreign policy.

First I was assigned to support the top secret Middle East peace negotiations that were under way. When the talks with Menachim Begin and Anwar Sadat took place up at Camp David that September, I shuttled back and forth, bringing members of Congress in to meet the principals. Probably the most important of these visits was when I brought Clem Zablocki, then chairman of the House Foreign Relations Committee, to meet with Begin, Sadat, and Carter.

Camp David is not, as some people might imagine, a luxurious country estate. It's a bunch of rustic cabins in the wooded hills of Catoctin Mountain

Park, about an hour's drive north of D.C. The three key figures—Begin, Sadat, and Carter—were outside talking when we arrived. Begin was kind of grumpy and seemed in a sour mood. Sadat was warm and cheerful. He got up and he wrapped his arms around me and said, "Nice to meet you, Mr. Beckel. It's a real pleasure." He then greeted Zablocki the same way.

The Jewish community had been very suspicious of Carter and of whether he was genuinely supportive of Israel. Ham Jordan had said a couple of controversial things, and APAC (the Arab-Israeli Political Action Committee) was down on both of them. I had good relationships in the Jewish community, largely because of my years at NCEC, which was heavily populated by Jewish contributors, so at times I acted as a go-between.

Today people jump on Carter because he'll say controversial things, like his comments about Hamas being legitimately elected representatives (which they are). But he was never afraid to say controversial things. And had it not been for the Camp David talks and the fact that Egypt and Jordan both established diplomatic relations with Israel, Israel would have found itself in a perpetual state of war. That was a big part of Carter's contribution as president, and I don't think he's ever gotten enough credit for it.

After the Camp David process wrapped up, I was assigned to work on the SALT II Treaty, which was the result of seven years of negotiations between the U.S. and the U.S.S.R. to reduce the manufacture of strategic nuclear arms. The treaty had been successfully negotiated and signed by Carter and Leonid Brezhnev in June of '79 and was now going before the Senate Foreign Relations Committee. I worked with John Glenn, who was deeply involved in the treaty, and learned a great deal about telemetry, trajectories, and all kinds of technical stuff I'd never have learned if they'd tried to pour it into me at school.

Unlike with Panama, we never had a chance with SALT II. That September U.S. intelligence discovered a secret Soviet combat brigade stationed in Cuba. Three months later the U.S.S.R. invaded Afghanistan, and President Carter staged an international boycott of the 1980 Olympics (which were held in Moscow) in protest. The Soviet bear wasn't very popular with Americans. No way were moderate Republicans going to risk the public's wrath on this one. A number of those guys had voted for the Panama Canal Treaty and got the shit kicked out of them back home as a result. (Howard Baker, for example, came out against SALT II, even though he privately admitted that he knew passing it was the right thing to do.)

SALT II never got out of committee. Although the treaty was never ratified by the Senate, its terms were still quietly honored by both sides through
the mid-eighties.

*   *   *

In November of '79, just weeks before the Soviet Union invaded Afghanistan, Iranian students staged a hostile takeover of the American embassy in
Iran and took fifty-two Americans hostage in retaliation for our harboring
their deposed shah, Mohammad Reza Pahlavi. The hostage crisis became a
dark shadow that loomed over the rest of our time in the White House. With
the 1980 presidential campaign season just about to begin, it also was a major
factor in the outcome of both the primaries and the general election.

In the spring of 1980 I took a little time away from Washington to go
down to Texas and work on the Texas primary campaign against Teddy Kennedy. (Yes, it was weird to be running *against* a Kennedy, but hey, Carter was
my boss.) As the hostage crisis wore on, the tide of public opinion was turning against Carter, and Teddy, who'd been trailing in the primaries initially,
had staged an upset and done very well against Carter in New York and Connecticut in March. Pennsylvania, in April, was close to a draw, with Kennedy
winning by a slight margin. Texas was going to be critical.

Meanwhile, we were working like hell to draw up a viable plan for getting those hostages back.

This was my bailiwick. When I got to the White House, the Intelligence
Oversight Committees in the House and Senate had just been established by
Frank Church's committee, in part as a response to Allende's being killed by
the CIA. The new law made it illegal for the CIA to conduct overseas assassinations. It also required the president to report to the Intelligence Oversight
Committees on a regular basis. As part of my job I was involved in a lot of
those reports to members of Congress, and for weeks I shuttled back and
forth between Texas and Washington.

A week before the Texas primary I was up in Washington listening as our
ultra-secret hostage rescue attempt, Operation Eagle Claw, got under way.

Charlie Beckwith, the Delta Force colonel in charge of the operation,
was keyed in by satellite and talked the president through the whole operation in real time. I wasn't in the Oval Office but was in Ham Jordan's office,
where we were listening to the same audio feed as the president. We could all

hear Beckwith giving a blow-by-blow account of what was happening. Then we heard an explosion as one of our helicopters blew up. That was the end of the mission. It was a terrible tragedy and huge blow to American morale. Our diplomats didn't come home and we lost eight servicemen in the attempt.

In that moment we knew we'd also lost the presidency.

A week later we beat Kennedy in Texas by a margin of more than two to one, but it was to a great extent a hollow victory. The moment Operation Eagle Claw went off the rails, the election was over. Even though we were able to beat back Teddy Kennedy and take the nomination, it was clear that we were doomed to fail in November.

Carter deserves a lot of credit for taking the risk and making the attempt. Its chances of working were actually pretty good. Intelligence estimates were that we'd probably lose up to four of our hostages in the process, which was judged an acceptable risk. Obviously we never had the chance to find out if we could beat those odds. We then began working up alternative plans, but none of them ever happened. By that fall it was clear that Iran was going to go ahead and release the hostages—which they finally did on January 20, 1981, the day Reagan was sworn in.

To this day I'm convinced that William Casey, the Reagan campaign manager who went on to become Reagan's CIA director, had made a back-channel deal with the Iranians, telling them, "Just hold on through this election, and we'll give you stuff you need." Which, of course, they ended up doing.

But we'll get to that part of the story a bit later on.

Those four years were an exciting time to be at the White House. History was being made on many fronts. At the same time, it was not really a time for a Democrat. Carter was a fluke in many ways. If it hadn't been for Watergate he never would have gotten elected. He ran on his pledge, "I'll never tell you a lie," and on the heels of Watergate that was of course a perfect message. Plus he was a successful governor and not a part of the Washington establishment, which the country deeply distrusted. It was the perfect convergence of events for Carter's bid, and I was incredibly fortunate to be part of the whole thing.

*   *   *

While I was at the White House two other significant developments occurred in my personal life.

The first was that I began talking to my father.

The second was that I was introduced to cocaine.

After leaving home and entering the wide open spaces of adulthood, we three Beckel kids had all sought out our own paths. My little brother escaped to Hollywood to chase a career as a film actor (successfully, as it would turn out). My sister went the other way, gravitating back to our family roots and relocating in Ohio. I staked my claim in D.C. and the world of politics. I stayed in touch with both of them, and with our mother, too, who lived out the rest of her days in Lyme, where I visited her often.

But my father? He was the one family member I most identified with the misery of childhood, the one family member I had never planned to stay in touch with. Evidently, though, life—and the old man himself—had other plans.

My father had continued to write me ever since the Peace Corps years. He was proud of my work in the '72 and '74 campaigns, and *very* proud that I'd now gotten a position at the White House. One day, for the first time since I'd barricaded myself into the college president's office in 1970, we spoke on the phone. Soon we were talking fairly regularly.

These phone conversations were extremely tentative at first, at least on my part. Every time I picked up the phone I braced myself, fearing that he would be drunk. But he was clear and sober, every single time, and I was not used to that.

As we talked, I finally learned what had happened to bring about this surprising state of sobriety and prompted him, years earlier, to start corresponding with me.

While living in Westfield he had kept up a subscription to his old hometown weekly newspaper in Huntingdon, Pennsylvania. One day he read that the richest guy in town, a man named Westbrook who sold shoes at outlets across the state, had died. My father decided to use what little money he had to hop a bus and go console the widow, whom he apparently knew from his early years in Huntingdon. Three months later the two were married and moved to Charlottesville, Virginia, into a nice condo overlooking the Rivanna River.

My father's new wife, Christine, whom everyone called Teenie, had grown up around the Beckel brothers and knew they were a rowdy crowd. She told him, "Look, Graham, you can drink one day a month, and that's it. If you drink more than that, you're out, and I keep the money." She was the one in the marriage with all the money, so my dad knew that this was no idle threat. From that day forward, he did exactly what she had demanded—although he did take serious advantage of that one day a month.

I didn't know about any of this when it happened. I had gone off to the Peace Corps, and in his letters to me this was one topic my father didn't write about.

I went at these calls very carefully. But I listened to him. We talked politics, which he loved, and he had some ideas on policy, which were very good. We gradually started to reintroduce ourselves to each other, and during the eighties we became consistent phone pals—though I still did not see him in person. That was still to come.

During my final week at the White House in January 1981 I was introduced to a guy I'll call Mark, who gave me my very first taste of cocaine. We did a line of the snowy white powder right there, on a mantel over one of the White House fireplaces—another transgression that our boss, President Carter, knew nothing about.

Cocaine was just starting to become a big deal in the United States. There were all kinds of stories in the press, including a cover story in *Time* magazine, detailing how this was a nonaddictive party drug (the *only* known nonaddictive party drug, in fact), and hey, everybody was doing it. I did that one line of coke and instantly fell in love.

My youthful affair with booze and drugs was now well on its way to becoming a committed long-term relationship.

CHAPTER SIX

Where's the Beef?

After leaving the White House in January 1981, I went back into the political business and had a good 1982 season—the season of Ike Andrews and many others. By this time I had been in the campaign business for a solid decade, and I'd managed or consulted with close to a hundred campaigns. I was starting to think about moving on to something else. But there was one thing I hadn't done yet. It is every political consultant's dream to someday manage a presidential race. That dream came true for me in November 1982, when I got a phone call from Jim Johnson.

I knew Jim from the Carter days, when he had served as the vice president's executive assistant; now he was heading up a consulting firm in D.C.

"Fritz is running," said Jim, getting right down to business. "You available?"

Walter "Fritz" Mondale was making a bid for the White House in '84. And Jim was inviting me to come run the campaign.

Johnson's call couldn't have come at a more perfect time. I knew Fritz Mondale from working in the White House, and I liked him a lot. In fact, I liked him more than any of the other likely Democratic contenders for '84, in part because he was a straight shooter and unabashed liberal who never equivocated or apologized for his positions. He was also considered the front runner for the nomination. I thought this would be a good way to cap off my political consulting career.

I said yes. By December I was working for Mondale.

*　　*　　*

There was one more reason the timing was good: In late '82, Reagan looked vulnerable. The economy had been in a deep recession for over a year, and he was struggling to convince people that his economic policies were not the cause of their hardships, that if they would just stick with him, he would turn things around eventually. He had come up with the phrase "Stay the course," which he used again and again. His vice president, George H. W. Bush, later picked up the phrase and ran with it. So did *Saturday Night Live*'s Dana Carvey in his hilarious and wildly popular Bush impressions. Back in '82, we Democratic consultants had been using the phrase against our Reagan-Republican opponents.

For example, I'd had a candidate during the '82 election season, Rick Boucher, running for Congress in Virginia's Ninth Congressional District, what they call "the Fighting Ninth." Boucher was considered a very long shot. He was kind of a dweeby, academic-looking guy from the University of Virginia who happened to come from a family in the Ninth with some money. He was running against a Republican incumbent named Bill Wampler who'd been in office for decades.

As Reagan's economic program continued to struggle, the president had been using the line "Just give my program a chance to work." Unemployment in the nation was up over 10 percent, and in this Virginia coal mining district it was running even higher. I put together an ad for Boucher that showed Rick walking out of a deserted coal mine and saying to the camera, "Reagan says, 'Give my plan a chance to work.' I say, 'It's time to give *people* a chance to work.'" It was so effective that it turned the tide in Boucher's favor. We'd been behind by thirty to forty points when we started. By the time we got up close to November we had closed the gap to within five points.

Here we ran into a snag. We couldn't seem to close that gap.

At this point Wampler had been around for nearly thirty years. The polls were telling us that people liked him but were getting tired of him, and that if we could figure out a way to get him a retirement watch they'd be happy about that and not beat him up. I decided we needed to do something to give voters the permission they were looking for not to vote for him.

We brought in a guy whose voice sounded just like Wampler's and recorded some phone messages and set them up as robocalls. (This was well before robocalls became more tightly regulated.) The night before the election, starting at 11:00 p.m., the calls started going out to voters in the district saying, "Hey, Bill Wampler here. I just wanted to ask you for your vote tomorrow, an important day for me . . . ," and so on, and then hung up.

An hour later, the same call: "Hey, Bill Wampler here . . ." One o'clock: "Hey, Bill Wampler here . . ." Two o'clock—"Hey, Bill Wampler here." And on and on throughout the night. Babies were being kept awake all through the district and people were boiling mad. The next day Wampler got literally booed at his own polling place. It was a shameless tactic and I was roundly (and rightly) chastised for it. Still, we won the race.

My bag of tricks aside, that outcome reflected the general mood of the voters in November '82. People were tired of the recession, tired of unemployment. They were ready for a change.

Maybe they would want Fritz Mondale.

I did have one concern about becoming Fritz's national campaign manager. An intensely loyal man himself, the former VP was surrounded by loyal staff who had been with him for many years; we called them the Minnesota Mafia. I was a bit worried that it might be tough for me to break into this crowd.

That turned out not to be the case. They were great. Since I had more campaign experience than most of them, they didn't hesitate to defer to me on political questions, and in fact we all got along very well.

Mondale and I hit it off right from the start. He was a hard worker and never whined (the way most presidential candidates do). Still, he was difficult to get close to. He was Norwegian through and through, and Norwegians did not wear their emotions on their sleeves. But he was a great stump speaker, an old-school politician who had come up through the ranks of the Democratic farm labor movement in Minnesota. Fritz knew how to talk to a union hall and burn the paint off the back of the room. That burning-paint approach doesn't work well on television, though, and I did worry about that. To his credit, he was aware of the problem and worked hard on having a more relaxed, natural delivery in front of the camera, but still, TV was never that kind to him. Or almost never.

*   *   *

There were a lot of people running for the party's nomination that year. There was Reubin Askew, former governor of Florida; Alan Cranston, senator from California, who was nearly seventy but colored his hair so it looked red;

Gary Hart, the handsome young senator from Colorado; John Glenn, former astronaut and now senator from Ohio; Fritz Hollings, the senator from South Carolina, who was a pretty strong candidate; the Reverend Jesse Jackson, who was an extremely compelling speaker; and George McGovern, who despite his epic failure in the '72 race was widely respected.

Among these seven, there were only three we were really worried about:

- Glenn, who had true American-hero status—the movie *The Right Stuff* had just come out, which was all about the American space program and starred Ed Harris as Glenn, and we thought that could get him some political traction
- Hart, though he was so young and not well known and thus considered a long shot, still had a strong streak of Kennedy-like charisma, which he obviously was going to play up as much as possible
- Jackson, who would have a lock on the black vote and played very well on TV. Even though nobody thought Jesse Jackson had a serious chance of winning the nomination, he clearly had the potential to rattle things up, soak up a lot more of our resources in the primary fight than we'd like, and make it a lot more difficult to come into the convention with the kind of unified momentum we were looking for

*   *   *

Running a presidential campaign is like living twenty-four hours a day in a Cuisinart with the power button permanently stuck on the ON position.

For one thing, it's a huge operation. In terms of personnel, logistics, and dollars spent over its two-year lifespan, a presidential campaign is the equivalent of a Fortune 500 company, except that you have to start it from nothing and have it fully operational in weeks. You have to put in headquarters, put in phone systems, hire (and manage) thousands of people, and plan an enormously complex nationwide strategy.

What makes it even crazier is that your product is not a widget, but a human being. And market conditions are changing on you constantly, sometimes dramatically, and often in ways impossible to anticipate.

And you are *on* seven days a week, twelve to eighteen hours a day. Make that twenty-four hours a day, because even when you're sleeping, you're obsessing about it all.

The campaign operation we put together was considered one of the best anyone had ever seen, at least among the political press. At the end of '83 *Newsweek* ran a cover story showing Mondale on a ski lift with the headline, "Mondale, Inc." The story inside was focused on three people: Johnson; his chairman and good friend, John Riley, who was counsel to the campaign; and myself. The piece talked about all the money we were raising and how well we were doing. Mondale was getting endorsements from all kinds of people, and was starting to look unstoppable.

But in politics, there is no such thing as unstoppable.

The first contest was the Iowa caucus. Mondale had been a senator for Minnesota, which borders Iowa, and Iowans considered him almost as the third senator from Iowa. Expectations for him to win in Iowa ran high. That feeling of inevitability could work for us, but could also work against us. To make it work for us, we needed not just to win, but to win big. In other words, to crush the competition.

There were limits placed on how much you could spend in each state. The spending limit in Iowa was something like $480,000; of course, we way overspent that. The way we got around the state limit was by setting up our phone bank operation in a neighboring state, either Minnesota or Illinois (I don't remember which), and stationing our organizers in the surrounding states so they could call in or drive into the state to work. Thus we could bill all those expenses against the other states' limits. Iffy, but technically legal.

Mondale won big in Iowa, as expected, with close to 50 percent of the vote and everybody else trailing way behind—except Hart, who came in second with a shocking 16 percent.

This is what makes campaigns such an interesting game: You'd think that if you won 50 percent of the vote in a particular contest it would be the death knell for everybody else in the race. But that's only math, and politics is not about math, it's about perception and expectation. Because this was Iowa and everyone's expectations were low for every other candidate but Mondale, the fact that Hart had done as well as he did had a lot of impact. Even though we'd captured well more than twice the votes he did, the psychological advantage now tipped in his favor.

Now Hart had a little head of steam going into New Hampshire, which was coming up in four days.

As the focus of the campaign shifted to New Hampshire, everyone was expecting Mondale to win there, too. On February 27, the night before the primary, we got the results of our latest poll—and it showed that Mondale had actually fallen *behind* Hart. I wasn't that surprised. Mondale was never a good New Hampshire candidate; there weren't that many labor unions there (labor unions being our strongest base of support), and he never felt very comfortable up there. But the campaign staff was caught completely off guard.

The next day, we lost to Hart.

We had rented the Manchester High School gym to hold a press conference for the thousand or so reporters who were in New Hampshire covering the primary. We had twenty seats set up on the stage for all the people who had played key roles in the campaign and wanted to take credit for winning in New Hampshire. Once it was clear our guy lost, of course, everybody split the state, and we ended up holding the press conference with just three of us up there: Peter Hart, the pollster; Paul Tully, the field director for New Hampshire; and me.

The press conference was blistering. They hit us from every direction. "What went wrong?" "Were you surprised?" "Can Mondale recover?" blah, blah, blah. A truly terrible experience.

The following week, in Maine, Mondale lost to Hart again—and now Hart took off like a rocket ship. Things started getting so bad for us that donations dried up. We didn't know how we were going to finance the rest of the campaign.

At this point, we came up with a novel idea. Each person running to be a presidential delegate at the convention is allowed to spend money on his or her own behalf. We put together delegate committees, then approached all the donors who had already maxed out what they could legally contribute to our candidate, and got them to start giving money to the delegates instead. Then we used that money to run our campaign.

We limped on into Super Tuesday, when nine races were all held on the same day. We were getting bludgeoned in state after state as the polls came in, and even with our borderline-legal delegate-committee tactic, we were almost out of money. If Hart rolled over Mondale on Tuesday, the way everyone was predicting he would, our candidate would be finished. It would be all over.

I decided it was time to roll the dice.

Quietly, I pulled every one of our organizers out of every state except for Alabama and Georgia, where there were a lot of labor unions and a fairly large black vote, and threw everyone we had into those two states.

On March 11, the Sunday night before Super Tuesday, the last debate with all the Democratic candidates would be taking place in Atlanta. I planned to go down the day before to help prep the debate and then come back up to D.C. headquarters. I never stayed for debates themselves; that was part of my superstition.

The night before leaving for Atlanta I was watching television with my girlfriend, and a commercial came on for Wendy's. There was this tiny, crotchety old lady yelling, "*Where's the beef? Where's the beef?*" My girlfriend commented, "You know, that reminds me of Gary Hart."

Bingo! The idea hit me like fireworks going off.

Our polling had told us that even though Hart was on fire, people still wondered just who this guy was. They didn't know him very well. His whole thing was his "new ideas" versus Mondale's old ideas. He was doing his best to project a sort of young-new-face, JFK-style image that would breathe fresh air into Washington's tired old politics. That was basically the theme. But we hadn't heard a lot of substance there, and there were still a lot of questions about him and what that all really meant.

When I got to Atlanta the next day I rushed over to Mondale's hotel and went straight up to his suite. As I walked in I called out, "Fritz, I've got it!"

"You've got what?" he said.

I stood still, looked at him, and said, *"Where's the beef?"*

He looked at me like I was out of my mind.

Wendy's had spent millions of dollars on this ad. It was hugely popular. Clara Peller, the little old lady in the commercials, had become a national icon. *Everyone* knew that slogan. But Mondale had absolutely no idea what I was talking about. He never watched television. He'd never even put out a political ad for himself until he was on the ticket with Carter in 1976.

I tried to explain it to him. I got down on my knees, trying to play Clara Peller. I said, "You get the idea? First this big boat comes by, and it sort of looks like Burger King, and then there's this big fluffy bun with nothing but this pitiful little beef patty inside, and there's Clara yelling, 'Where's the beef? Where's the beef?'"

Mondale looked at me again, then shook his head and said, "Nah, that's not going to work. I don't get it."

"Look, Fritz," I said, "just do me a favor and think about it."

He must have thought about it that night, because the next morning, when Fritz was on his way to church and I was outside my hotel on my way to the airport to fly back to Washington, his motorcade pulled in right next to me, and he yelled out the window, "Bob, come over here!"

I went over to his car, leaned down to his open window, and he said, "I think you're right." And then, enunciating each word carefully, he goes, "Where—is—the beef?"

I said, "No no no, Fritz—it's, *Where's* the beef?"

"That's not proper English," he said. "It's, 'Where *is* the beef?'"

I wanted to pull my hair out. Our entire campaign was standing on its tip-toes at the edge of the precipice, about to fall into the abyss. Within forty-eight hours we were almost guaranteed to run smack into the dead-end conclusion of our bid for the White House, unless we could pull off some kind of eleventh-hour miracle. And he was concerned about proper English?

"Fritz," I said, "trust me when I tell you this. *Where's the beef?* You've got to say it that way. You've got to look for exactly the right moment, turn to Hart when he talks about his new ideas and all the rest of it, and say, 'Senator, where's the beef?'"

He goes, "Where—is—the beef, Gary?"

"No, no, no, no, no," I said. "Gary, *where's the beef?*"

He grumbled a little and waved his hand, annoyed, like he was waving away the whole silly idea. I gave up. Clearly this just wasn't going to work. I started to walk away—and he said, "Wait a minute. Wait a minute!" I turned back and looked at him. "I got it," he said. "You're right. *Where's—the beef?*"

I said, "You've got it, Fritz. Go with it. It's going to turn this race around."

Nobody in the campaign thought a win was remotely possible at this point. Somebody on the staff had even written a concession speech for Mondale to read on Tuesday evening. But then, nobody but Paul Tully had really caught on to the fact that we'd moved all our organizers into those two southern states.

And of course, nobody knew that our candidate was going to try to pull off a Clara Peller impression on national TV.

That evening on the debate stage, the millions of people watching all saw what happened. Right on cue, Senator Hart started talking about his "new ideas." "I've made quite an issue of the need for a new generation of leadership," he said. "I think there is a fundamental difference, for example, between Vice President Mondale and myself," and he launched into a discourse on his "new thinking" on jobs creation.

Mondale, who was sitting right next to him, turned in his direction and said, "You know, when I hear about your new ideas, I'm reminded of that ad—" and he looked directly at Hart and said, "*Where's the beef?*"

It was Mondale's TV moment—and it was magical. It has since become one of the iconic moments in the history of American presidential debates. You can find it online and watch it.

Mondale is looking at Hart, completely deadpan, and the moment he says the line the whole audience starts laughing—and as Fritz hears the audience's reaction his face lights up with this big delighted grin, like he's thinking, *Hey, this is working!*

Hart struggles to get on top of it—"Well Fritz, if you'd listen for just a minute, I'd think you'll hear it," he says with a forced-friendly grin—but he doesn't have a chance. From that point on, Mondale's body language completely changes, and he's beaming and looking around, suddenly as relaxed in his chair as a king at home in his castle.

It couldn't have gone more perfectly. Mondale seized the moment, and the moment carried the evening.

Back in D.C. two days later, on Super Tuesday, reporters from all the big papers and all the networks gathered in Washington in a large hotel ballroom to witness the election returns. I was busy working the room, playing the lowball position—not outright pessimistic, but very tempered.

This was strategic. I wanted to build essentially the opposite condition to the one we'd faced in Iowa. I wanted to keep everyone's expectations as *low* as possible. As I went around the room people were telling me, "Bob, you don't have a chance. Hart's going to kill you, you're going to be out of the race." And I admitted to everyone I talked to that, yes, if Mondale lost Georgia, that would pretty much mean he'd lost the race. Of course the subliminal message I was really hammering home, without anyone realizing it, was the other side of that statement: What if Mondale *won* Georgia?

Chris Matthews wrote about my strategy and this very press event in his book *Hardball* as an example of managing the expectation game in politics. I've always believed that the key to success in politics is to maximize your own assets and minimize your deficits, and to maximize your opponent's deficits and minimize his assets. In this case, Mondale's deficits were obvious.

He was going to be killed on Super Tuesday. His assets at the moment were virtually nonexistent. So I had the press exactly where I wanted them: They had the lowest possible expectations for our candidate.

If we hadn't won anything at all that day, that would have been the end of it. But secretly, I felt certain we were going to win Alabama and Georgia.

And we did. What's more, Alabama and Georgia were the first two states to report their closing tallies, and once that happened it was such a big deal, especially because it ran completely contrary to everyone's low expectations, that suddenly the other seven states didn't matter. The reporters and media people in that press room were all congratulating me, saying, "Mondale, what a comeback!"

The next day, as I was waiting to go on the *Today Show*, Gary Hart walked in. Judging by the look he gave me, if he'd had a gun in his hand, I'd be dead. Hart went out first, and Bryant Gumbel asked him, "What happened, Senator?"

Hart said, "What do you mean, what happened? I won seven out of nine states!"

"No, no," said Gumbel. "I mean the big ones—Alabama and Georgia."

Hart sat there and fumed. When he walked off the set he shot me a homicidal glare.

I walked out onto the set and sat down, and Gumbel said, "Great comeback, Bob!"

*   *   *

After Super Tuesday we continued to roll over Hart. By this time Glenn had withdrawn from the race (that *Right Stuff* film never did make the political splash we'd worried about) and so had all the other candidates—except for Hart and Jackson. The last thing we wanted, in the next three months leading up to convention, was a costly and contentious three-way race. We had to find some way to narrow the field, if we could.

Mondale had a very close friend in Georgia, Bert Lance, who had been Jimmy Carter's director of management and budget but was forced to resign in his first year in office after being indicted as part of a banking scandal. (Bert was later cleared of all charges.) Bert had a very good relationship with Jesse Jackson—in fact, he later served as Jackson's campaign manager in his second presidential run in '88—and he helped me forge a working relationship with Jesse and the Jackson campaign. I met with Jesse more than forty times during that year, and we established a very good relationship. But we simply could not talk him out of staying in the running.

Whether we wanted it or not, a three-way race was what we had.

In order to seal this thing, we needed not to make many mistakes. To get a majority of delegates in a three-way race, we had to not just win but win big, every week. The Illinois primary was coming up on March 20, just a week after Super Tuesday, and the polls showed Hart even with us. We had to focus everything we had on Illinois.

And then something happened, one of those completely unpredictable and unplannable things that happen in campaigns, and that can break either way, in your favor or against you.

There was a young intern in our campaign who happened to be walking by the room where we were editing some man-on-the-street-type ads about Hart. The ads featured brief clips of people saying things like, "I don't think this guy Hart knows what he's talking about. Where does he come from? What's he about?" They were pretty negative.

This kid went out that night and had a drink with one of Hart's young aides. Probably hoping to come off as a big shot, a guy who was on the inside of things, he told the other aide about the ads we were working on. This filtered up through the Hart campaign, and eventually came to Hart's attention on his plane as he was on his way to Illinois, the day before the primary. The moment he touched down he started going on the air saying, in effect, "Mondale, I demand you take these ads down! These are horrible ads. This is *not* the way to win a campaign!"

The thing was, the ads hadn't aired yet.

Once we finished them, we put them in the trunk of a staffer's car, so he could drive them off to get them shipped to Illinois. On the way, his car broke down.

When I heard what was happening I immediately called the staffer, caught him just in time, and said, "Don't ship those ads! Bring them back." Meanwhile I called Mondale and said, "When you get off that plane in Illinois, go on the air and tell Hart, 'Hey, you've got to play this thing straight. There are no ads like that.'"

That cost Hart Illinois.

Then, a few weeks later, the delegate committee story broke.

We were staying at some rich, Oscar-winning director's house in New York City, getting ready for the New York primary. Our host had a screening room in his home, with one of those pull-down movie screens, which was where we were meeting to talk about strategy when Mondale learned about what I'd done with the contributions through the delegate committees.

He was not happy about it and demanded we take them down right away.

"We can't do that, Fritz," I said.

He grew furious. I'd never seen him like that before, have never seen it since.

"I don't give a shit what you think," he yelled at me, "you close it down!" Then he hurled his cigar at the movie screen and said, *"You take those fucking things down!"* The cigar was burning when he threw it. The screen burst into flames. Fritz was so mad, I thought the screen might have caught on fire even without the cigar.

So we had to close down the delegate committees. We took some hits about it in the press for a few weeks. But we managed to survive it.

We battled it out with Hart for the next two months, until the last big contests on June 5, which were California and New Jersey. These two states were significant prizes because they went by proportional representation, meaning whatever percentage of the vote you got, you'd get that percentage of that state's delegates. If Mondale won at least one and did reasonably well in the other, we'd be in good shape.

The run-up to that contest was absolutely grueling. We were crisscrossing the country, back and forth between California and Jersey, Jersey and California. It was a brutal pace. Hart was doing the same thing. At that point it was a dead heat, and nerve-racking as hell. Then, about a week before the primary date, Hart was at a fund-raiser in Beverly Hills with his wife, Lee, and was overheard making a comment to someone: "Here's the good news: Lee gets to campaign in California. The bad news is, I've got to campaign in New Jersey."

Someone caught it on tape, and it made its way to us. Bingo.

Within forty-eight hours we had it on the air all over New Jersey. Hart got beaten like a drum. And Mondale came within a few points of beating him in California. That put us over the top.

However, we still had to contend with Jesse Jackson, who refused to bow out. And even though Hart now had no chance of winning, he stayed in, too.

It was going to be a three-way slugfest right to the bitter end.

*   *   *

By the end of June we were in the final run-up to the convention. I had lost count of the number of times I'd met with Reverend Jackson by this time. He was a frustrating man. You could never get him to close a deal. He talked a good game, but most of the time that's all it was: talk. I had by now heard his bullshit so much and so often that I didn't hesitate to cut him off to get to the point.

By this time I'd also gotten pretty good at doing an imitation of his rap: "From the outhouse, to the courthouse, to the state house, to the White House." Often I'd end up standing on a chair yelling, "Our time has come." Jesse would laugh.

Usually I had at least a good half a buzz on when I met with Jesse, to ease the pain of listening to his sermons. Contrary to rumors, Jackson did not drink or use drugs. He just drove others to it.

On this day we were heading to a meeting in Kansas City, Missouri, just before the annual conference of the NAACP. Both Jackson and Mondale were speaking. We were pushing for a meeting between the two with the aim of getting Jackson to endorse Mondale. Another hopeless task.

At six-thirty that evening I showed up at Jackson's suite, ready for a two- to three-hour meeting, and stepped right into the chaos that was the Jackson presidential campaign. For starters, three meetings had been planned at the same time. Jesse didn't mind this confusion at all. He reveled in it. To Jackson, chaos was an ally that allowed him to gain the upper hand and keep other people off balance.

I sat there for a while, waiting for the other two meetings to be finished, and when they both finally wrapped up I started going over Mondale's plans for the next day. Frank Watson, Jackson's white aide (and professional Jesse ass-kisser), interrupted to tell us that the motorcade was ready to take Jesse to a fund-raiser at some barbecue joint deep in the Kansas City ghetto.

I lost it.

"What the fuck is this, Frank? I fly out here early to have this meeting, and now you tell me you've scheduled a fund-raiser at the same time?"

"It came up at the last minute," was Frank's lame response.

That did it.

"Everything in this fucked-up campaign is last minute! I'm out of here." I started out the door—and the next thing I knew Jackson had got me in a big bear hug. He got me calmed down and urged me to come along with him.

"You and I can have our meeting there," he said, then added his usual closing line, "you'll learn something."

And this time, was he ever right about that.

From the car window I could clearly recognize the point where our motorcade left the safety of the city's business district. We started out on streets that were clean and well policed. As we moved toward the ghetto the number of broken streetlights steadily increased and boarded-up buildings became the norm. On hot nights like this one everyone was out in the street. Air-conditioning was still a luxury here.

The barbecue place was well lit and still impressive through the grime covering its walls, a sad reminder of a neighborhood that at one time had been prosperous. By 1984 the place was surrounded by dilapidated public housing projects. We pulled up to the front door where several preachers and other local dignitaries met Jesse. After briefly shaking hands, he told the welcoming group that he had to speak with me alone for a few minutes before they got rolling.

This last bit of information did not exactly make me an instant favorite with the crowd. But what was I supposed to do, turn down the meeting? Catch a cab back to the city? What cabs?

We went inside and sat by ourselves at a two-person booth looking out on the parking lot. The topic, of course, was the convention, which was now just a few weeks away.

As the two of us started talking over the issues involved, word quickly spread that the Reverend Jesse Jackson was right there in the neighborhood. Within minutes the parking lot, which had been nearly empty when we got there, was teeming with folks trying to get a glimpse of Jackson. Obviously we weren't going to be able to get that far with our meeting.

Here I was once again, on Jesse's turf and on Jesse's terms.

Yet with all the frustration, as infuriating and exasperating as the situation was, at one point during our inconclusive conversation I got a rare glimpse of the other Jesse Jackson. The one with his mask off.

A kid in the crowd outside, no more than four or five years old, was being held up by his daddy to get a better look at Jesse. As the kid waved he accidentally hit his hand on his father's cigarette. We could hear the poor kid's screams of pain through the window. Jackson called over one of his Secret Service agents and told him to bring the boy and his daddy inside and over to our table.

Jesse had a way with young kids that bordered on the magical. I'd seen it before, but never so vividly or with such dramatic effect. He sat the little boy on the table and talked to him so softly that, sitting right across from him, I couldn't hear what he said. I saw Jackson grin and kiss the little boy's burned hand. Within a few minutes the kid began to smile, then laugh. Jackson then took one of his ever-present silk hankies from his breast pocket. On it, with a pen, he wrote something for the boy and his family, and gave it to him. That was one happy kid when he and his daddy departed from the table.

After the two had left us alone, Jesse seemed almost embarrassed. Maybe he felt exposed, showing his vulnerability to another pol. But to this day I believe that the Jesse I saw with that little boy was closer to the real Jackson than the public Jesse who causes so much fear and loathing among conservatives.

By this time the parking lot crowd had grown in size and was getting louder. Well over a thousand black folks were out there now, yelling, *"Jes–se, Jes–se, Jes–se."* The Reverend Jackson was never one to walk away from a crowd. He got up, grabbed me, and went outside to speak. Our meeting was over.

Standing on a milk crate in the parking lot, Jesse started out softly, as he usually did. His voice then built and built, working the crowd into a frenzy. I'd heard it all before, but tonight there was more to it than usual—more soul. As he closed with his "Our time has come" the crowd surged toward him. His Secret Service agents pulled him off the crate straight to his car. With sirens blaring they took off, chariots a-blazing.

I was pretty blown away by the whole scene. In fact, I was so impressed that it took a moment before I remembered something that Jesse and his entire entourage had apparently forgotten.

Me.

And now, in an inner-city crowd of hyped-up black folks, in a parking lot at night in the ghetto of Kansas City, in the dark, some of them drunk and all of them mighty riled up, there stood this one city-slicker-looking white guy.

Smiling, with fear written all over my face.

In an instant I'd put on my racial sympathy mask. Which was strange, when you stop to think about it, because the real me—if there was such a thing anymore as the real me, I honestly wasn't sure about that—was genuinely empathetic to the black community and everyone in it, and had been since as long as I could remember. So why did I need to put on a mask? Or was the mask actually who I really was? And if it was, then what was it that I was putting the mask on to cover up?

But I wasn't thinking about any of that, because a) being that introspective was of no interest to me in those days, and b) there wasn't time anyway. I was about to be swallowed by a mob that was turning angrier by the second.

My mind raced to find the right words to start a dialogue with some of the young brothers in attendance. My solidarity with the community went something like this:

Me: Hey, Bro.
Dude: Yo Mama sucks, just like you.
Me: How's it hangin', my man?
Dude: Get de fuck outta here, you bitch.

This was not the response I was hoping for. A circle of dudes was now gathering around me, closing in like a noose. My voice shrinking into itself, I tried again.

Me: Ain't that Jesse sumpin else?
Dude: You da ugliest fat white boy I eva seen.

Okay, this was not working.

Some sort of thrown object flew past my head. A hand reached out. Right then I wished I believed in God. I felt myself being pulled into the crowd. I smelled death. My luck had finally run out.

My eyes found the person holding my arm—and it wasn't some big angry dude about to stomp me, it was one of the gray-haired ministers Jesse had snubbed earlier that evening, pulling me out of the crowd and into his car. To me he looked like an angel.

Once we were in the car I looked at him and saw genuine concern in his eyes.

"Why you hang around like dat, boy? You coulda got yourself killed."

"It wasn't my idea," I replied. My terror hadn't backed down yet, but it was quickly being overtaken by anger at having been left behind. "Please don't take offense, but that sonofabitch Jackson—he left without me!"

The minister nodded and replied, "I know the feeling."

He put the car in gear and started driving me into the safer parts of downtown. The closer to downtown we got, the angrier I got. Jackson had been a pain in the ass on more than one occasion, but there was something about being left behind that caused my rage to grow by the minute, even more than I'd expected it to.

"People like Jesse don't see beyond what's right in front of them," the minister said. "He loved the crowd, and they loved him. Don't hold it against him, he just plain forgot you."

He kept talking, but by this time I was barely listening. Outside in the streets of Kansas City it was a boiling hot July night...but inside the car it was a bitter cold February day in 1963, and I'd been left to freeze in the car while my old man sat on a barstool in Middletown, Connecticut.

I noticed there were tears on my cheeks.

I will never, ever, let anyone abandon me like that again, I remembered whispering furiously to myself as I sat shivering in rage in the bathtub that day.

"Sorry, Reverend," I whispered as the kindly minister drove on. "Not on your life will I forget this one."

*　　*　　*

By this time, the general election was looking like a lot tougher battle than it did back in November of '82. The economy was experiencing a robust recovery, and Reagan was shaping up to be a much bigger problem than anybody had expected.

When we asked Jackson to release his delegates to Mondale the night before the convention, he said that in exchange for his delegates he wanted to give a prime-time speech. We had a huge argument about this among the campaign staff. Nobody but Bert Lance and I wanted to give it to him. Bert and I finally prevailed, but it wasn't easy.

I went over to see Jackson at Tip O'Neill's suite (O'Neill was still Speaker of the House in those days), and the two of us went out onto the balcony to talk.

"Listen, Jesse," I said, "this is really important. I mean, *really* important. Mondale's agreed to let you have a prime-time speech—but you've got to do it right, or I'm dead."

He said, "Beckel, I ain't going to tell you what I'm going to say, but I'll tell you this—by this time tomorrow night, you're either going to be a chimp, a chump, or a champ."

Well *that* was comforting. I went back to my suite.

When the convention began, I didn't go down onto the floor. I watched the entire thing on TV from my suite. Jackson gave a magnificent speech, released his delegates, and said nice things about Mondale. That put Mondale over the top and was considered a big coup on my part.

Jackson is an extraordinary human being in many ways. He was basically a gofer for Dr. King in Memphis on the day King was killed. Jesse ran up to King and cradled his head in his lap, got the dead man's blood on him, and then went on all the TV shows the next day as King's aide, wearing that same bloodstained shirt. Bert Lance put it best. "Bob," he said one day during the thick of the primary season, "you've got to remember that this is the same guy who rode to the top on the blood of Martin Luther King. You think he cares about some stiff honky from Minnesota?"

That business with the bloody shirt infuriated a lot of the King people. But that's Jesse: He sees an opening, he's going to take it. It was the King assassination that made Jackson a national figure, and he never let anybody get in front of him from that point on. He became *the* black leader in the country. Among the black community there were a lot of people who didn't like him, but he was strong enough that they weren't going to take him on. And he has essentially maintained that position for forty-five years. To this day, it's hard to think of another black leader in the country who would be the equivalent of Jesse, with the possible exception of Al Sharpton—and now, of course, Barack Obama.

I remember watching television the day Obama was sworn in and seeing clips of Jackson with tears in his eyes. The commentators were all saying, "Look at this, look how emotional Jesse is, how happy he is to see this day finally come." And I knew full well what was really going on in Jackson's mind: *Sonofabitch! That should be* me *up there.* There's never been a lot of love lost between those two guys. I think Jackson knew full well that he couldn't win the presidency in the eighties, but he certainly thought he should have gotten a lot more credit for it. He never thought the Obama people acknowledged him sufficiently for paving the way. He believed that Obama could never have made it without him and his trailblazing, as he says. And there's probably some truth to that.

There are a lot of things about Jackson that I admire. He is an unquestionably great speaker, and a good minister. And yes, he was a guy who saw opportunities and took them, but he's done much good for the black community. Those on the right accuse him of being a "professional civil rights leader" who wants to keep things stirred up so he can go on being in front of the cameras. And he does have a tendency to show up on camera whenever there's any kind of racial incident in the country. But I think that Jackson's motivation has always been fairly pure.

I never forgave him for leaving me behind that day in Kansas City. But I've also never forgotten the kindness and tenderness he showed that little boy.

*   *   *

Although we had safely reached the goalpost of the nomination, we were badly beaten up by the time we arrived. We were out of money and had lost precious ground battling Hart and Jackson right up through the convention. And Reagan was gaining ground. The only solid good news, beyond the fact of the nomination itself, was Mondale's choice of running mate.

Fritz had been interviewing vice-presidential candidates at his house in Minneapolis. (It was a Frank Lloyd Wright house, the most uncomfortable home I've ever been in in my life—everything squared off, the furniture built into the walls; it was terrible.) It was the same deal every time: The candidate came, went inside, came back out, met the press on the driveway, left...and the next one pulled up. It looked like a cattle call, and Mondale took a good deal of heat for that.

One day he called Johnson and me into the room and he said, "What do you think about naming a woman vice president?"

We both looked at him and said, "You know, that's a great idea. But who are we going to pick?" This was about a week before he needed to make his announcement.

He told me to go out and check out a list of women candidates, which I did—and every one of them had a problem. There was Martha Layne

Collins, who was governor of Kentucky, but she had some baggage; Dianne Feinstein, from California, who was a big Carter-Mondale supporter and a strong candidate, but there were financial questions about her and her husband, who was a wealthy investment banker. When you're vetting a possible candidate for an office like vice president, the level of scrutiny is intense. It has to be. Not many people would make the cut, no matter how strong their qualifications.

Finally we looked at Gerry Ferraro—and she looked great. Solid Italian-American candidate, great background, public school teacher, worked in the New York DA's office, good member of the House. She was Tip O'Neill's choice, and it wasn't hard to see why.

Mondale looked everything over and said, "All right, I've made my decision. We're going with Ferraro. Don't anybody say anything." He'd made a truly smart choice.

We took a private plane out to New York to pick her up and fly her back into San Francisco. When they walked out onto the convention stage and Fritz introduced Ferraro, she shouted to the crowd, "If we can do this, we can do anything!" and the place went absolutely nuts. She was terrific, and it was a smash success. It got a fantastic amount of press attention. We couldn't have asked for a better boost to our embattled campaign.

They went out and campaigned together for a short while, and everything was going great. Then we started setting Gerry up for her own campaign trip to California—when we ran into a problem.

In the process of vetting our VP candidates we had sent our lawyers to scour everyone's background and make sure we knew everything we needed to know (which was *everything*, period). Gerry's husband, John Zaccaro, owned a bunch of real estate in Little Italy and other parts of New York City and had a number of businesses there. I told her, "Gerry, you're going to have to release your taxes, or else the press will hound you."

She said, "Well, I'll talk to John about that, but it's John's call." I knew they had a very traditional Italian sort of marriage, and that the decision was going to be up to him. But what was he going to do, say no? I figured we were good to go.

Meanwhile a more pressing perception problem was pestering for my attention.

At the San Francisco convention, Mondale had announced that he was naming Bert Lance as the new Democratic National Committee (DNC) chairman. It's the candidate's right to name a party chairman, but when it started circulating that Lance was his pick, it caused a firestorm. The media caught the scent of blood in the water and immediately jumped on it. I had to hold a press conference with about a thousand reporters, trying to explain the wisdom of our candidate's choice.

We had just left San Francisco basking in the warm afterglow of our enormously popular and successful Gerry Ferraro announcement when the Bert Lance thing blew up. After going round and round on it, Mondale and Jim Johnson finally made the painful decision that Lance had to go. Someone needed to take on the unpleasant task of going out to New York, where Bert and his wife were then staying, and telling him in person. You can guess who got that job.

I flew out to New York and met with Bert, his wife, Labelle, and one of their sons, in their suite.

"Bert," I said after a bare minimum of uncomfortable pleasantries, "I hate to ask you this. You and I are old friends. But, Bert...you've got to resign."

His son looked at me like he could have killed me. Labelle had tears in her eyes. Bert said, "I don't know what I'm going to do, Bob."

Then Labelle said, "Why don't we all pray on it?" Bert was religious; his wife was *very* religious.

There we all were, down on our knees in this hotel suite, holding hands, and Labelle was praying out loud, and Bert was praying out loud, and I was thinking, "This is crazy, man—you couldn't *write* this script."

The praying eventually came to an end, and Bert said, "I've got the message. I heard it in my head. I got the message from the Holy Spirit. I'll resign."

He wrote out a letter of resignation, by hand, and gave it to me to deliver to Mondale: "I'm requesting—solely directed by my own initiative—that you allow me to relinquish the title of general chairman of the Mondale-Ferraro campaign."

I took it, read it, and looked up at Bert.

"Thank you, Bert," I said. "You're making the right decision."

I put the thing in my pocket, said my good-byes, and grabbed a taxi to get to the airport, to fly back to Minnesota and report to Mondale and Ferraro.

On the way, though, I had to make a quick stop.

I needed some booze.

The thing was, I hated flying. All my life I'd been desperately afraid to fly. (It was one of the reasons I was looking forward to giving up the campaign business.)

Plus, I was deeply upset about what I'd just had to do. Bert Lance was one of the finest human beings I'd ever known. I knew this was a terrible blow for him and his family. He'd already been drummed out of the Carter administration, and now he was being drummed out of the Mondale campaign. The thing was, he was innocent of the charges against him and had been acquitted in a jury trial. But baggage is baggage, no matter what the outcome is. Once you've got it, you never get rid of it.

As I would learn in the course of my own career, a number of times over, in several cases quite painfully.

I had my cab driver pull over in front of a liquor store, got out, went into the store and bought a bottle of booze, then came out and got back in the cab. We took off again for the airport. About eight blocks later I reached into my pocket to take out Bert's letter and read it over again.

It wasn't there.

"Oh, my God," I said. "What the hell happened to the letter?" I explained to the cabbie what happened.

"I dunno," he said, "maybe you dropped it when you got out of the cab to go into the booze store."

We circled back, pulled back up in front of the same store again—and there was Bert's handwritten letter, sitting in the gutter. I picked the thing up, jammed it back into my inside pocket, buttoned up the flap over the pocket, and said, "Thank you, Lord."

That was probably my very first conversation with God, and He came through for me. Although I wouldn't look at it that way until many years later.

Asking Bert to fall on his sword was, for me, the lowest point in the campaign. Even lower than losing.

*   *   *

By this time I was drinking heavily, I mean *heavily*, and it got progressively worse throughout the rest of the campaign. The pressure was so unbelievably intense, and the only medicine I knew to take to calm down was booze. I kept a bottle of booze in my desk at all times. I wasn't *drunk* drunk, but I was drunker during the day than I had been in a long time. And at night, Katy bar the door, I'd get loaded and sleep with any woman I could get my hands on. We had a third-floor apartment on Wisconsin Avenue, in the building that housed Mondale headquarters, and that became my secret tryst site.

By day, I was doing my level best to get a deeply honorable man elected to the presidency of the United States.

By night, I was steeping myself in a vat of unbridled drunken debauchery.

Somehow, I honestly don't know how, I kept getting away with it.

*   *   *

About a month after the convention, in late August, I was driving to a meeting with all the state directors we'd picked for the fall campaign. I turned on the car radio, and there was Ferraro on the news saying, "We've decided not to release our taxes."

What? I couldn't believe what I was hearing.

I pulled in to the hotel where we were meeting and sat there, fuming, as I waited for her motorcade to arrive. When they pulled up I got out, went over to her car, and told the Secret Service guys to stand back. I needed to talk to Gerry. Alone. I slid into the backseat next to her, told the driver "Get out" and then let her have it with both barrels.

I had huge respect for Gerry, and by this time we had an excellent relationship. I could tell her exactly what was on my mind. Which I did. I yelled at her so bad the windows got fogged up.

"Bob," she said, "I can't do anything about it."

"Gerry, I am telling you, you *have* to release your taxes, or we're fucked. It's the only question they're going to ask when you go around the states and talk to the press. The *only* question."

"Well, John won't do it," she said.

So I called John and told him, "John, you've got to do this. You've just got to."

"Bob, I'm not doing it," he replied. "Our taxes are nobody's business but mine and Gerry's."

"John," I pleaded, "you have no idea how crazy the press corps is going to go on this."

But he wouldn't budge.

It was, of course, a total disaster. On her next campaign trip the questions about her taxes absolutely consumed every moment of press exposure.

Finally, she was forced to hold a press conference about it. We asked every press person to come in, and she said she'd stay and answer every question they had, and she did, going through the whole grueling process, addressing every single detail the press could think of to bring up for scrutiny. The event lasted for more than two hours. It felt like two years.

In the end, they released their taxes.

Not only was there absolutely no impropriety at all, but it actually turned out that they had paid *more* in taxes than they had needed to pay. I called John and said, "John, you paid 43 percent in taxes. What are you, kidding me?" He was stubborn, but he was one honest guy.

But the damage was done and, just as it was for poor Bert Lance, it was going to stay done. Even with that press conference, the cloudy financial questions never really went away, and the issue dogged the rest of the campaign.

I loved Gerry Ferraro. She was an excellent candidate, and she would have made a hell of a vice president. She died after a battle with cancer at Mass General in Boston, in 2011. I miss her badly.

*   *   *

One morning that fall I woke up and turned on the television, and there was a beautiful ad playing that looked like it was about that summer's Olympics, which had been held in Los Angeles that year and had generated an enormous groundswell of national pride across the country. The ad started out in this quiet rural area, and you saw a farmer and his kid standing up on a hill, looking way down the road, and in the distance you could see police lights flashing in slow motion, and you knew immediately that this was the Olympic torch being run to California. It was so beautiful, the music was great, the thing was just mesmerizing. When the flag started to wave, without even thinking about it I automatically stood up and put my hand over my heart, watching that convoy go by. And in the closing seconds of the ad these words come over the screen: "It's morning in America. Reagan for President."

"Oh, *shit*," I said to my empty hotel room.

That was the theme the Reagan campaign had come up with. The economy was bouncing back. Things were looking rosy. It was morning in America. And here I was standing up there saluting this fucking television commercial for my opponent. I fell back on my bed and just about cried.

As the election d   near it was obvious that Reagan was growing stronger by the day. The only good thing I can say about the fall campaign was that we were so far behind, nobody gave us any odds at all. If lowered expectations were all there was to it, then we were in great shape.

Although there was one moment there that was sort of hopeful.

There were two presidential debates that fall. The first, held in Louisville, was the one where perceptions really mattered. At this point people's expectations of Mondale were so low that just getting on the stage with Reagan gave him a big boost. We actually measured this. We had monitors running in real time, recording whether people watching thought each candidate was doing a good job or a bad job from moment to moment. These monitors were finely calibrated and reacted to every single statement or gesture.

The moment Mondale walked out onto the stage, the dials all jumped to the right.

When your candidate gets high marks from the public just for having the balls to show up at all, that is not necessarily a good sign.

Before the debate started, I talked to Reagan for a few moments. Seemed like a nice guy. "Bob," he said when we were introduced, "so you're the one kicking my ass all over the place?"

"Yes, Mr. President," I said. "It's my job."

He smiled and said, "Well, you're doing a good job of it." I wished it were true.

The debate wasn't very eventful; both candidates were doing fine. I was standing off on one wing of the debate stage, and Ed Rollins, Reagan's campaign manager, was off to the other side. All of a sudden, right at the tail end of the debate, when each candidate was given ninety seconds to close, Reagan started off on a long, rambling, incoherent pitch about all the good his administration had done for the country. It went all over the place. He stumbled in a number of places. It was a train wreck. As I watched it unfold I thought, "This can't be really happening." I looked over and caught the expression on Mondale's face: "What the hell's going on?"

When it was over it was obvious to all that Mondale had won the debate handily. The press corps jumped all over that rambling closing statement of Reagan's. "It's his age," they said, "Reagan's starting to lose it." Reagan slipped seven points in the polls, and for the next two weeks he got beat up from every direction. All the people who had deserted Mondale and had been ignoring him were now suddenly his close friends. Typical politics.

It was all just too good to be true.

And it was, in fact: too good to be true.

During debate preparation for the second and final debate in Kansas City, two weeks later, Mondale said to me, "Bob, have you got another 'Where's the beef' for us?"

"No, Fritz," I said, "I don't. Those things only work when you've got a setup like we had with Hart. And we don't have it."

But ultimately it didn't matter, because nothing Mondale could have said would have changed the outcome of that second debate. The Gipper had got his mojo back. When Reagan got the dreaded question from one of the panelists about his age, he replied:

> I will not make age an issue of this campaign. I am not going to exploit for political purposes my opponent's youth and inexperience.

Boom. There it was—another iconic moment for the history books, and this time we were on the receiving end.

I was sitting there with other people from the campaign, watching the whole thing, and when Reagan delivered that line even Fritz couldn't help laughing. It was Reagan the actor at his best, and the moment was as devastating to us as "Where's the beef?" was to Hart. Right then I stood up and quietly said, "Okay, that's it," and started to walk away.

"What do you mean?" the others said. "We've still got half the debate left!"

"No," I said, "that's it. Forget about it. It's over."

And it was. Sure enough, we got crushed. Out of fifty states, we lost *forty-nine.* The only state we won was Mondale's home state, Minnesota— and that by less than four thousand votes.

Mondale knew he was not going to win the race; we all did. After all, the economy was growing at 7 percent and Reagan was now extremely popular. Beyond that, the country was weary of politics. We had been through Watergate, runaway gasoline prices, the Iran hostage crisis, and a general feeling everything was going in the wrong direction—until Reagan took office.

Hell, with things as good as they were in 1984, my guess is a lot of people didn't want to see any more campaigns, period.

Fritz Mondale and I have stayed close ever since the White House days. Now in his late eighties, he still has a great laugh and can poke fun at himself better than any of the rest of us ever could. I was proud to work for him, and I'm proud to call him my friend.

*   *   *

As crushing a defeat as it was, I rode "Where's the beef?" for the next twenty years on the speaking circuit. It was like the term "Watergate": After the Watergate scandal, every new scandal was called *something*-gate. "Where's the beef?" became a standard piece of the political vernacular in campaigns forever after, and because I got the credit for it, this helped me tremendously with my speaking engagements. To this day, every time I am introduced before giving a speech, the host will refer to me as "the guy who ran Mondale's campaign," which everyone knows lost in the biggest landslide in U.S. presidential election history.

In fact, sometimes I tell my host beforehand, "When you introduce me, make sure to remind people that I ran Mondale's campaign." Then after my intro I'll get up to speak and say, "It's so nice to see so many liberals in one room." That line goes over like a lead balloon, because these are typically very conservative groups.

Ahh: low expectations. Gotta love it.

Then I say, "Thank you, Mr. Chairman, for mentioning the Mondale campaign," and everybody laughs. And then I say, "I don't know why you guys are laughing. I managed a forty-nine-state loss, which was a record in presidential politics—and you're paying *me* to be here to give *you* political advice."

That gets an even bigger laugh.

CHAPTER SEVEN

TV Lights

"Ed, what the hell did I say in there?"

This was the question I posed to Ed Rollins as we exited the TV studio together. It was election season, 1984, and every week NBC's *Today Show* would host the two presidential campaign managers to talk about the state of the campaign. Ed was Ronald Reagan's campaign manager; his opponent, the campaign manager for Walter Mondale, was me. I was thirty-five years old, in my prime, my star on the rise...and completely blasted.

On this particular *Today Show* appearance I had been drinking and using cocaine pretty much right up to the moment I took a shower to get dressed and go do the show. Everything seemed to be going fine—until I walked off the set when our spot was over and realized that I could not remember a single thing I'd said the entire time we were on camera. I'd been in a complete blackout.

Thus my question to Ed.

Ed laughed and said, "The same bullshit you always say, Bob."

I didn't believe him. It wasn't that I didn't trust him. I liked Ed; we'd been good friends for years. It's just that when you are in the middle of a campaign, you always have to be careful. And among all campaigns, presidential campaigns are the highest-stakes game in politics. If I had committed a major blunder on the show, it wasn't Ed's job to tell me any more than it would have been mine to tell him if he had messed up.

I had to assume I'd said something bad and that, more than likely, I was screwed.

I went home, got out a hammer and some nails, and nailed blankets over my bedroom windows—don't ask me why, drunks do strange things—and crawled into bed, waiting for the phone to ring saying I was fired.

After not hearing from anyone for two hours, I finally got up the nerve to call campaign headquarters and ask them to courier over a tape of the *Today Show*. The tape came within the hour, and damned if I hadn't said everything exactly right. To this day I don't remember a word of it.

The next fifteen years of my life were a period of rising fame and deepening drunkenness, of brighter brights and darker darks. TV lights—and alcoholic blackouts.

*   *   *

Before 1984 I had done plenty of local television in locations around the country where I was running races, but I had not done national television, which is a very different experience. With the Mondale campaign, that all changed.

The first national spot I did was a segment on CNN very early in the campaign called "The Campaign Managers." With the colorful range of Democratic candidates running in the primaries, they thought it would be good television to bring on camera all the different campaign managers. This was going to be my first national exposure—in a sense, my first *real* television.

I still remember sitting in the studio, getting ready to go on the air, live, coast-to-coast, for the very first time. The producer, who knew I'd never done this before, came over to me and quietly said, "Now, Bob, when that red light comes on, that means we're on the air...but don't get nervous. You'll do just fine."

But I *wasn't* nervous. I *knew* I would do fine. When that red light came on I felt like someone had given me a Valium: relaxed and utterly at ease. From my first instant in front of the TV camera, I felt completely at home.

The thing for me about television was that I never *felt* like I was "doing television." A lot of people, when they get in front of that TV camera, start straightening their ties, and changing their voice, taking on a false air of authority, and in general do their best to become someone else. For whatever reason, I didn't do that. When I went on camera, people would see the same guy they'd see if they met me on the street. Throughout my waking life I was walking around wearing a mask, one of the skills at which survivors excel, and I would protect that façade ferociously if it were ever threatened. But the moment I went under those TV lights, I always felt perfectly at home just being myself.

I also started getting positive feedback from people right away about my TV appearances. That didn't have as much impact on me as you'd think, because I never did take positive feedback very well. (I tended not to believe it.) But I did have the sense that there was more television in my future.

Throughout the '84 campaign I did a lot of TV, and despite the absolutely crushing pressure involved in running a presidential campaign, most of the time I managed to keep my drinking reined in during the day to the extent that I could continue to function. That blackout with Ed Rollins on the *Today Show* was the exception, not the rule.

I was doing fine.

I had it all under control.

*   *   *

After the '84 election I more or less disappeared from television for two years. It was time to figure out what to do next. I'd promised myself that I would get out of the campaign business after the Mondale campaign, but what was my next act? I only knew I didn't want to go to work for anybody else. I wanted to work for myself.

Of the thousands of organizers around the country who had worked for Mondale, some were still in town in early '85. We got together and I asked them, "What are you guys going to do now?" They said they really weren't sure, but they figured they'd go looking for something, maybe find a campaign to work on.

One of them said, "You know, Bob, why don't you think about using us as a resource?"

I thought this was a great idea. We could build a type of grassroots company that hadn't been done before. There was already a type of grassroots component in lobbying campaigns, then done strictly through direct mail. There'd been one company that would send mailings out to voters, who would then send mail back to their member of Congress. Instead of lobbying Congress themselves, these guys were lobbying indirectly, through the voters. But it was sort of crude. I had a huge Rolodex of organizers spread out all over the country. Why not turn that into an altogether new kind of business? We could help lobbying campaigns by getting organizers in a particular congressional district or state to get significant numbers of people in that area to contact their member of Congress over whatever the particular issue was.

And there was nobody else in a position to do this but me—and, of course, the Reagan people. But they weren't about to do anything like that. Their guy had won the election. They were in the government business now.

I hit the bank for a business startup loan (I'd put some money away during the campaign years, but not much) and established Bob Beckel & Associates. With a staff of eighteen or twenty people, I moved into a wonderful office space overlooking the Potomac in Georgetown. In a sense, I was still doing campaigns, but now in a completely different way.

We built BB&A into a very successful business, and I relished every minute of it. We were breaking new ground, and the excitement was tangible. At the same time, the atmosphere at our office was casual and carefree. We all wore jeans and dressed up only to go to the lobby meetings once every two weeks or so. We loved what we were doing, and we were good at it.

Everything about the next few years was wonderful...except that during that time I also drank more and more. It reached the point where I had to keep some level of alcohol in my system basically twenty-four hours a day. As soon as I got up in the morning I would start the day with some Greek liqueur. Which sounds terrible, I know, but it had a licorice taste to it and I figured people around me would just think I was eating licorice. In fact, I carried a bunch of licorice around with me wherever I went to substantiate my cover story. During those years I kept licorice in my office, in my car, in my pocket, everywhere I went. Years later I learned that I'd fooled no one.

*   *   *

Toward the end of 1986 a new topic erupted in Washington and quickly captured everyone's attention. A story coming out of Lebanon alleged that there had been a weapons-for-hostages swap set up between the U.S. and Iran. Ten days later Reagan was on national television explaining himself to the American public.

When the Iran-Contra affair blew up I was not at all surprised. As far as I was concerned, what we were hearing just validated my earlier suspicions about the Reagan people and a back-room deal with the Iranians to keep the

American hostages on ice till after the 1980 election. They insisted it wasn't true, that it was bullshit, but I still have serious doubts about that.

In any case, the more immediate point was that Iran-Contra was big news—and big news needs big television personalities. When Iran-Contra hit, the producers of all the TV networks scrambled to find commentators who could talk about it effectively. Television producers are always under a great deal of pressure to deliver, and they like to play it safe. In other words, to go with proven commodities rather than try something new. If they know somebody who's been good on television before, that's who they'll grab to go on again this time. So they all ran to their Rolodexes to pull out the people they were comfortable with from the previous election cycle.

My TV career was off and running again.

Throughout December 1986 and all of 1987, at the same time that I was quite busy with BB&A, I was also doing lots of televised commentary on the Iran-Contra affair.

Then, one cold day in the fall of 1987, nearly a year after the Iran-Contra boom began, my phone rang at home. I picked up and a clear baritone said, "Bob? Peter Jennings, from ABC." I was floored.

Jennings was a rock star. When ABC first put him at the helm of its evening news program, at age twenty-seven, he was the youngest person ever to anchor a U.S. news spot, still a record today. By the time his voice showed up on my phone he had been sole anchor for ABC's premier nightly newscast, *ABC World News Tonight*, for four years, and in those four years he had singlehandedly pulled ABC News out of a ratings slump. By the end of 1989 his show would pull ahead of CBS for the first time ever to claim the number-one spot.

As it happened, Jennings and I had worked together briefly a few years earlier. In 1983 the Kennedy School of Government at Harvard held a mock crisis session and invited various people to role-play different White House staff members. I played the role of political advisor to the president; Peter played the role of press secretary. They presented us with some sort of crisis, and because the political office needs to work closely with the press office Peter and I spent quite a lot of time together that day. We came up with a good crisis plan and had a good deal of fun doing it. (I had been through crises in the real White House, and let me tell you, when they're real, they are not nearly as much fun.)

Apparently Peter had enjoyed the experience and remembered me from it.

"Why don't you come on the air with us, as an analyst for the presidential campaign in '88? We can start in Iowa and New Hampshire."

No hesitation on this one. "Sure!" I said. In one sense, Jennings's offer was exactly like being invited to run the Mondale campaign: It meant that I had hit the big time. It also marked a turning point in my career, the moment when the center of gravity in my world began shifting from campaign work to television work.

I followed the Iowa and New Hampshire races for ABC in early '88, and continued right on through the rest of the year. This was my first real experience with a big-time network, and it gave me a lot of exposure. And I was not exclusive to ABC. Another television gig soon came up that put me front and center for the entire '88 election season.

There was a new company out of Minnesota, called Conus Communications, that had pioneered the development and use of satellite uplink trucks as a tool for news gathering. Conus provided satellite uplinks for small and medium-sized markets that couldn't afford to have their own satellite trucks at the various primary and debate sites. They asked me and Haley Barbour, who was to become the chairman of the Republican National Committee and later governor of Mississippi, to participate together as political analysts for their various client stations. Which we both thought was a fantastic idea. Haley and I had met on the *Today Show* and had clicked instantly. Conus then said, "We can do this one of two ways. We can pay you a flat fee, fifty thousand for the year; or we can pay you on a per-shot basis, at two hundred per shot."

Haley and I talked this over and both had the same view. We felt pretty good about the assignment and thought we'd work well together. We said, "What the hell! Let's roll the dice and go for the per-shot basis." That turned out to be the right call: Over the course of that campaign season we did more than a thousand shots.

The coast-to-coast work for Conus was a fascinating experience. We would start at the 6:00 a.m. hour for the local stations on the East Coast, then do seven o'clock, eight o'clock, nine o'clock, then move through Central and Mountain time zones, continuing straight through the day as our broadcasts moved across the country, and go all the way up until two in the morning (that is, two in the morning for me in Washington) for the West Coast stations' 11:00 p.m. newscasts. Every time we did a spot we would change out the logos on our microphones so we reflected that station's identity. It went very well; we got a lot of good feedback, including a remarkably positive piece in the *Boston Globe*, which helped the show gain more visibility and got still more stations to sign on.

During the course of '88, still another television opportunity opened up, when I was invited to do a guest spot for CNN's *Crossfire*.

Crossfire was the mother of all political adversary shows. Premiering in 1982 with hosts conservative Pat Buchanan and liberal Tom Braden, the show broke all the rules for political and current events programming. CNN was barely two years old when *Crossfire* first aired, and it was not constrained by the standards of the network shows. It was definitely not *Meet the Press*. It was in-your-face politics: right versus left in a pitched battle for the high ground—or, depending on how you looked at it, the low ground.

The format was two hosts, one conservative and one liberal, and two guests, representing opinions from the right and left. The topics were selected specifically to evoke debate from both ends of the political divide. *Crossfire* was not a show for the fainthearted. If you wanted to be *in the crossfire*, you had better be ready for battle. The audience for *Crossfire* was the political equivalent of the viewers of the World Wrestling Federation. They were mostly men, over thirty, who were very partisan and, judging by the show's mail over the years, with very strong opinions about issues and hosts.

After that first guest shot I did another, and another. I ended up doing quite a few spots with *Crossfire* during 1988. Then they asked me if I would substitute host when Michael Kinsley, who was then their *Crossfire* host on the left, was not available, and I agreed. That was my first real step into the CNN world, as well as my first experience with the type of show that would become my bread and butter for years to come.

Crossfire was designed to generate strong feelings in its viewers, and that it certainly did. The mail I received was always genteel. The typical letter began, "Beckel, you big fat commie pig," or, "You're an asshole and a liar," or my favorite, "YOU ARE BORN FROM THE ROTTING RECTUM OF A DEAD SKUNK." Gotta love the fans.

Over the years I appeared with many conservatives both as a host and as a guest. For three years I cohosted *Crossfire Sunday* with Lynne Cheney, wife of Bush 41's secretary of defense, who would later become 43's vice president.

Lynne was smart and I liked her. In fact, I can honestly say—perhaps with the exception of the Prince of Darkness, Bob Novak—that my conservative cohosts were always good company. But my favorite of them all was columnist, talk show host, and two-time presidential candidate Pat Buchanan.

From the first day we met in 1983, Pat and I hit it off. Despite our obvious and wide political differences, we had much in common. We were both former athletes, both rabble-rousers with the same take-no-prisoners approach. As a viewer once wrote, watching Pat and me going at it was "like watching a good fight at the local bar." We both took this as a compliment, because in our younger days we both rarely had an argument inside a bar that didn't end up outside in a brawl.

My favorite Buchanan story was about the night during his college years at Georgetown University when Pat and some others were bar-hopping on M Street, a favorite watering-hole neighborhood among college students. With each passing bar, the boys got more rowdy. Finally the cops were called and Pat was thrown in a paddy wagon. When the wagon's door opened to let in another drunk, Buchanan came out swinging and belted a cop. My kind of guy.

Viewers of *Crossfire* may think they are seeing a completely unscripted verbal boxing match, but it's a bit more scripted than it looks. To make a good show, cooperation and coordination between hosts is essential. *Crossfire* encourages lively debate, but sometimes the debate can get out of hand and turn into a screaming match fairly quickly. The hosts can fuel the fire, or calm it down. The key is to have both hosts working together to keep order. Before airtime Buchanan and I would talk through that show's topics and discuss how to keep the shouting to a minimum without taking the edge off the show. When the debate got too heated, one of us would be the lead fireman while the other backed off. If one guest persisted in being out of hand, we would jump in together and double-team the offender. You did not want to be the focus of a Buchanan-Beckel tag team.

Hosts and guests may not be able to stand each other's politics, but their personal relationships are often pretty good. Don't get me wrong. *Crossfire* is a serious show, about serious issues, among serious people. The debates are very real. But to be successful, it also needs to entertain.

Opposing opinions are at the heart of the *Crossfire* format. Without clear and unambiguous differences, *Crossfire* would not work. Sometimes, however, the best-laid plans can go awry.

Take the case of the nuns at Auschwitz. In 1984 the Polish archdiocese and a group of Carmelite nuns established a convent in an old theater building that had been commandeered by the Nazis for their use during World War II. The building was on the outskirts of the infamous Nazi concentration camp at Auschwitz. After the war Auschwitz had been declared a memorial to the million and a half Jews who died there, along with hundreds of thousands of other eastern Europeans. The Jewish community wanted the convent moved to a new site, well outside the area of the camps. The nuns and others in the church didn't.

It was one of those *Crossfire* moments that gives producers heart palpitations. Pat was the conservative host that week; I was in substituting for Mike Kinsley on the left. Each morning the *Crossfire* producers would have a conference call with that night's hosts to go over topics and guests. On this day a number of issues were on the table, including the convent, but no firm decision was made during the call.

At the time Buchanan was hosting a radio talk show for Westwood One called *Buchanan and Company*. Three days a week, from noon till three, I was the Company. The radio show allowed callers to set the agenda; given Buchanan's audience, the issues were usually incendiary. That day on the talk show a caller raised the Auschwitz convent controversy, suggesting that certain Jewish groups in the U.S. were behind the effort to oust the nuns. Buchanan, a strong Catholic, was ballistic on the issue. He said the Jewish group could shove it and defended the nuns' right to stay. On certain issues Buchanan would not give an inch. The convent was one of them, and it smelled of trouble.

Pat had a reputation among Jews for being an anti-Semite. His support of a Detroit auto worker fighting extradition to Germany on charges of being a Nazi guard at Dachau was still a hot topic when the convent story broke. I am a strong supporter of Israel and know an anti-Semite when I hear one. In all the years I had been around Buchanan, I had never once heard him utter an anti-Semitic word. Many of my Jewish friends were adamantly convinced that Pat was anti-Semitic and constantly berated me for defending him. The convent issue had the potential to add fuel to that fire.

In his eyes, Pat wasn't attacking Jews but fiercely defending his own religion. And I sided with Buchanan on this one—not because I was gung ho for the nuns' position, but because I frankly didn't want to see Pat branded with the anti-Semitic label again. If I was on the same side, it might take a little heat off Pat. So we sang from the same hymnbook on the convent issue that day, and agreed on the air that the nuns should be allowed to stay.

But we had forgotten that the convent issue was a possible topic on *Crossfire* that night. It wasn't until we were on our way out of the radio studio that the thought even occurred to us. And if it was a topic that night, I was toast, since the assumption would be that I would side with the Jewish community.

Sure enough, the producer greeted us with a big smile and her idea of a joke.

"It's the nuns, boys. Bob, you take the Jewish side, Pat has the missionary position." Ho, ho.

The entire show was put together around that battle. To make matters worse, a good 50 percent of each *Crossfire* episode is produced before the hosts even show up for work. Videotape footage of the relevant news stories is edited into the program, with room left for voiceover by the hosts. To undo a show just a few hours before airtime would be a major undertaking, not to mention an expensive one.

The Voice of God announcer at CNN Atlanta had already done the introduction to the show hours earlier. In his deepest Charlton Heston basso he began: "Tonight, should Catholic nuns have to abandon their convent so that the Auschwitz memorial to the millions who died can stand alone? Tonight Pat Buchanan and Bob Beckel face off on this explosive issue."

Buchanan and I got together to bravely prepare our pitch to *Crossfire's* executive producer.

Me: You tell her.
Pat: No, you tell her.
Me: You tell her. The only reason I went in the tank was to keep you from another Jewish attack.
Pat: I didn't ask you to do that.

Unbeknownst to us, our producer was standing outside the open door of Pat's office and had heard this entire conversation. "Tell me what?" she demanded.

Me: You tell her.
Pat: No, you tell her.

Neither Pat nor I was what you would call an armchair pugilist. We had both been through more than our share of bar fights, and some pretty nasty ones. But neither of us especially wanted to face the wrath of the woman we called El Jefe.

You cannot imagine the look of irritation and loathing on her face when we explained what had happened at the radio show.

"Well, we seem to have a problem, don't we?" she said, as if we were two kids who'd been caught looking at porn magazines. "I guess I could change the show. After all, I've got sixty minutes to find a new topic, find new guests, recut new video, get the Voice of God back in the studio, and rewrite the open."

"That's good of you," I said sheepishly.

"I could, but I'm not!" she screamed. "The show's going ahead as is—and you two better figure out how to make this topic into a *Crossfire* moment."

Pat, demonstrating the kind of flexibility I fully expected, said he wasn't about to change his position.

Our producer turned to me and said, "Well, Bob, I guess it's up to you then. Somehow you're going to have to figure out how to completely change your position without looking like a total turd. Have a ball."

One of the benefits of growing up in a volatile family is that you learn how to turn on a dime and adapt to whatever situation is thrown at you. As we took our seats and got ready for the red light to go on, I flashed back to a memory from when I was ten years old:

I come into the kitchen and say, "Mom, Dad's drunk again and he's having trouble getting out of the car." Then I go back to the front door.

The first thing the old man tells me when he reaches the front steps is, "Don't tell your mother I was having trouble getting out of the car, or I'll kick your ass."

Time to completely change my position.

I dash into the house and tell Mom that Dad's home, and he's just fine after all. "I thought you said he was so drunk he couldn't get out of the car," Mom says suspiciously.

"Well I was wrong," I say, the lies flowing along smooth as the Connecticut River, "he was just cleaning out a bunch of old papers from the back of the car."

As the old man comes in Mom asks, "So where're the papers?"
I don't miss a beat. "I threw them in the trash outside."
Ducked another one.

If you can do that at age ten, then as an adult, Auschwitz nuns versus Jews on live national television is a piece of cake.

After opening the show I turned to my guest, a rabbi, and said, "Rabbi, I'm going to play devil's advocate tonight…" and went on to lay out the pro-nun argument—positioning myself as a good, professional, objective journalist and completely sidestepping the question of where I personally came down on the issue.

As I talked, Pat shot me a look of genuine admiration, and El Jefe said in my earpiece, "Nice move for a dumb shit." I was humbled by the adoration.

Ducked another one.

*   *   *

In the last weeks of 1988, after the Bush-Dukakis presidential contest had wrapped, an upstart new TV network invited me to do a show. When it aired its first broadcast in October 1986, nobody thought the new network, called the Fox Broadcasting Company, had a chance of lasting. A year later opinions hadn't changed much. But by the end of 1988 it had been on the air for more than two years (albeit with only two nights per week of programming), and it was surviving against all odds.

My kind of success story. Nothing I love as much as an underdog survivor.

At this point there was no such thing as a national newscast or public affairs program on Fox. (The Fox News Channel wouldn't come into existence until nearly a decade later.) Some of the handful of locally-owned and -operated Fox stations ran local news programs, but Fox was a bit player in the world of news. By late '88, however, Barry Diller, the CEO of Fox Broadcasting, decided he wanted to have a weekly national public affairs program that would go out to all the owned-and-operated stations as well as the ninety or so affiliates nationwide. He decided it should be produced in Washington and called it *Off the Record*.

Their idea was to do a new kind of talk show format, with their panel sitting not around a table but in a living room–style venue, with younger people, in a looser format and with a greater range of topics. I was called in to do an interview with them as a possible panelist. After all the interviews were all completed they called me back in and said, "Listen, why don't you host this thing?"

To be honest I was surprised that of all the available on-air talent, they were asking me. To them I said, "Why not?"

They added, "We'll have you be the host, and we'll give you a cohost, Tony Snow."

"Great idea!"

I liked Tony. He worked as chief speechwriter for George H. W. Bush and later became press secretary to George W. Bush. He also became one of my best friends. Sadly he died of cancer in 2008 at the age of fifty-three, way too young.

We had a great cast of people for that show. We had Susan Molinari, a congresswoman from New York; Michael Barone, a noted conservative political expert; Jim Glassman, a noted business writer on economic issues who was also president of the *Atlantic Monthly* and executive vice president of *U.S. News & World Report*. It was a great lineup. The problem was, it aired on Saturday nights, right between *America's Most Wanted* and *Cops!* Not exactly the kind of audience lead-in you would want for our show. Even though *Off the Record* was critically acclaimed, it just couldn't hold the ratings. It ran for only a few years before they took us off the air. It was a very good show, but Fox wasn't ready for it and the Fox audience definitely wasn't ready for it.

I was sorry when it got canceled and I said good-bye to the fledgling network. Little did I know that these people would in time become the only network on television that would touch me.

I continued doing CNN, and in 1990 I was also picked up by CBS to do their morning show, *CBS This Morning*, with Fred Barnes, who was a conservative.

The timing, again, was perfect: I was ready to take on more television. After the '88 campaign season had come to an end there was a shift in the nature of the work and client load we were getting at BB&A. Suddenly we were no longer working for political candidates, but for lobbying efforts around specific issues and, in some cases, for big corporations. Which I couldn't stand. The grassroots business was starting to feel like the wrong place for me, and I was spending more and more time on my television career.

Now, between CNN and CBS, I had television work morning and night.

Fred and I did *CBS This Morning* together for an incredible nine years, and it was on this show that I started becoming known as a guy who was outspoken and a little outrageous. In fact, CBS played to that. During the Olympics in '94 Barnes and I went ice skating on the air at a rink in D.C. We staged a lot of things like that, occasionally on location but often just with some kind of backdrop they would rig up for us, so it would be something more interesting than two guys sitting in a studio talking back and forth.

This all required more acting than your typical straight news analysis— and I loved it.

My brother, Graham ("Buddy") Beckel, is an actor, and a very good one. He graduated from the American Academy of Dramatic Arts in New York in 1972, just as I was getting my start in campaigns; his very first movie was *The Paper Chase* (1973), the classic legal drama with John Houseman. Since then he's been in a ton of movies, television movies, and television shows—*L.A. Confidential, Leaving Las Vegas, The Practice, Battlestar Galactica*, the list goes on and on. He's a well-known character actor, which means you've never heard of his name but you'd recognize his face if you saw him. (For example, he played Anne Hathaway's character's father in *Brokeback Mountain*.)

Like Buddy, I had always loved acting. I even got the Best Actor award for a high school play. For me, the choice between being an actor and being a politician was almost like flipping a coin. The survival skills I learned as a kid fit in perfectly with both professions. As an actor, your job is to hide behind the mask and be somebody different. Which is exactly what you do to get away from being in the middle of horrors in your household. It was perfect. So my brother went that direction and I went into politics. But I always had a little bit of the ham in me.

On the CBS show I started developing my own TV persona. Not that I was trying to be something I wasn't. I just wanted to emphasize the part of me that was a little bit edgy, a little bit outrageous and controversial.

*   *   *

Not long after I got the CBS gig, I was sitting in for Kinsley on *Crossfire* one day when the producer for Larry King came running in and said, "Bob, you've got to do Larry's show tonight. He can't make it in. He's sick."

Larry's show? What the hell did I know about doing Larry King's show?

Larry King Live was then the top-rated program on CNN. It was an hour long and required the host to work with all kinds of different guests and topics. As far as I was concerned, King was the best interviewer there was, probably the best there *ever* was. And now, boom! there *I* was, sitting in Larry's chair. And the little red light was on.

It was a blast.

After that first guest spot, they started having me on regularly. Now I had yet another TV gig on my docket.

Doing *Larry King Live* was a very different experience from anything else I'd done. Being a host and interviewer, rather than a political analyst, was a whole new territory. I did this for several years and gradually got more and more comfortable with it. (By the way, that was where I picked up my habit of wearing suspenders, which have since become so much of a trademark that if I went on the air without them today, viewers would write in saying, "Hey, where did Beckel go, and who's the new guy?")

Under his contract, Larry could take off any night he wanted, and any time there was going to be a particularly bad show they'd end up calling me because he didn't want to do it. I noticed that whenever they had starlets or other beautiful women on as guests, Larry would always manage to do those shows.

One day they called me and said, "Can you sit in for Larry tonight?"

"Sure," I said. "What's the topic?"

They said, "Well, one segment is the Dallas Cowboys cheerleaders."

"Man," I thought, "I'm surprised Larry didn't get out of bed for that."

Okay. I went in and started the show. Larry's set was a big, black room that looked like a warehouse, and the host sat at a desk with an old-time microphone sitting on it and a map of the world in lights behind him. You couldn't really see your guests walk in until they got close enough to break through the camera lights. So here came the Dallas Cowboys cheerleaders, with me craning and squinting, trying to see them—and when they broke through the lights, I realized they were the *original* Dallas Cowboys cheerleaders. As in, from 1960.

"The sonofabitch," I thought, "he must have known."

One day they called me in to do a show on exorcisms. ABC had done a spot on some teenager in Florida who had been exorcised. TV being the fanatically competitive industry it is, the networks all watch each other, and if they see a story on one of their competitors' networks that looks good, they feel they have to go with it, too.

When I asked who the guest was, the *Larry King* people said, "The lead exorcist in the country."

"What do you mean, lead exorcist?" I'd never heard of such a thing.

"The Catholic Church has six hundred exorcism-trained priests," they told me, "and this guy's the top guy. It's a bona fide part of the Catholic Church."

You've got to be kidding me! But they weren't.

Okay, lead exorcist it is.

At a break halfway through the show, the door opened and I could vaguely see this collar coming across the room. Then the guy broke through the TV lights, and I looked into his eyes—and I'll tell you what, that sonofabitch had seen the Devil, no question about it.

We had a short time before we were going back on, so I said, "Father, what's the longest exorcism you ever did?"

He said, "Oh, thirty-some days. In Maryland. I did it with another priest."

I said, "You've got to be kidding me!"

He said, "No, no. That was it. It took more than thirty days."

At this point I had no faith and really didn't believe in God. I didn't especially believe in anything. I said, "Father, just out of curiosity, where *is* the Devil?"

He looked at me and said, "Son, he's right here, right now. He's at my house, he's at your house."

"Really," I said. I did my professional best not to roll my eyes. Still, it made me uneasy.

Then the show came back on. I asked him a question, and he started answering, and about a minute into it, I heard the producer's voice in my ear saying, "Bob, the microphone."

That old-time microphone Larry had on his desk didn't actually work. It was just there for art's sake. I looked at the microphone—and it was moving. Slightly, but no question: It was moving. I stared at it and thought, *Uh-oh.*

I got off another question to the Father, and fortunately this guy liked to talk, so he was going on and on. Before long the producer said in my ear again, "Bob, *the microphone.*" The microphone was now moving, jittering along the desktop's surface about three inches in either direction, as if it had a mind of its own. I have never walked off the set of a TV show in my life, but at this point I was getting ready to bolt.

Finally, just before our next break, I asked him one more question, and the voice in my ear yelled, "Bob, that microphone's got to stop!"

That was the moment I realized what was happening: I was so nervous about what this sonofabitch was saying that my knees were going back and forth under the desk, and I was hitting the microphone's cable.

For the rest of that show I was about six inches shorter, holding on to my knees so I wouldn't bang against the microphone cord.

My house was undergoing some renovations at the time, and the whole back half of the house was covered in a big plastic sheet, ruffling and flapping in the wind. All that night, with every sound I heard, I kept thinking about the Devil being in my house. I didn't sleep a wink that night. If I could have had that exorcist guy with me, I would have shot him.

*   *   *

Back in 1987, when Peter Jennings called and touched off a tectonic shift in my professional life by inviting me onto ABC, I was also in the midst of a revolution in my personal life. For the first time since my teenage years, I wasn't drinking.

After steadily increasing for years, my level of alcohol consumption had escalated to the point of crisis. I was aware of this. On some level I knew that it was putting me on a collision course with my mortality. But I was able to keep that knowledge stuffed away in some deep place where it wouldn't bother me, as survivors know too well how to do.

Finally it jumped out and slapped me in the face so hard that even I couldn't ignore it anymore.

One Sunday morning in early January 1987 I was driving back down to Washington from New York City on the New Jersey Turnpike when I fell fast asleep at the wheel.

I had come up from D.C. to go to a party the previous Friday and hadn't slept all weekend. The party was on a fifty-five-foot boat owned by a friend, and it was the picture of decadence: women, drugs, booze, and no rules. By the time Sunday rolled around I was in no shape to leave. My friend begged me to sleep before I left, but, of course, something as sensible as that suggestion was lost on me.

Within minutes after getting on the turnpike, I started nodding off. Instead of pulling off the road I just rolled down the windows, hoping the cold air would keep me awake, and kept on going.

The next thing I knew a truck driver was pounding on my door with one enormous fist. A chorus of horns cascaded from the dozens of cars backed up behind me. The trucker was yelling at me to pull off to the side before a cop came along. He didn't look angry—just worried.

My senses slowly returned, and as they did I realized that my car and I were sitting in the second of four lanes, smack in the middle of the pike, at a dead stop. Apparently when I passed out, my car had stalled and simply rolled to a stop, without hitting anyone else or careening off the road.

How lucky was that?

I started my car and looked at the guy. "Thanks for helping me, man," I stammered.

And I'll never forget what that trucker said: "Son, you need to get some help before you kill yourself."

I couldn't remember being that shaken up since I was a kid. Anyone who knows the Jersey Pike knows how dangerous it can be rested and sober, let alone tired and hungover—let alone literally asleep at the wheel. The chances of avoiding a collision were a thousand to one; by any measure, I should have been dead or at least seriously hurt. But somehow I'd defied the odds. I managed to tell the trucker that I was fine, that the only problem was I hadn't slept in three days.

I exited the turnpike and pulled into a nearby motel, still shaken. I told the desk clerk I needed a room for a few hours to sleep. He was used to dealing with tired drivers.

"You don't want to fall asleep on the pike," he said.

"I already did," I replied, and I told him about what had happened on the pike, concluding with, "I'm one lucky guy."

He shook his head. "That's not luck, friend. That's pure grace."

I didn't forget that, either.

The crazy thing was, I couldn't sleep. It felt like the night terrors I used to get as a kid: too tired to stay awake, too scared to fall asleep. After a few hours I gave up trying, got up, climbed back into my car, and headed home. It was a frightening drive. One long anxiety attack held me in its clutch for the entire trip. I gripped the steering wheel so hard it bent. I didn't start to relax until hours later, when I caught my first glimpse of the thing I'd been desperately waiting to see.

The Washington Monument.

There it was, that beacon of marble that said, "You're home."

When I got inside my house, the tears poured. Tears of relief, tears of fear, and tears of anger, too. I couldn't deny the obvious anymore. The drinking and partying were out of control. For the first time in my life, I was afraid that drinking would eventually kill me, and that made me angry. Angry because I was in the middle of something I couldn't control, and worse, because I was in the middle of something that was controlling me.

I called my brother, Buddy, in Los Angeles and told him I needed help. He told me something that added one more shock to a day already rich in shock value.

"I'm an alcoholic, Bob. I've been in Alcoholics Anonymous for over a year now."

I groped to find my voice. Buddy? An alcoholic? "Why didn't you tell me before?" I said.

"Because," he replied in a sad, tired voice, "I was embarrassed. I never thought I'd end up with the old man's curse."

Hey, I didn't think I would, either.

Buddy told me to go get a drink, and he'd call back. Now, that was strange. Get a drink? That was the whole problem, right? He read my mind and told me if I quit drinking cold turkey, I'd get something called the DTs.

"Let me tell you, bro, you do *not* want the DTs," he said, clearly the voice of experience talking. "We'll find someone who knows how to take you off booze the right way."

I hung up, then threw down three Scotches while I waited for him to call back.

"What took so long?" I asked when he finally called again.

He said, "It's only been five minutes. About the time it takes you to drink three or four Scotches, am I right?"

Wiseass. I didn't say anything. Didn't have to; he knew he was right. He gave me the address of an AA meeting in Georgetown, close to my house, at noon the next day. He made me promise to go or he'd bug me till I did. And I knew he would, so I did.

When I woke up the next morning I needed a drink in the worst way.

The phone rang. Thinking it was my brother, I picked it up. It was some dude whom I'll call "Franklin." He said he was in AA and my brother had called the Washington office of AA to tell them to follow up with me. The boy truly had no confidence in his big brother.

Franklin gave me the same Georgetown address Buddy had given me and said he'd keep an eye out for me. Then he asked me when I had my last drink. I lied and said, about two days ago.

"Right," said Franklin. "But just in case you forgot and had a few last night, you might want to have one or two this morning to keep the DTs away."

"I understand those DTs can lay some hurt on you," I said, a bit of the know-it-all in my voice.

"No, they don't hurt you," said Franklin. "They kill you."

*   *   *

For some crazy reason, I decided to put on one of my tailored, two-thousand-dollar, three-piece suits for my first AA meeting. (Like I was going to impress someone?) I found the address in Georgetown and saw a sign pointing to the second floor. It read The Westside Club. Nice name, but I already belonged to lots of clubs and wasn't sure I needed another one. Who was I kidding? I was nervous as hell and just using that who-needs-another-club thing as an excuse to cut out. I sucked it up and headed up to the second floor.

Opening the door on the second-floor landing I was immediately attacked by clouds of cigarette smoke. The room was big and dark. That, along with the smoke and the hangover, made seeing a little tough. I groped my way toward a seat in the back and let my eyes adjust to the dark. When they did I saw that the place was dirty and decrepit. The people in there all looked like they were on their last legs. But what the hell. I was there; I decided I'd stick it out and give it at least one try.

A few of the people there were staring at me. *Must be the TV personality thing*, I thought. I smiled and puffed my chest out some. Now I was thinking, *Hey, this isn't so bad*. I had a whole group of new people to listen to stories of my successful life. Hell, I'd have them all liking me in no time.

They kept staring and turned away only when the chairman called for order. I was sitting next to a bucket of water, hoping it wasn't the AA equivalent of a drinking fountain. Then I felt a drip of water on my head. Then another splash on my suit, and another on my tie.

Suddenly I was paralyzed with fear. It was the damnedest thing. I knew I should move—but I was afraid to embarrass myself in front of all these people. What would they think? It would show weakness, and that was not acceptable. It was crazy, but I was frozen to the damn chair.

I was flooded with the memory of my first day of fourth grade, when we had just moved to Connecticut, the day we wore our Sunday best and all the other kids mocked us. Sitting at my little desk, I'd realized I badly needed to pee—but I was too embarrassed to raise my hand and ask the teacher for permission. Frozen to my chair in terror, I finally couldn't hold it any longer. Pee soaked my pants and began spilling over down the sides of my seat. The girl behind me screamed out the news, and seconds later the entire class was pointing, gagging, and laughing. I was so humiliated I wanted to die—

"Son?" My reverie was broken by an old guy who had come over to my chair. He leaned down and said quietly, "You should move to another chair before that leak in the roof ruins your nice suit. Better to have the bucket catch the water than you." He said this last with a smile. I realized I was sitting right where the roof was leaking.

My paralysis eased up. This time, I moved—and this time, no one made fun of me. It felt good.

At halftime they asked if there was anybody there new to the program. I raised my hand.

After the meeting Franklin, the guy who had called me that morning, came up and introduced himself. He was a producer for one of the major networks and I liked him right away. I told him I thought people in the room were staring at me because of my suit, and knowing me from television, before I realized it was about the water. Franklin said, "Yeah, we don't see many suits like that in here. As for the TV thing, most of these people don't own TVs anymore."

That was my first lesson in AA humility. It wouldn't be the last. The problem was, I didn't like feeling humble. Which probably had a lot to do with the fact that I wouldn't get the AA program right for quite a few years to come.

Franklin gave me a ride home, and as he drove he talked about the program and the twelve steps. He said he'd be back to get me for another meeting, but in the meantime I should read the steps.

"Pay attention to the God steps," he said.

He gave me a copy of *The Big Book*, the original book of Alcoholics Anonymous, written by AA's founder, Bill Wilson, and some of the earliest members of AA, and first published in 1939. Once back home, I read the three "God steps"—and they stopped me cold. They are, in order:

- *Step 2:* came to believe that only a power greater than ourselves could restore us to sanity;
- *Step 3:* became willing to turn our will and our lives over to a power greater than ourselves; and
- *Step 4:* turned our will and our lives over to a power greater than ourselves.

The thought of turning my will, let alone my life, over to anyone or anything other than myself was ridiculous. In my precious, all-knowing mind, doing something like that was the equivalent of pushing the key to my bedroom under the door to my old man when he was roaring drunk. *Just turn it over to your father. Everything will be fine.* No dice. Not going there. No way.

As a kid, keeping that key away from my father was absolutely the right choice. For years afterward that mindset had kept me from trusting most people, let alone some "higher power" I could neither see nor touch. Give up control? Are you kidding? For survivors, maintaining control is the central operating principle of life. For a survivor, control is like oxygen.

This, too, had a lot to do with why it would take me years to begin getting this thing right.

Meanwhile, though, I was determined to give it a serious try.

In AA you typically see a wave of new people coming to the meetings in early January. It seems to be a time when a lot of people make a commitment to stop drinking. Within two or three months that wave dies out as those new people drop away one by one. I was not one of them. By this time the specter of dying from booze had become my most terrifying fear. I hung around with people like Franklin and went to lots of meetings. It turned out there was a core group of people in AA whom I already knew pretty well as colleagues. Over the months, we grew fairly tight. I stayed sober. In fact, I felt better and better each day I didn't pick up a drink.

The next twenty months or so was a wonderful experience. As my TV career grew—from Peter Jennings, ABC, and Conus, to *Crossfire*, *CBS This Morning*, and *Larry King Live*—I was also experiencing my own *pink cloud*, that initial period of sobriety that is such a relief after the constant circus of endless drugs and alcohol. Once you've stopped drinking for a while you get to this point where you start feeling healthy again, alive and alert. That's what happened now.

People in my office could sense it right away, and I felt very good about it. When I went to Scotland for a vacation, taking a woman I'd met at AA, I went to AA meetings in Scotland. I even went to an AA meeting on the Hebrides Islands, which is about as remote as it gets. You can find an AA meeting anywhere in the world. Although I couldn't understand a fucking word they said, because the Scottish brogue was so thick. But at least I was there. That was the important thing.

The thing about a pink cloud is that it feels so solid, so dependable, and so permanent—and it is none of those things. Fear of death and a good pink cloud can keep you sober for a while, but the problem with pink clouds is that they eventually go away. And when they do, the combination of feeling healthy and relying on yourself to stay that way—in other words, refusing to accept a higher power—makes staying sober very hard. They say in AA that you have to stay sober a day at a time. As a survivor, living in the moment like that just wasn't part of my makeup.

I felt good about the AA program, but in time the old fears returned. No matter how many meetings I attended, no matter how many sober friends I made, without faith in a higher power to overcome my personal demons, I was destined to fail.

And I did—over and over.

*   *   *

By the fall of '88 the presidential elections were in full bloom, and I was doing a lot of TV with Haley Barbour. I was home one September night, sitting in my living room—perfectly content, sober now nearly two years. I stood up, walked into my kitchen, reached under the sink where I had somehow kept a bottle of booze hidden back in there, brought it back into the living room, and sat down with it.

Why? I have no idea.

Ask any alcoholic who starts drinking again, "Why? What was the reason you started again?" and if he's at all honest, he'll probably tell you, *there's no reason*. You just do it. Maybe part of it is that you start feeling so much better while you're sober that the little alcoholic voice in your head starts whispering, "You're doing great, Bob. You've got it together. You can drink now, it's okay." But whatever the reason, or lack of reason, the stark reality of it was that I was sitting there, and then the bottle was empty, and I was drunk.

And totally horrified at what I'd done.

I had never forgotten the soul-crushing disappointment that descended on me as a kid when my father went out and got smashed on his one-year anniversary. And now here I was, almost at my own two-year point—and I was drinking again. Just like my sixteen-year-old world had come crashing down then, my newfound and still tender sense of self-esteem and achievement suddenly crumbled into dust and despair between my fingers.

There was only one thing to be done.

Drink more.

And I did.

And now I really found out, for the first time, just why it is that people describe alcoholism as a progressive disease.

Because when I started drinking again, I needed to drink a greater quantity than I did when I quit in order to maintain the alcohol level I needed in my system. Soon I was drinking a quart to a quart and a half a day—a staggering amount that I was able to keep up only with the assistance of generous amounts of that wonder drug I'd discovered in my last week at that place that I can no longer refer to as the "White House" without a clear tinge of snowy irony.

For me the draw of cocaine was not the experience or the fun of the drug itself as much as the fact that it allowed me to drink more. After I went back out from the haven of sobriety in the fall of '88 this became my new pattern: I would get drunk, then use cocaine to level me out so that I could get that much more alcohol into me, and then drink more.

A few years later, I got sober again, and stayed that way for months. Then

I went back to drinking. Then I got sober again. And so on. Between January 1987 and the end of the century I was in and out of sobriety, in and out of AA meetings, a handful of times. I'd get a little bit sober, enough to start feeling great, and then invariably I'd pick up a drink. Ironically, it was the feeling healthy that was the biggest danger to my sobriety. That's when that devil whispered in my ear, "Yo, Bob, feel great, dontcha? Got money in the bank. Liver's all better. Man, you ought to celebrate. Go get one drink. That's all, just one. Hey, you've earned it. Just one little drink, and then you can come right back to AA."

Over and over, I listened to that voice and bought into what it said. Of course, believing I would have "just one drink" was crazy. As they say in AA, "One drink is too many, and a thousand are not enough." That slogan didn't just fall from the sky; it crawled into being from the pain of the gutter. There are plenty of field agents like me who have put that theory through some pretty rigorous testing, and damned if it isn't true.

And every time I went back out, it was worse.

Alcoholism is a progressive disease. Every time I started drinking again, I was drunker and more lost than before. It couldn't go on; it couldn't get any worse than it already was. Yet it kept doing exactly that.

TV lights, and alcoholic blackouts. The cycle consumed me, growing steadily more extreme by the month.

CHAPTER EIGHT

Crash and Burn

In early 1989, just a few months past my fortieth birthday, I woke up one day and realized that I wanted to have kids. I was a lifelong, committed bachelor. I had no interest in getting married. Not only had my childhood home provided no kind of role model for it, but on top of that most of my friends over the years had had pretty rough marriages. The whole institution felt suspect to me, and not like something that I wanted to pursue. I didn't want any commitment. But suddenly, I wanted kids.

In those days if you were going to become a parent, it was important to get married. It wasn't as easy then as it is today to have kids out of wedlock and have those kids be considered normal. And there was no way I was going to raise these kids I wanted under that kind of stigma—or any kind of stigma, if I could help it. One of my strongest desires was to bring these kids up in a home that was as different from my own upbringing as Miami Beach is from the moon.

So I started thinking seriously about something I had never in my life thought I would ever contemplate: having a long-term relationship with another human being. Specifically, with a woman.

This was not easy for me to do. In fact, it probably would have been impossible without some professional help.

Which, fortunately, I had.

Not long before this somebody had mentioned that there was a psychiatrist in Washington, Steven Wolin, who worked with people who came out of abused homes. I called Dr. Wolin and went to see him. That first meeting was the first time I'd ever heard the word "survivor" used to describe a life like mine.

According to Steve, going through an abusive, dysfunctional, and sometimes terrifying childhood like mine didn't just do lasting damage. That much was obvious. What was not so obvious, and almost universally overlooked or ignored at the time, was that a horrific background like that could also produce tremendous resilience and inner strength, and lead to a life of significant abilities and accomplishments.

This clearly was not the prevailing view, and when Dr. Wolin and his wife and colleague, Sybil Wolin, first presented their ideas to their peers in the mid-eighties, the establishment was none too thrilled. Conventional thinking said children who lived through abusive and dysfunctional childhoods were irreversibly injured and more or less destined to fail. For years these people had been told they were wounded and emotionally crippled. The Wolins' research revealed a very different scenario. As they later wrote in their 1993 book, *The Resilient Self*:

> While early hardship can cause enduring pain, often it is also a breeding ground for uncommon strength and courage. If you are a survivor, you probably already know about the pain. This book is about the strength and courage.... [There is] a widespread image in our society of survivors as damaged goods. Here you will read about survivors' aspirations and accomplishments, which are often remarkable and just as often overlooked.

As I listened to Steve Wolin talk about their survivor theory, it made a hell of a lot of sense to me. I started meeting with him regularly and began gradually developing a new perspective on my own past.

After we'd been working together for a while, we moved on to the question of whether survivors could maintain long-term relationships. He explained some of the reasons survivors have such a difficult time with this. For survivors, it's very difficult to commit, not just to another human being, but to virtually anything that requires a long-term involvement.

To some degree, the reasons seemed fairly obvious: We never had any very solid relationship role models to begin with. But there's also a question of self that survivors always seem to have: Am I a real person? Or am I a complete fake in every way? And if I'm not a real person, then if I have children, am I going to breed aliens?

Dr. Wolin made it clear to me that in the process of dealing with those demons from the past that I was starting to learn how to manage, there were going to be aspects of myself that *were* going to change and grow. He wasn't giving me any guarantees, but he thought marriage could be something that would work out for me. Over time, I came to the point where I thought this might be true, and that I might actually consider getting married. (Though to whom, I had no clue.)

I have to thank Steve Wolin for that. If we hadn't had those sessions, if I hadn't been given the gift of his insights, I honestly can't say that my kids would have ever been born, and the brightest lights in my life might never have come to exist.

But there was one question Steve Wolin couldn't answer for me: Who the hell would I marry?

*   *   *

That spring, I was playing golf at Columbia Country Club in Maryland with two other guys. We'd just driven our balls off the first tee when this good-looking blonde woman walked up and said, "Do you guys mind if I play with you?" One of the guys there knew her. Her name was Leland Ingham.

She put her ball down at the men's tee, and I said, "Don't you think you ought to hit from the ladies' tees?" She looked at me like, *You dumb sonofa-bitch*, and then, ba-boom, she blew past me by sixty yards on her first drive. Fast-forward to the eighteenth hole: I pulled a five-putt or something, and she beat me by twenty-two strokes. She took my ball out of the cup, looked over at me, and said, "Next time, maybe *you* ought to play from the ladies' tees."

Ha! I loved that. I thought it was ballsy.

It turned out Leland was a very talented golfer. That "meet-cute" story of our first conversation quickly made the rounds; the following year, when she played the finals Mid-Am national title to national coverage, the sportscasters covering the event recounted it on CBS.

It also turned out she was a big drinker. This was good news to me; it would make our relationship an awful lot easier. We started going out together.

Over the next few years we partied and partied. Her grandfather had died and left her a lot of money. We bought a house in Jackson, Wyoming. I'd been to Jackson Hole before, and I'd always loved it there. It's a stunning location. She liked to ski, but I couldn't ski worth a damn, so we bought the house there essentially as a summer home, but soon we were spending a great deal of time there throughout the year.

In the early nineties, Jackson had not yet become the kind of fancy destination it is today. Back then it had lots of cowboy bars. If you wanted to get drunk, that was the spot to do it in. In fact, Jackson had one of the few retail establishments left in America where you could still get drive-through drinks. You would motor right up to this liquor store, like you were ordering a burger and fries at a McDonald's, they would mix your drink for you and hand it out the window to you, and off you drove with it, sipping to your heart's (and liver's) content. I used to go through that thing five or six times a day.

My kind of place.

By the time the 1992 campaign season arrived, two big things had changed that made this different for me from any other presidential election season since 1976.

The first big change was that, even though there was now an influx of political campaign work available, I was no longer interested in being involved—at least, not from the campaign-consulting end of things. I had been doing increasingly more television now for a few years, and working less and less with our grassroots business. I brought on a partner, Glenn Cowan, to run things at BB&A, while I spent the majority of my waking hours on television, covering the campaigns as an analyst.

The second big change was that I was engaged to be married. Leland and I had been partying together for three years now. It was high time to tie the knot and make an honest woman of her, as the saying goes.

Bill Clinton was elected on November 3, and on November 14, exactly one day before my forty-fourth birthday, Leland and I celebrated our nuptials in D.C. It was an enormous wedding, with about four hundred friends flying in from all around the country. I was eighteen years older than Leland, which didn't bother me at all and didn't bother her at all—but it bothered her father a bunch, apparently, because he refused to put a dime toward the event. It cost me upward of three hundred thousand dollars.

*   *   *

I said two big things changed that year. Actually, it was three.

I saw my father.

I'd had fair warning. The old man had told me he'd be coming to my wedding. I wasn't sure if it was really true. We had now been talking on the phone with some regularity for fifteen years, and corresponding even longer. But my wedding would be the first time we'd actually seen each other, live and in person, in more than a quarter of a century. It was also the first time he and my mother would be encountering each other since that day in mid-1965 when he hit her and then drove away in the family Studebaker. The thought of the two of them being in the same room was terrifying.

On top of all that, he mentioned that he was not bringing his wife, Teenie, along with him. Which meant no official reins on his drinking. Which meant, I guessed, that he would probably get loaded. Which, of course, he did.

Mardi Gras, baby, Mardi Gras.

Although I'll have to admit, he did so gracefully. That frightening night-time dad-beast, with its slurring and growling and screaming and beating, never did put in an appearance. Perhaps that beast truly was gone. Perhaps. But my guard was up for the entire event, all my senses quietly on DEFCON 1, just in case.

He was a perfect gentleman, charming and entertaining as he ever was at his best of times. Hilarious, too—not always intentionally. At the reception he came up to my mother and said suavely, "Hi, I'm Graham Beckel. And you are...?"

She looked at him with weary deadpan eyes and said, "I'm your former wife, Bud."

He said, "Oh, my God, I'm *sorry*, Ellen. Well! We've aged, both of us, haven't we?"

I put up all our out-of-town guests at a pricey hotel in Bethesda. Unbeknownst to me, my father held forth in the bar there for two nights running with my friends, who all fell in love with the guy. He was such a great raconteur. Nobody knew how to tell a good joke like my pop.

After the whole thing was over quite a few of my friends told me, "Damn, Bob, your old man's such a great guy! Man, weren't you lucky to have an old man like that!"

At the reception he danced with my wife and was the life of the party. He even danced with my mother, briefly. It was the last time they ever saw each other.

*   *   *

Leland and I honeymooned in Maui, where we ran across Stephen Stills, of Crosby, Stills, Nash & Young, who came out and played golf with us. Stills was a dedicated Democrat and a big fan of Jimmy Carter's, so we got along famously. He also happened to be a heavy cokehead, so we got along *very* famously.

Leland and I hadn't carried any cocaine on the plane with us when we flew out to Maui. It didn't seem prudent. Happily, with Stills in our midst, we had a ready supply.

Two months later, in January, Leland got pregnant, and immediately quit drinking, which was the responsible thing to do. I, of course, did not.

On the evening of November 27, 1993, a year after the wedding, my son, Alex, was born. His birth was one of the most incredible moments I've ever experienced. Once he came out, and he was breathing, and they said he was healthy, and I was sure he had ten fingers and ten toes (and that he was *not* an alien), I was ecstatic.

By the time they got the baby wrapped up and off to the nursery and Leland cleaned up and all checked out, it was late, close to midnight. My wife was exhausted and needed to go to sleep. I said, "I'll go look in on him."

When I tiptoed into the nursery and looked down at our newborn son, I felt for the first time in my life something that I thought must be close to what people meant when they said they were "in love." I had never understood the phrase; up to that point, it had meant nothing to me. I'd heard people say this many times, but I honestly didn't know what they were talking about. Now, looking down at this tiny little person, suddenly I understood why people say "I'd take a bullet for my kid." I didn't think I'd ever felt so happy before in my entire life.

And I cannot tell you why I did what I did next.

I left the room, left the hospital, got in my car, went out and got drunk, found an escort I knew, and took her home with me. I did this on the night of my son's birth.

After the woman left, I stood in front of the bathroom mirror and stared bleary-eyed at the haggard face looking back at me. "This is the most important day of your life," I told the sorry-looking sonofabitch in the mirror. "And what do you do? You get drunk. And you sleep with a prostitute."

How can I adequately describe the wave of self-loathing that swept over me in that moment? Shame, humiliation, guilt, and disgust, all wrapped in together, maybe seasoned with a bitter sense of hopelessness.

But I knew how to get rid of that feeling. I knew just what to do.

I drank more.

*   *   *

A few months after Alex was born I decided to sell the grassroots business to a big company in downtown Washington, Cassidy & Associates, one of Washington's largest lobbying firms. Our piece of the business would still be run by Cowan and myself (in other words, by Cowan), only under a new roof and new ownership. The whole operation moved out of our relaxed Georgetown offices down to Thirteenth Street in D.C., on New York Avenue, into this stuffy corporate world that was the absolute antithesis of what my people and I were used to.

The day I first walked into our new offices, I instantly regretted the decision.

They had given us the whole floor. I went into my office and sat down. On my desk was a copy of the rules for Cassidy & Associates Companies, which included wearing a tie and a jacket every day. This I refused to do, outside of special situations that absolutely required it.

Not that it really mattered. By this time I had grown so disengaged from the business that I was hardly ever there. Between CNN and CBS, my television career was in full bloom, and I was doing quite a bit of public speaking, too. Both were quite lucrative. Also, I was able to fit both around my busy drinking schedule. First thing out of bed in the morning I'd have a drink to get the blood levels going, so I could function and go do *CBS This Morning*. I could modulate things during the day with cocaine as necessary, and the speaking gigs typically wrapped up by midevening, plenty of time to get to my late-night appointments with recreational ethanol.

Meanwhile, Leland and I spent more and more time at our party pad in Jackson, when she wasn't away traveling on the golf pro circuit. BB&A had been doing so well that I had made a lot of money. We had full-time nannies and nurses, so my responsibilities and child-care duties were minimal, although I did spend lots of time with our son. I made sure to take time with him every chance I got, and put him to bed at night whenever possible—right before I started my serious drinking.

In July of '95 we had a second child, a daughter, MacKenzie. Fortunately this birth happened in the afternoon, so I didn't feel the need to go running out immediately and get loaded. There were also complications with Kenzie's birth and her mother required further surgery, so it was a difficult time for us for a few days.

Our marriage was starting to show signs of strain. During the nine months when my wife was pregnant with Alex, and then again during her pregnancy with MacKenzie, she gave me a ton of grief about my drinking. Her being sober and my being constantly drunk created an enormous amount of friction. However, she took up drinking again after each pregnancy, as soon as she'd made it through childbirth, so I no longer had to worry about being hassled by my partner. After MacKenzie's birth, with Leland now back on the sauce again, things went more or less back to the way they had been...except that I was getting increasingly drunker, and increasingly more isolated from my friends.

I had also virtually abandoned the grassroots business. And that now came back to bite me.

*   *   *

At the time, there was a big move in Congress to overhaul the federal telecommunications laws. One of our biggest clients was a coalition of the big long-distance companies, including AT&T, MCI, and other corporate telecoms, who hired us to help them defeat the bill Congress was considering. I didn't have the slightest interest in it.

Our company succeeded in generating a massive amount of mail from people to their elected representatives, something like half a million pieces. Which was great work. Except that it soon came out that there were all sorts of quality control issues. Serious questions were raised about some of the boiler room operations tasked with calling people and polling them to see if they were in opposition to the bill. Evidently a bunch of the mail Congress received came from people who said they had never given permission to have their names used at all. One of the vendors we used, a firm that kept and managed the actual mail lists, used an old list. Some of the letters Congress received came from people who were dead.

I hadn't been watching the store—and the store had fucked up royally.

I could protest all I wanted that I hadn't had anything to do with the problems, that it was our vendors, that Cowan had been in charge. But it was my name on the door. And besides, I was the face and the name that the media knew. They had a field day.

When the story broke, it was a true shit-hitting-the-fan moment. The thing went on *Nightline*. We were crucified. More to the point, *I* was crucified.

The day the story broke, I went into a meeting with my old friend Howard Baker, who was heading up a congressional coalition to get the bill passed. Howard handed me a really nice-looking box, all wrapped up and tied up with ribbon. It was a present for my newborn daughter. The warmth in his face was genuine—but I could also see the alarm and concern. He didn't say it in so many words, but there was a message there I couldn't fail to pick up on: *Beckel, you really need to get your shit handled.*

By this point it had become painfully apparent to people in Washington that I had a serious drinking problem. Whenever anyone brought it up (always quietly and discreetly), I'd shrug it off and say, "Don't worry, it's not a problem." The truth was, I didn't much care what people said or thought.

After the telecom scandal I was completely fed up with the business. "*Screw it,*" I said one day, "I'm leaving!" I walked out the door and never went back. I sold my interest in the company, which meant I had a lot more money in the bank, and also meant I now had free rein to go hog wild.

Which I did.

By the end of the nineties I was no longer being invited anywhere. Everyone knew that if I came to their party I'd get embarrassingly drunk. I found myself going out more and more to crappy hole-in-the-wall dive bars in Washington and the surrounding areas. I call this the "dark world." You go into these bars and everybody's a con artist, everybody's an alcoholic. And every one of them is convinced they could stop if they wanted to. Which is complete bullshit.

The schizophrenia of my life became extreme. I was on television, I was maintaining a busy calendar of professional speaking gigs, and I was taking my kids to school and picking them up, spending every waking hour I could with them. Every daytime waking hour, that is.

At night I went out and plunged into the dark world, an ethanol vampire.

*   *   *

As the century crawled to a close, I spent more and more of my time in the dark world. I got into what seemed like a never-ending series of bar fights. AA was a distant memory.

In early 1999 I traveled to New Orleans, where I was scheduled to give a speech. My friend and longtime TV partner Haley Barbour was on the roster as well, and we'd agreed to meet there. Haley was a big drinker—not an alcoholic, but a big drinker—and we planned to do some serious partying.

New Orleans: a city full of drunks, con artists, whores, and a lot of survivors. Nobody wanted to know where you came from, what you were doing, or where you were going. It was always Big Easy time. I'd always loved the place. My speech was on a Monday morning so I decided to go down there the Friday before.

I got drunk on the plane, of course. When I got into my hotel room, in a rare display of common sense, I decided to sleep off the juice. I left a wakeup call request for eight o'clock Sunday morning. That would give me a full day to party before the speech.

My dreams that night were unbelievably realistic. Partying in a cemetery (which happens a lot in New Orleans), taking a cruise on the Mississippi, and banging two hookers in a seedy hotel. Somewhere a phone was ringing, and someone was pounding on the door.

Hang on. That last part wasn't a dream.

I eventually answered the phone and a very relieved operator asked if I was okay. Fine, I said, I'd had a good sleep. She told me it was 8:00 a.m.

Now that damn knocking on the door was getting unbearable.

I fell out of bed, feeling a lot more hungover than usual. Which was funny, because I'd only had eight or ten drinks on the plane. Not enough to make me feel this lousy. "The booze must be catching up to me," I thought as I opened the door.

A security guard was standing there with a ring of keys out, obviously about to use them to come in through the door if I hadn't answered.

"What's up, my man," I said.

"We were worried about you, Mr. Beckel. You disappeared on us."

No, I explained, I hadn't disappeared, I was just sleeping in and had asked for an 8:00 a.m. wakeup call, which in fact I had just now gotten.

"I know that, sir," he said, "but that was scheduled for Sunday."

Now I was getting a little irritated. Was this guy dense or what? I told him I knew that, I'd ordered the call for today, Sunday, and I'd just gotten it.

"Yes, sir," he said, with a pained look. "But...today's Monday, sir."

I thanked him, gave him twenty bucks, and asked him to get me a cab in forty-five minutes so I could get to my event. Then I fell back on the hotel bed and tried to pull my thoughts together. This wasn't a dream. What the hell had happened here? I reached for my wallet in the suit pants I had apparently been wearing since Saturday. No cash. Damn, I must have been robbed. Then I found all my credit cards, ID, and the rest. That was strange. Why would someone take cash and leave all this good stuff? I dug deeper into the wallet and came up with a handful of receipts. One for a limo for thirty-six hours. Another for a boat charter up and down the Mississippi, one for booze, a bartender, a caterer, and a band.

A band, a boat, booze?

Then I realized what must have happened. I'd had another blackout. The worst ever. For thirty-six hours straight, I had partied all over New Orleans—and I couldn't remember a thing.

I was furious at myself. I was angry with the vendors who signed up someone who was obviously out of it, and upset that I would have to give a speech to three thousand people in an hour with no preparation. Most of all, I was terrified.

I sat on the edge of the bed and sobbed.

So now I was losing my mind. My body and soul had begun leaving me years earlier, but my mind had been pretty dependable. Now it, too, was turning on me. Without a creative mind, I couldn't keep flipping masks at the right time and place. How could my mind shut down for thirty-six hours, yet still send signals that allowed my body to function? What the hell could I do about this?

For the first time in my life, I started getting honest with myself about the cost of booze.

It was time to go to rehab.

There are two kinds of rehab programs: inpatient and outpatient. They're not that much different, in terms of the content: what you do, what they tell you, the routine of it. Except that as an inpatient, you're stuck there twenty-four hours a day—no home, no work. I had too much going on in my life. I couldn't afford to just unplug from it all for a month. As far as I was concerned, outpatient rehab was the way to go.

When I got back home from New Orleans I went to an outpatient rehab facility in the Washington area. Later on that year, I went to another one.

Both times, I drank straight through the treatment.

That's the other thing about outpatient rehab. You can go home, you can go to work—and you can slip out and drink. I went in every day, listened to everything they said, behaved myself like a model citizen, and then went home at night and drank. It cost a lot of money, and I never got sober, not even for a day.

*   *   *

That December, while I was still doing *CBS This Morning* along with CNN and other TV shows, I met a girl at a bar near the White House. We got drunk and went out to her car.

I said, "You ever been to London?"

She said, "No."

I said, "You got a passport?"

She said, "Yeah."

We drove out and got her passport, then my passport, then went to Dulles, where I bought two tickets on the Concorde (which cost something like seven grand per seat), flew over to London, checked into Claridge's, a magnificent luxury hotel in London.

The first thing I did was to secure an ounce of cocaine. We then partied for the entire weekend. We had people coming in and out whom I'd never met and had no idea who they were, escorts coming and going...it was total debauchery. Eventually the hotel began to signal that they wanted us out of there. After three days we finally got out, went to Heathrow, and flew back to Dulles. I was exhausted and sick as a dog.

As we were passing through immigration, the woman turned to me and said, "What's your name again?"

As I left the airport I had just one thought: *This has really gotten out of hand.*

*   *   *

Based in Pennsylvania, with additional locations in Florida and Texas, the Caron Foundation is considered the best alcohol and drug addiction rehab facility in the eastern United States, on a par with Hazelden in Minnesota, which is the gold standard. Caron has an excellent track record with alcoholics from dysfunctional families. In mid-December 1999 I voluntarily checked myself into Caron—this time as an inpatient.

The day I packed my bags for my extended stay and walked out of our home is a day that still hurts to think about. As I stood there by the front door, my bags in my hands, my two little kids looked up at me. Alex was six, Kenzie was four.

"Daddy's got to go away for thirty days," I told them. "I'm going to the North Pole to help Santa make your toys for Christmas." I'd told a lot of lies in my life, more than I could ever count. That one hurt the worst, maybe more than all the rest put together.

When I arrived at Caron I immediately requested a single room. Survivors are loners by nature. They don't get up close and personal, for fear of being discovered. "Discovered" at what, exactly, isn't all that clear to me. My best guess is that successful survivors truly, deeply believe that our apparent success is not real. That we are just skilled enough at the deception to make people *think* we're successful, but that it's all a lie. Not surprisingly, I don't do roommates well.

This was a challenge, though. There was only one single room in the men's building, and while it was intended for handicapped patients, it was also the room of choice for the occasional VIP who passed through Caron. I was determined to get that room. The only question was the best approach. Which mask would be the most helpful and which con story would be the most persuasive?

Most of the counselors were all recovering addicts themselves. All had been clean for years. One advantage this gave them was that they could relate to the patients' experience, especially in their early days of recovery. Another advantage was that it also meant they knew every trick and scam any drunk or druggie might try, and plenty more.

Very few rehab patients check in entirely voluntarily. Some are there under court order, or because their employer made attendance mandatory as a condition of continued employment. Most, like me, were there because spouses or parents had made staying clean a condition for continuing family relationships. In other words get clean or get your ass out. I immediately put on my "defeated and rejected" sad mask. I soon realized, though, that most of the other convicts were wearing the same mask. A change of tactic was required. So instead, I switched to my VIP mask, and went to approach the head counselor about the single room.

When you go into VIP mode, the best approach is to do so with understatement and modesty. Understatement and modesty: I was a master at that. I knocked on the door and when it opened I gave the counselor a self-deprecating smile. He did not reciprocate. The conversation went something like this:

Me: Hey, how are you sir?
Counselor: Call me Larry.
Me: Sure, Larry. I don't know if you've had a chance to read my file, I know how busy you must be.
Larry: I read it, what about it?
Me: Well, you notice I'm in politics and on TV a lot, and I wouldn't want that to have an impact on the other patients.
Larry: Why would it?
Me: You know, they might be afraid to speak up. It would be particularly tough on my roommate. Can I have the single room?
Larry: Not a chance. That's one of the reasons you can't stay sober, Beckel. You're so far up your own ass you can't hear anyone else. I've seen guys like you, Mr. TV Man. I can't think of one of them that got clean. If you got any shot at all, you better stop thinking you're any different than any other addict in here. Got it?
Me: Sure do, Larry, sir.
Larry: Remember, big shot, the only person who cares about politics around here is the director. He needs politicians to get government money. I don't. So save the breath on politics.
Me: Sure thing, Larry. Thanks for the advice.

I should have said, "Thanks for the inside information, big boy," but that would have been plain dumb. Not that I wouldn't have loved to tell him that he had just given me a "pass go and go straight to the single room" card. But I just quietly closed the door and took off on the next phase of my mission.

Quickly finding an empty counselor's office, I ducked inside, picked up the phone, and called the director's office. When I asked for an appointment his assistant said he was busy, and besides, he didn't meet with patients one on one.

"This is urgent," I said. "Would you give him my name? You spell it B-E-C-K-E-L," I added. "I'll hold."

The assistant was back on in a few seconds, and she didn't sound pleased. "Come over right now, but only for five minutes."

I was over there in about one minute—not five—because I had some important homework to take care of. The first thing I always did was get right with the assistant. If you ever want to be a real success in life, always, *always* be nice to the assistants. They can help you or castrate you.

"You are very nice to arrange this, Betty," I oozed. (First thing I did once inside the door was check the nameplate.) "I know I wouldn't have a prayer of seeing the director without your help. Really, thank you so much. By the way, my mom's name is Betty." (It's not, of course, it's Ellen.)

A smile spread across Betty's face, and she told me to go right in.

The director turned out to be a wonderful guy. I almost felt bad I had to con him.

We talked politics for forty-five minutes. The guy knew his business. He had lots of friends in Washington, especially senior members on the appropriations committees. Most of the rehabs wouldn't stay alive without federal money. If your director wasn't good at politics, chances were good your rehab would fold. But this guy was *good*. No wonder Caron was supported with federal bucks at higher levels than most rehabs. I made a point of dropping the name of the chairman of the House Committee on Ways and Means. "A very powerful guy," he commented. He also clearly loved to talk inside politics. I give him some good gossip and assured him there would be more over the next twenty-eight days.

As our chat was winding up, I asked if I could explain some personal issues I had. No problem, he said.

Me: Mr. Director, I've got a problem.
Director: What's that, Bob?
Me: Well, sir, you know I'm on TV and in the public arena all the time.
Director: I know you are, must be a lot of pressure.
Me: It is. I think it's one of the reasons I drink.
Director: I'm sure it contributes to your problem. What can I do?
Me: Well, I was wondering if I could have the single room in the men's dorm for some privacy.
Director: I think we can arrange that, Bob.
Me: Thank you so much, Mr. Director.

I stood up to leave, thinking, "Well, that wasn't tough at all!" Just as I turned toward the door, the director spoke up again.

Director: One other thing, Bob.
Me: Yes, sir?
Director: The chairman of Ways and Means?
Me: What about him, sir?
Director: I could sure use his help in next year's budget. You know, that single room is the only one with a private phone. Why don't you use it and give the chairman a call on behalf of Caron? I mean, after all [here he gave a wry smile], you can give him a firsthand account of how good we are.
Me: I'll do that, Mr. Director, first thing.
Director: Enjoy the room, Bob.

I walked out of that room thinking, "Now *that* was a good con." Not mine. His.

As I began unpacking in the single room, Larry, the head counselor, came in. "You must have a lot of pull, TV Man." He said it with more sorrow than anger.

"So you're not mad at me?" I said, feeling a little self-conscious.

"No, I'm not mad, I'm worried," he said. "I'm worried because you don't stand a chance, and frankly, I don't want to see you die."

That first week at Caron I went out of my way to charm the other patients and the staff. I've always been good at turning on the charm. Growing up in my house, if you didn't charm the old man, you were staring at a beating. As a consequence, I was always desperate for people to like and admire me. Without the attention, I felt empty inside. When I felt empty I drank. So I tended to make short friendships quickly and easily—an asset in politics, a necessity in a survivor's life.

Nine out of ten of the men at Caron came from dysfunctional families. Half these guys were street people, the other half successful survivors. The street guys seemed to get with the Caron program fast. The survivors had heard it all before, or so we thought.

After a week in my private suite, my counselor told me I had to move to a double room. Thrown out of the VIP room? Impossible. Who was coming, Prince Charles?

His response was straight Caron talk. "No, asshole, someone who needs help badly, but is in total denial that he's an alcoholic. Just like you. By the way, we made you his buddy." Caron had a buddy system that assigned a veteran—someone who had been there at least seven days—to a new guy. "You'll meet him this afternoon," he added. "But be gentle. He just got here. He won't be in the mood for Beckel humor."

I went down to lunch (a big deal when you're confined to a rehab) to see if I could find my new buddy. Looking over at the director's table I saw a guy engaged in an animated conversation with the director himself.

It was Ron Ziegler. Richard Nixon's former press secretary. What the hell was *he* doing here?

And then it hit me: Ziegler was the new guy. My buddy. And the son-ofabitch was horning in on my VIP status and trying to take my single room! Who the hell did this guy think he was?

Then I remembered the first time I'd met Ziegler, and the kindness he'd shown me.

*   *   *

April 1992. I'd been invited to speak at the annual meeting of the National Association of Chain Drug Stores (NACDS), one of hundreds of organizations of well-paid executives in the Washington trade association world. The event was taking place at the Grand Hyatt Wailea Resort & Spa on Maui. Although by now I was a well-established speaker, this was the first time I was matched up with the big boys. There was General Norm Schwarzkopf, the recently returned hero of Desert Storm; conservative columnist George Will; Pulitzer Prize recipient William Safire; and ABC's over-the-top correspondent Sam Donaldson, among other big names. These guys' speaking fees dwarfed mine, although they were chump change compared to Liza Minnelli, who got $250,000 for one night of song and dance.

My accommodations were first class, my fee doubled because of the distance, *and* I was invited to spend the entire five days there gratis, staying on even after my speech. *This* was living at the top of the Washington food chain! How proud I was of myself. At least until they handed out the speaking schedule.

The event ran from April 25, a Saturday, through the following Wednesday. My speech was scheduled for 7:00 a.m. on Saturday, the first day of the meeting. An hour when all the executives who'd flown out to Hawaii for the event would no doubt be sleeping off their jet lag. For those unfamiliar with the world of paid speakers, this wasn't even equivalent to the top bleachers. More like standing outside the ballpark, listening to the game over a bad radio.

My event was billed as a breakfast meeting of the industry's political action committee. The setting was an outdoor patio. The turnout was embarrassing. It didn't take more than five minutes to realize that I was about to become roadkill for about twenty hungover conservative businessmen.

At the appointed hour, I was introduced by the president of the NACDS: Ron Ziegler.

Ron was best known for his role as Richard Nixon's press secretary during the Watergate scandals. A thankless job if ever there was one. Even after all the rats had deserted that sinking ship, Ron had remained firm in his resolve to support Nixon to the bitter end, and it was a pretty bitter end at that. Ron was also one of the few members of the Nixon White House staff who was never indicted for any wrongdoing. After Nixon left office Ron became president of the National Association of Truck Stop Owners for six years, after which he became president of the NACDS.

(Strangely enough, I was already connected to Ron by an odd sort of family thread: Three years earlier, in 1989, my brother, Graham, had played the part of Ziegler in a made-for-TV movie based on the Woodward-Bernstein book *The Final Days*. I never knew about this out-of-left-field connection until the process of writing this book.)

Ron was most gracious in his introductory remarks, but clearly embarrassed by the turnout. The outdoor podium where I was to speak happened to face east, putting me smack face-first into the rising sun. In fact, I was so blinded by the sunrise I couldn't see my notes. Ron came back to the podium and lent me his sunglasses. It was a little thing, a small gesture, but one I wouldn't forget. Sometimes the littlest gestures reveal the most about who a person really is.

*   *   *

Now, here was Ron, an inpatient drunk, just like me. I needed to cut him some slack. And after all, just the week before, I'd been the one in the director's office, shamelessly manipulating him in order to negotiate my VIP room. Ron was only playing the exact same game I'd played. And he'd been at the game a lot longer.

Later that afternoon I knocked on Ron's door. When he opened it and saw my face, he looked stunned. "What are you doing here, Bob?"

"What are *you* doing here, Ron?"

"I'm writing a book," he said.

"Yeah," I said, "and I'm recruiting bartenders for the next Republican convention."

We stared at each other, realized how ridiculous both our answers were, and laughed our asses off for the next ten minutes.

This being a Sunday and a relatively free day, Ron and I spent hours talking about...everything. We covered childhood memories, how we got to where we found ourselves now, our love of politics, our wives, kids, and life itself. No partisan politics stood in the way that afternoon. We were two drunks who both needed someone to relate to. Someone who understood Washington and its pressures. Two guys who had known fame and were no better off for it.

That was the first of many intimate conversations to follow over the next three weeks. One of the bedrock principles of Alcoholics Anonymous is anonymity, being able to share your most intimate feelings and histories with other drunks and knowing for certain that the information will never get out. There's a saying in AA, "Who you see here, what you hear here, let it stay here." I will honor that commitment to Ron even now that he's gone.

However, I do want to relate one conversation that I'm certain Ron would want written. It was about the fear of imminent death, a fear that virtually all drunks I know live with every day.

If you are alcoholic and actively drinking, your body is subjected to constant attack. An alcoholic needs booze in the system to operate. Few practicing alcoholics' bodies ever get away from having some level of alcohol in the bloodstream. The heart, liver, brain, and stomach struggle constantly to deal with this toxic substance, day after day without letup. Over time, even the biggest and strongest drunks fall prey to the physical ailments of the disease.

The body, meanwhile, is constantly sending ominous warnings about the damage being done. The drunk feels the damage growing, but is powerless to stop drinking. Imagine what it would feel like to know that what you are putting in your body every day is killing you, yet you are powerless to stop putting it there. This is psychologically devastating. As a result, alcoholics typically loathe themselves. They feel inadequate and cowardly. They also feel physically sick every day—at least until they ingest more poison to numb the body and brain.

Ron and I talked about this every day we were at Caron together. Why didn't we stop something that was not only ripping us apart from our families and friends, but killing us as well?

We also talked a lot about our wives. It had begun to dawn on both of us that our wives were at the limits of their patience. Now why would anyone want to give up on two bright, successful men like us? All Ron did was go into an alcoholic coma with a blood alcohol level of 0.49. And me? All I'd done was...well, that list was too long.

Nonalcoholics cannot understand why we subject ourselves to such torture. Why not just stop? After all, if a nonalcoholic was drinking something that was killing him, he would stop it immediately.

Why *couldn't* we stop?

If we knew the answer to that question there would be far fewer drunks in the world. All we can say is that we honestly try. I don't know of a single drunk who is deep into the disease who doesn't want to quit. The only real hope is AA. That program has saved millions of lives. The one catch is that the twelve-step program requires a belief in a power greater than yourself. For survivors, that is a foreign concept. It would take me years to accept, let alone understand.

Ron was a survivor and he, too, had difficulty with the idea of a greater power. He asked me one day if I worried about death. I said, just about every day. He wondered if it was possible to stay sober without that higher-power business. I didn't have an answer, except that I, too, could not get my arms around the idea of a higher power or a God.

"I want to believe in God," Ron said one day. "If for no other reason than to get the nightmares away from me."

"Which nightmares are those?" I asked.

"Just about every night I have a dream that drinking is going to kill me soon if I don't stop. How about you?"

"I think about dying, too," I agreed. "I don't have dreams about it, but my body tells me every day that it can't handle much more. How do you die in your dreams, Ron?"

"I'm drinking Scotch. I don't believe in God. I'm scared, and I'm alone. I know that if I can't find God soon, I'm going to die from a massive heart attack. And then I wake up in a heavy sweat."

"Ah, Ron, don't say that, man. We'll both find God and kick this thing," I said, unconvincingly.

"I hope so, Bob, I hope so," said Ron, staring off into the distance.

A little over three years later Ron Ziegler died of a massive heart attack at his home, in his sleep. I don't know if he was scared, or alone, or whether he had come close to knowing God. I only know he was a good friend, and I miss him.

*   *   *

I emerged from Caron truly committed to staying sober. And I did. I was sober throughout the 2000 Bush-Gore contest, stone cold sober through all the television commentary I did that campaign season.

Then Election Day happened, and the controversy over the vote in Florida erupted.

I was outraged by the whole thing. Having worked in Florida a lot politically and having looked at some of the returns there, I instinctively knew that Gore had won the thing. On my own dime, I commissioned a statistical analysis of the vote in Florida, conducted by a firm in St. Louis, that proved Gore had won the state by thirty to forty thousand votes. The president is not officially elected until the state electors meet in Washington in January. My plan was to send this report to all the Republican electors in Florida, hoping I could find one or two who would be persuaded on moral grounds that they shouldn't be voting for Bush. God knows why I thought I could actually convince these people, but that was my plan.

It was an insane idea from the start. I don't mean that as a figure of speech. It was an act conceived and executed in a state of literal insanity. As a seasoned political operator I was far too experienced ever to think I could possibly change an elector's mind, let alone change a Republican elector's mind based on a study commissioned by a Democratic political consultant. But when you're a drunk you slip into fancifully inflated notions of the extent of your personal power. And being in politics also tends to give you that same false sense of elevated impact. You start thinking that your very spoken words are listened to with rapt attention, that people change their whole lives based on what they hear you say. I know politicians who go through their careers actually believing this.

At the time, I believed it.

The moment this leaked out it blew up like a firestorm.

I went on NBC News to make my case, which was a terrible mistake. I said something like, "If I could hold these people hostage to get them to understand, I'd do it," which was edited (of course) in a way that made me sound like a total whacko, like I was actually talking about holding the electors hostage.

I got absolutely bludgeoned.

My car and office were both vandalized.

For the first time in my life, I started getting serious death threats.

The Republican National Committee sent out a mailing to millions of people, urging them to give me a call and tell me to stop what I was doing. At that point I had a small office in Virginia with maybe six people working for me and six or seven phone lines, and every phone was lit up from morning till night. For days stretching into weeks, they didn't stop ringing. These were the days when faxes were the big thing, and we had another half dozen fax lines. They spewed paper nonstop for days.

It didn't stop. For weeks, the pressure kept building.

People started showing up at my house late at night, spray-painting our windows and all kinds of crazy things. I had to hire security people to protect my family. I moved out, knowing that would make things safer for my wife and kids, and rented a little farmhouse in Maryland to hunker down in until the storm passed. At this point my wife had just about had enough of being married to a public figure and our relationship was in real trouble, which only added to the drama. Her mother moved in with them for a while, and police kept a twenty-four-hour watch on our house.

Finally it all came crashing down on me.

On January 19, I climbed into my car and thought, "This is all just too much." I started to drive, and just kept driving, until I ended up at an extremely sleazy bar, a dump in Prince George's County that I'd been to before.

Back into the dark world.

I walked into the place, sat down at the bar, having been stone cold sober for a year since going through Caron, and said, "Give me a drink." And proceeded to get blazing drunk.

At some point in the evening I tried to pick up a good-looking woman sitting next to me at the bar. Suddenly a guy burst in behind me, screaming.

The woman was married. This was her husband.

When I turned around to look he had a .45 pointed directly at my face.

He pulled the trigger.

Click!

For what reason no one will ever know—like that third grenade at the Plaza Miranda thirty years earlier—the gun did not go off.

An instant later somebody grabbed the guy from behind, yanking his gun arm up, and he pulled the trigger a second time. This time, the gun *did* go off.

And blew a gaping hole in the ceiling.

The bar's owner, who had no interest in the cops' getting involved here, grabbed me, hauled me off my stool, and had his bouncers throw my ass out onto the back parking lot asphalt in the freezing cold, where I passed out. A perfect candidate for death by exposure.

But I was not out there long. Somebody came out to where I lay prone and unconscious, went through my wallet, stole nothing, found Steve Wolin's number, and called him. To this day I have no idea who that person was—good Samaritan, angel, or fellow alcoholic. Maybe a combination of all three. Whoever he was, he probably saved my life.

Dr. Wolin got the call and immediately sent an ambulance to pick me up.

I awoke the next morning, Inaugural Day, the first day of George W. Bush's presidency, in a private room in the psychiatric ward of George Washington University Hospital, staring out the window at that familiar obelisk.

The Big Pencil, as my kids called it.

Welcome to the nuthouse.

CHAPTER NINE

Hitting Bottom

Being a VIP in the psycho ward meant VIP treatment all the way. It meant I was given a cover name to protect my identity. (Which meant absolutely nothing; my real name would be hitting the hospital gossip mill in a Washington second.) It meant that when I was being quietly wheeled in the night before through the rear entrance, the hospital administrator had leaned down over my stretcher and assured me I would have no contact with "those people." Comforting to know that while I was going crazy, I wouldn't have to sit with the nutjobs in the cheap seats.

Once my gigantic prison-guard-suicide-nurse had settled back in her chair and resumed paging methodically through her year-old *People*, I looked around and took stock of my VIP room. Worn but adequate. The pink-purple-green wallpaper had an acid-flashback flavor to it. A threadbare oval rug defied identification of its country of origin. My best guess: Trenton, New Jersey. Matching leather couch and armchair, both looking suspiciously like Naugahyde. Visible cuts on the armrests; the result, no doubt, of suicide attempts by previous tenants. Or maybe just fits of self-flagellation.

In midafternoon I had a visit from Steve Wolin. He asked my grizzly-bear sentry if she could leave us alone for a few minutes.

As the door closed behind her, the sound of marching bands playing Texas songs started pouring in through my window. I leaned over and looked out. There on the street, directly below us, was some Texas band loading up after their boy's inaugural parade. They were playing "The Yellow Rose of Texas," so help me God.

We were being serenaded by George W. Bush himself.

I was convinced that this was intentional. It had to be. Bush's people had heard about my clandestine incarceration and arranged to give me a victory serenade.

When I shared these thoughts with Dr. Wolin, he voiced the opinion that this was clearly delusional—that is, the part about its being intentional. But the Texas marching band was no illusion. Steve heard it, too, so I knew I wasn't hallucinating. He sat there next to me, looking out the window and shaking his head.

That evening my night nurse, smaller and much nicer than her daytime colleague, agreed to take me outside for a cigarette. Bless her. I didn't even have to listen to the old "I feel so much better since I quit smoking" routine that seems like a mandatory hospital staff recitation these days, even from the staff members who smoke. She brought me upstairs to an open deck on the top floor of the hospital.

We were overlooking the Mall, the Central Park of the nation's capital. The rain had stopped and the clouds had lifted. The entire Mall was visible, from the Lincoln Memorial clear over to the Capitol building. To me, there is nothing in the world as beautiful as the great Mall and its monuments on a clear night. The Washington Monument, all 555 feet of her white marble, was fully lit by banks of fluorescent lights.

How strange, I thought, that in a psych ward where you're under a twenty-four-hour suicide watch, they would let you smoke, out on an open balcony seven stories up, with nothing but an eighteen-inch railing and a whole lot of air between you and the concrete below.

Smoking that cigarette, staring at the Big Pencil, I reflected very briefly on the arc of my life, or at least, of my life so far. I grew up in a loony bin where generous portions of pain and suffering were on the menu every day. Hell, that was why I ran away to Washington in the first place: to get away from the madness of my family. For nearly thirty years this city had rewarded me handsomely. But now it seemed I'd ended up more or less where I started.

From the nuthouse to the White House to the nuthouse.

Who says you can't go home again?

*   *   *

About a week after my release, once I'd gotten settled back in my rent-by-the-week place in Maryland, a friend called and asked if I could come over to his place. When I got there I found my brother, Buddy, sitting in my friend's living room. My sister, Peggy, was there, too. So was Jim Cando, my old friend and NCEC cameraman from North Carolina. In fact, the room was full of old friends going back years, people who'd worked for me in politics, good friends whom I'd lost contact with because of my drinking. There were maybe a dozen people in all, and they'd come from all over the country. And there was one guy there I'd never seen before.

Oh, shit, I thought. I knew exactly what this was about. *They're here for a fucking intervention.*

They sure were. Peggy was the driving force behind it, because she'd seen how heavy my drinking and cocaine use had gotten. They'd raised the money to hire a professional interventionist to take us through the whole process. That was the guy I didn't recognize.

It took them about three hours to break me down. Finally I said, "All right, what do you want me to do?"

They said, "We want you to go to Hazelden." The granddaddy of all rehab facilities, the original and still one of the very best there is.

"Okay," I said, my voice thick with…with what? Resentment? Gratitude? Fear? Relief? Probably all of the above. Then I added, "Can I fly first class?" Buddy thought that was pretty amusing. He may have been the only one.

Jim Cando went with me over to my place, helped me pack up all my stuff, and brought me back to the house to drop everything off and say good-bye to MacKenzie and Alex, which my wife had agreed was okay. I had thought the day I went off to Caron was the lowest point of my life, but I was wrong. This was worse.

I flew to Minnesota with the interventionist. I had asked him if I could drink on the plane. "You can drink all you want," he said, "until you get to Hazelden." So I did. I drank the whole way there.

Hazelden is about sixty miles north of Minneapolis, sitting out on a bucolic lake in the middle of nowhere. It was cold. (Minnesota in January is not for sissies.) But the clear air felt wonderful. Although, not at first. First they checked me in, stashed me into the hospital wing, and waited me out while I detoxed.

At Hazelden, as at Caron, many of the counselors were recovering alcoholics and addicts. They didn't give a shit who I was. They treated me like everybody else—worse, in some cases, because I had some notoriety and they needed to knock that down.

I was defeated, and I knew it. I'd had this incredible run for all these years, but at Hazelden they broke me down to the point where I finally had to face the full reality of what was going on. I turned around and with the good psychiatric help there I faced my demons from the past and understood what the survival thing really meant.

For the past decade Steve Wolin and I had been talking about this stuff, so I was aware of it, but I was not aware of how much it was an enabler for my disease. All the skills I had as a survivor had made me an incredible amount of money, gotten me extremely well-known, and put me on television. They also allowed me to become horribly addicted to alcohol.

When the thirty days was up I extended my stay for a few weeks more, because I knew this time I had to make it.

When I finally left Hazelden I felt much stronger entering my life sober than I had when leaving Caron the year before. This time, I knew, my life as a drunk was over. It was either that, or I truly would die.

The doctors at Hazelden had made that last point very clear. They put me through a rigorous series of physicals and showed me the results, scans of my liver, blood work, everything. "Bob," they said, "you're only fifty, and you've got the body of an eighty-year-old. Your liver's shot. Any more drinking and you're going to get cirrhosis."

Cirrhosis: I knew all about that. That's what finally killed my uncle Sam.

They said, "You're killing yourself, day by day. If you go back to drinking, you're not going to last much longer."

"How long do you think I'd live," I asked them, "if I did go back to it?"

They said, "Maybe a year, if you're lucky. You should have been dead by now. But you're not. You've got one more chance, and that's about it."

Many of these doctors were recovering alcoholics, too. They knew what they were talking about. They'd seen it all. I believed them. I thought about my kids. I just couldn't wrap my mind around the fact that I'd put myself in this situation, that my kids were on the verge of losing their father. Yet here I was, worse off than my own father had ever been.

I came out of Hazelden with a resolve that I was going to stay sober. And this time, I did. To this day, I still am. By the grace of God, one day at a time. As I write these words, that was thirteen and a half years ago.

Haven't had a drink since.

*   *   *

Much to my surprise, though, my successful course through rehab did not mark the end of the downward spiral my life had been following. Much to my surprise, getting all those years of drinking and drugs and decadence and poison out of my system wasn't the hard part.

The hard part was what came next.

After fourteen years of trying on and off, I had now gotten truly and sincerely sober. But getting sober, as tough as it was, was one thing. Staying there was about to get a lot tougher.

In AA they talk about hitting bottom. They say an alcoholic doesn't have much of a chance of staying with the program and genuinely turning his life around until he has hit bottom. I thought that by this time, I had hit bottom pretty hard. And maybe I was right. Maybe I had, or at least, maybe I'd started.

But if I thought I was *finished* hitting bottom, I was quite wrong.

After Hazelden I continued living at the rented farm in western Maryland. I saw my kids on and off and spent as much time with them as I could swing, driving into Washington to pick them up at school and take them home. My wife and I were seeing very little of each other. I knew the whole thing had been hard on her.

Leland still traveled a fair amount with her golf career, and although I was living at the Maryland farm I would stay at the house with the kids when she was gone. One night, when she was away traveling with her golf team, I was home with my son, who was then seven years old. The phone rang and I heard Alex say, "Oh, hi, John, she's not here. I'll have her get back to you."

"Who's John?" I asked.

He said, "That's mom's friend, John. He comes to see us a lot. He was there with us on vacation."

There with us on vacation. In other words, a year earlier—when I was going through rehab at Caron.

I went down to the office in our house and started looking through the cell bills. There were literally hundreds of phone calls between my wife and a man named John Keyser.

Keyser was a wealthy guy out of Chicago who had recently sold his very successful international insurance company, had lots of money, and had decided to become a philanthropist. He funded the Georgetown University girls' golf team and had met Leland when she applied for a position there as golf coach. She gave up pro golf, took the coaching position, and she and Keyser started a relationship. He was about twenty-three or twenty-four years older than she was, an even bigger age difference than ours.

When I confronted her, she said, yes, she'd found somebody who was stable, and she thought it was in the best interest of the kids, and it was time for us to consider getting a divorce.

When my family was setting up my intervention and stay at Hazelden, Leland had told the people organizing the whole thing that she was going to try to make the marriage work. I now realized she'd had no intention of doing that at all. At that point, she had already decided to move out.

This probably should not have come as such a big surprise—but it did. The idea of divorce hit me like a blow to the solar plexus with brass knuckles. (I'm talking from experience.) This may seem strange. After all, I'd never thought I really wanted to be married to begin with. And to be perfectly honest about it, Leland and I never really got along very well. We were both devoted to our kids, and we'd been great at partying in our day. There wasn't a great deal more to the relationship.

And I understood that this was my fault, to a significant degree. My actions toward her in the latter half of the nineties were not good, to say the least. I cheated a lot. I came home drunk, often very drunk, very late at night. She had finally quit drinking well before I did, so that was an additional strain on things. I knew that being married to me was no picnic, and I didn't blame her for wanting out.

Yet despite all that, the news that our marriage was over badly shook me up.

For survivors, rejection can be an intolerably painful thing. It strikes all those abandonment chords that are still echoing from the earliest days. When somebody turns you down or leaves you, it suddenly feels much more painful than you ever would have imagined it would be. I mentioned earlier that I had a relationship with a girl, back in my college days. That relationship hadn't lasted long, but when Rosie Lee decided to call it quits and separated from me it hurt like hell, and I spent the next year and a half trying to get her back.

Still, the personal rejection divorce represented and the stinging sense that I'd failed (survivors are allergic to failure; I *hate* to fail) were only part of it. Probably the worst part of it was the fear that we had irrevocably screwed up our kids.

There was nothing in the world more important to me than our two children. All my life I'd been dedicated to myself and my career, but when those two entered my life I found a higher priority. At that point my highest aspiration, the thing I wanted more than anything, was to give them a life that was not the life of scarring and suffering that I had experienced.

The absolute worst part of the whole debacle was the day Leland and I had to tell the kids we were getting separated. I would take any number of beatings from North Carolina rednecks, any public pain or national humiliation, over having to repeat that day. We got them together out by the pool we'd built behind our house, sat them down, and told them. Of course, they both started to cry. We tried to do the textbook thing, "This has nothing to do with you, and we're going to try our best, we'll always love each other, but this is best for right now." It was a terrible day.

The kids had never seen us argue. We had always gone out of our way to avoid fighting in front of them; that was something I insisted on, after all the experiences of growing up in my house. One night, though, when I was down in our home office going through a stack of bills that Leland had run up, I started yelling at her about spending money, and in a fit of fury I swept everything off her desk with one arm and sent it all crashing to the floor. I heard a noise behind me, turned around, and realized to my horror that my son was standing there.

He looked up at me and started backing away, saying, "Dad, don't hit me! Don't hit me!"

I walked up to him gently and said, "Alex, I would never hit you. I'm mad at your mom, but I'm not mad at you. I would never, ever do that."

To this day Alex remembers the whole scene vividly. It's still painful to write about it.

You could say that because we divorced early, when they were still young, it was easier for them than if our marriage had continued for many more years. And I do think there's some truth to that. I think in some ways it would have been even harder for them if they were twelve or thirteen when we split up. But it would be a very big mistake to assume that it didn't leave scars. It always does.

*   *   *

On top of the emotional pain, I quickly realized I had also entered a world of hurt financially. That disastrous Bush-Gore fiasco had badly damaged my reputation. When it first blew up in the press at the end of 2000, my bosses at CNN warned me that I was going too far. I now discovered that they were absolutely right. It cost me, big-time. Most of my speaking engagements came from business groups, most of which were naturally Bush supporters. After my pro-Gore flameout I was not exactly high on their list of matinee idols to have at their conventions.

My speaking calendar dried up.

The old grassroots business was gone (Cassidy & Associates got fed up with it and dissolved it at the end of the nineties), and although I'd made a pretty penny when I sold out, I'd long since burned through most of that.

And now I was looking at a divorce—potentially a very costly divorce.

As Leland and I got into the process we soon decided we didn't want to go to trial. Our lawyers wanted to, I suspect, so they could rack up some good bills. But we opted instead to go through mediation with a retired family judge rather than the contentious and inevitably ugly path of litigation. (A good decision, and one I strongly recommend if you are ever in that situation.)

Mediation went fine. Child custody and visitation were never issues for us; we didn't do the "You get every other Saturday" bullshit, and agreed from the start that we would both continue to be full-time parents to the best of our ability, and both be flexible about schedules and accommodations. (And have pretty much continued to do so ever since.) We divvied up the property pretty quickly.

The big question was, what kind of cash alimony was I going to have to pay?

After everything else was completed, the judge looked at me and said, "All right, Bob, until Leland cohabits with someone else or remarries, your alimony is seventeen thousand dollars a month."

Seventeen thousand dollars a month?

"Your Honor," I said, "that's almost a quarter-million dollars a year! I don't even make that much."

"Well, you did last year," he replied. "Sorry. That's the law. That's the way Maryland works."

For the next few months I was bleeding bad. Every bit of cash I could pull in was flying out the door in alimony payments. I hadn't had much to start with. Soon I was down to just about nothing.

About three months later, John Keyser called me. He sounded very nervous. He was probably worried that I was going to have him assassinated or something. By this time we had put our house on the market and Leland had moved into another house near her mother.

John said, "Bob, I hate to ask you this, but... I'd like to move in with Leland. I want to make sure that's okay with you."

"John," I said, "can I rent the truck? Can I buy you some furniture? Is there any way I can help?"

"Gee," he said. "Thanks, I'm surprised you're taking it so well."

I said, "Far be it for me to stand in the way of love, John. When can you go? Can you move in tonight?"

He moved in with her the following Wednesday, and that was the end of the alimony. I don't know how I would have made it much longer than that.

*   *   *

Fortunately, right about then someone tossed me a life preserver.

I was at a dinner party in Washington in 2001 when I overheard a gentleman named Alan Blinken talking with another gentleman about guns. I knew Alan, though only vaguely. A very wealthy man, he'd made an unsuccessful run for New York State Assembly in 1990, and then served as Bill Clinton's ambassador to Belgium through the nineties.

I was drawn into conversation with Alan, and he told me he was thinking about running for a seat in the U.S. Senate.

"New York already has two Democratic senators, Alan," I said. "Hillary Clinton and Chuck Schumer."

"Not New York," he replied. "Idaho."

I just about spat out my food. Idaho? *Alan?*

"You know I have a place there," he said.

Yes—a beautiful vacation home in Sun Valley, a relatively isolated little resort community in the middle of a very big and very Republican state. Here is this incredibly wealthy guy who's been a New Yorker all his life, degree from Harvard, wife the daughter of a big Hollywood film producer, and he's Jewish to boot. You go up into northern Idaho and you can't find a single

Jewish name in the phone book. I couldn't even count the number of ways I couldn't see this happening. I thought nothing more about it.

Late the following spring Alan and his wife invited me over to their beautiful townhouse in Georgetown. When I got there he said, "We've heard great things about you. We wondered, would you run our campaign for the Senate?"

Me, run a campaign? At this point I had not been in the campaign business for nearly two decades. Still, I really needed the money.

"Tell you what," I said, "let me go out there, take a look at the state, and see what I can come up with."

What I found was that the Republican incumbent, the guy Alan was running against, was pretty popular. He'd held office there for three terms, and in Idaho they don't tend to throw people out of office. Our candidate was a Jewish millionaire who'd run for public office once—in New York—and lost. Who was using his own money to buy a Senate seat, was how the opposition was putting it. And of course, they were absolutely right. Even getting the Sun Valley place to count as in-state residency was going to take some fancy footwork.

When I got back from Idaho I said, "Let me tell you something, Alan. Your chances out there, even with every possible factor lining up in your favor, are ten to one against you."

He said, "That's fine. We can do that."

I said, "You sure?"

He was absolutely set on it. I told him I wouldn't move to Idaho, but I'd do the consulting and the advertising and come out there every few weeks to scope out how things were going on the ground. So that was that: I was now Alan Blinken's campaign manager.

Here was how the *New York Times*'s Timothy Egan put it:

> As if to make his run for office a perfect long-shot fantasy, Mr. Blinken has drawn Bob Beckel out of semiretirement to run his campaign. Walter F. Mondale lost every state but one when Mr. Beckel ran his 1984 presidential campaign.

Gee, Tim, thanks for the vote of confidence.

Alan's magnificent Sun Valley house was a lot of fun to visit. This is something I've noticed about rich people: Everything they have is incredibly high quality. The towels are luxurious, the sheets are soft like doeskin, the food is amazing. I wasn't used to this level of high living—waiters and waitresses, housekeepers, doormen, and all. It was a little out of my league. But I managed to pull through.

Blinken fancied himself a sportsman, which I figured was good because this was Idaho, right? When I got there he said, "Hey, every town we visit, why don't we go to the local gun range and shoot?"

"That's a hell of a good idea, Alan," I said. "I hadn't thought of that."

The first time he did this, I happened to be there with him. We were getting ready to leave for the day, and down from his master suite came Alan dressed in this Teddy Roosevelt, African safari kind of jacket, one of those handmade ones with the leather in the armpit for the gun, and he had on pants that fluffed out at the sides, and big, beautiful, German boots. He had his rifles in cases that cost probably forty thousand dollars apiece. It was like he was trying to look like a caricature of a rich guy trying to look like a sportsman.

We went out to the first gun range. We'd worked this out ahead of time, and the guy who ran the place had agreed to get a bunch of the boys out there to shoot with my guy. We arrived and got out of the car, and these boys just looked at Alan. One of them said, "Are you shittin' me?"

While Alan started getting out his guns I pulled these guys aside and said, "Just go along with this, okay? Boys, look, I know this guy probably isn't going to win. I know he's the wrong candidate for your state. But please, give him a break. Just shoot with him. The guy's a great shooter."

They grudgingly agreed.

Blinken came over and introduced himself, and they all headed out onto the range. They had it set up at something like fifty yards, and one of the boys said, "Why don't we drop that back to a hundred yards, see how good old Alan here is."

Blinken is a pretty good shot and did a decent job—but these Idaho guys were all Second-Amendment NRA types who shot every day. They were hitting bull's-eye after bull's-eye after bull's-eye. A few of the candidate's shots missed the target entirely.

Blinken turned to them and said, "Boys, I'm really sorry."

No, wait—actually, that's not what he said. That's what *I* would have said. But not Alan. He said, "Gentlemen, I apologize for my lack of dexterity."

I just about died right there on the spot. *Oh, dear God,* I thought, *please, no, he can't be saying that.*

Now I don't want to give the wrong impression here. Alan is a tremendous guy, lovable as they come, and I liked him a lot. But you couldn't have made a more perfect choice if you were *trying* to put exactly the wrong person in this race. It was ugly. And it just got uglier as we went around touring the state, visiting different cities in the campaign bus he'd bought. Boise and Sun Valley were lovely places where Alan could buddy up to people, but get outside that limited area and you are in some very rough places. Beautiful, but rough. At night, people would paint swastikas on the side of the bus. He got a lot of death threats.

There's a city in the northwestern corner of the state, Sandpoint, where I heard the post office received the largest number of police retirement checks in the country outside of LA County. That was no coincidence: That region was home to all these ex-cops who would leave Los Angeles and move to northern Idaho so they wouldn't have to be around any blacks, gang members, or anything else that reminded them of LA. Mark Fuhrman, the detective on the O. J. Simpson case, lived up there.

I went up to Sandpoint to check things out and do a little advance work before I sent Alan up; I didn't want us to embarrass ourselves too badly. I met Fuhrman, and he and I actually hit it off. In fact, we became good friends. I explained to him what we were doing.

He said, "Bob, I can tell you everything you need to know about Alan Blinken. Which is this: That boy can't get a vote out here. Not one."

I said, "Not even yours?"

"The last one would be mine," he said. "Hey, you've read the stories about me."

"Yeah," I replied, "but I don't believe them. I don't believe you're a racist, Mark." And I don't think he is, either. He's just a guy with right-wing convictions. Hell, everyone there was right wing.

He said, "C'mon, let's take a walk around town. Let's have a conversation with some people."

So we started walking. The first guy we met up with, Mark said, "I want to introduce you to Bob Beckel. This is Alan Blinken's campaign consultant."

The guy looked at me and said, "You supportin' a fuckin' *Jew?*"

"I wouldn't exactly put it that way," I said. "That's not very kind."

He said, "I don't give a shit. That's why I moved up here—so I don't have to be kind."

Back down to Sun Valley. Told my candidate he needn't bother going up to Sandpoint at all.

He said he *had* to go. "If I don't, I'll look like I'm chickenshit."

"I'm telling you, Alan, it's a bad idea. I'm a blue-collar guy, and I barely got out of there alive. And you, you're to the manor born." And he absolutely was. Alan was the epitome of elegance. He had perfect Brooks Brothers suits, and he *always* wore a suit and tie. I could never convince him to get into jeans or anything like that. He occasionally still wore *top hats*, for crying out loud. (Though not in Idaho, thank God.) I kept trying. "Alan, this is just the wrong place. There aren't going to be that many votes up there anyway, and I promise you, you aren't going to get any of them."

He said, "Well, let me give it a try."

I'll have to give this to him: The man had guts. He was not afraid of anything, and not about to back down from anything. There's a reason people like Alan are successful. He might not be northern-Idaho tough, but underneath the gentlemanly veneer there was a tough spirit there.

Not that the good people of Sandpoint saw it that way. I didn't go with him on that trip, but apparently it was even worse than I thought it would be. Blinken had a big rally set up, and maybe three people showed up.

That summer wasn't easy. The divorce was in process, I was struggling financially, and while Alan's campaign was sustaining me for the time being, it was a one-off—I wasn't about to get back into the full-time campaign business. And the campaign itself was going from bad to worse.

It was an ongoing battle not to succumb to the pressure of the time and the seduction of alcohol and take a drink.

That battle was about to get worse, by degrees of magnitude.

*   *   *

Late one night in early July I came back home from two weeks in Idaho. As I started going through my stacked-up mail, I noticed a Federal Express envelope. Only it hadn't actually been sent through FedEx. Someone had just slipped it into my box. I opened it and took out a letter. It said:

> We see you getting back from Idaho late. We know that you
> screwed around with one of our girls. We're going to tell your
> wife's lawyer, unless you pay us fifty thousand dollars and drop it,
> tomorrow, at [a particular location in D.C.].

The letter also told me to go listen to my answering machine, in case I doubted they had proof of my illegal activities. I listened to the message. There were two voices. One belonged to a woman evidently named Tiffany. The other was mine.

God knows I'd been with enough hookers, but this was one woman I'd never even heard of, let alone slept with. They had spliced my voice, taken from TV broadcasts, together with hers to make it sound like we were having a conversation. I knew right away it was a fake, but it certainly made the point that they were paying a lot of attention and going to a lot of trouble to pull this thing off.

By now I'd had enough of dealing with the dark world. The next day I went down with my lawyer to the Bethesda Police Department and reported what had happened.

They said this was the biggest extortion they'd ever heard of in Montgomery County. "We want to pursue this and track these people down. Will you help us?"

My lawyer said, "Maybe—as long as he's not described in any of the legal papers and is not publicly associated with the case."

The police agreed to our terms. They said they would describe me only as Victim X, and the only time I might have to appear would be if these guys actually went to trial, which I knew was quite unlikely, because nine out of ten cases like this get plea-bargained and never see the inside of a courtroom.

So I agreed.

The police said, "All right, now let's see if we can find out who these people are."

The note told me to drop the money on a little street overlooking the Potomac River, in the District of Columbia. It happened to be on park service land, which was federal land, so we had three police departments involved: the Montgomery County police, from Maryland, where I lived and had received the note; the District of Columbia police; and then there were the federal police. When I drove my car down to the stated location, I'd never seen so many telephone repairmen in my life, guys riding innocently by on bicycles, and guys out for walks. The police had commandeered a house right on the corner overlooking where the drop was to be, with video cameras trained on the spot.

I took the bag down and dropped it at the given location. Inside the bag was a few hundred dollars along with a note saying I needed a little more time to put together the whole fifty grand. This was a Friday; the note said I needed till Monday.

After I left, the police observed a car that kept driving around the block. Obviously the pick-up car. They had to smell cops. Anybody in their right mind would smell them.

They took off without retrieving the bag, but the cops got their license number and were able to trace it back to an escort agency in Virginia, right across the river.

They asked me if I'd be willing to get one of these girls to come meet me in Bethesda. They said, if I could get her to meet with me, they'd pick her up and see if they could turn her and get inside information on the outfit. I agreed.

As I was about to make the phone call, one of them said, "Do you know how to conduct this conversation?" Yeah, I said, I was pretty sure I knew how this went.

I got this woman to come meet me in the Hyatt in Bethesda. We sat there for half an hour making conversation that came down to "You're a cop," "No, *you're* a cop," "No, *you're* a cop..." We finally decided neither one of us was a cop, so she said, "All right, it'll be two hundred fifty dollars," at which point the real cops came in and arrested her. Once they booked her they found she had several arrests for prostitution and some pending cases. They cut a deal with her: They would wipe off those arrests and pending cases if she would report on these guys' activities and testify. She agreed.

I then gave her two checks that she could take back and give the guy, and say, "He wants me next week, and he gave me these checks just to confirm it." Of course escort agencies don't take checks, and we knew that—but the guy went out and cashed them anyway, and his picture was caught at the bank when he did.

The police thanked me. "You did a good job, Bob. We appreciate it. You've done the community a fine service."

"Happy to help," I told them, and that was the end of that.

Until six weeks later, at the end of August, when I came back from another trip to Idaho and found my phone ringing off the hook. The woman on the other end introduced herself as Lauren Dunn, a reporter from the *Northern Virginia Journal.*

"Are you the same Bob Beckel that's on CNN and is a well-known political operative around Washington?" I said I was, and she said, "We have a story that you were with a hooker at the Hyatt Hotel in Bethesda six weeks ago—"

"Whoa, whoa, wait a minute," I said. "Wait. You need to understand something here. Do *not* print that story, because I need you to get some clarification."

I went right down to the police and said, "Look, this story can't run. If it runs, I'm screwed."

They said, "Bob, there's nothing we can do about it. It's been turned over to a federal judge now, because it's a multistate operation." The way these guys were operating, they would look up people who were filing for divorce, which is a matter of public record, and then extort five thousand a whack from them. Or, in my case, fifty thousand. Since this thing crossed state lines it had left the Montgomery County judge's hands and was now under the jurisdiction of a federal judge.

Okay, federal judge it is.

I went to see the federal judge in charge of the case and explained to him that the police had asked me to do this, and had promised that I would be identified only as Victim X.

The judge walked me through what had happened:

One of the guys who ran the extortion racket, who was also the owner of the car they'd traced, lived in Alexandria. In order to get a search warrant on his house they had to involve the Virginia police. When they sent their paperwork over to the Alexandria cops, there was a right-wing cop there who saw my name on the thing. This cop didn't like me. So he deleted the name "Victim X" from the search warrant and put in my name instead—so my name was part of the official search warrant, which also became a matter of public record after the search was completed. This Dunn woman was crawling around the courthouse in that area and saw the thing come through. She was twenty-two years old, a cub reporter. She figured this was her big break. Her Woodward and Bernstein moment, I guess.

I went to see the judge again, this time with my lawyer, and said, "Your Honor, I can't let this thing go out like this. I'm going to lose everything I've got."

"I'm sorry, Bob," he said. "I've got to keep this under a gag order on everybody until we wrap this up."

It hit like a firestorm. It was all over the Internet, all over the blogs. They set up a site called "Bob's Hookers Alley" with a picture of the woman. And because of the gag order, I couldn't say a thing. I couldn't talk to Lauren Dunn to clarify the story; I couldn't talk to any other journalists; I couldn't talk to my bosses at CNN; I couldn't do anything but sit there and take it.

CNN called me up and suggested I "take a few weeks off the air." Which was a polite way of saying, "Clean out your desk."

That was the end of my career at CNN.

And all the other networks.

At that point I had about ten speaking gigs set up. All ten were canceled. Suddenly I was radioactive. Nobody would touch me. The parents at my kids' school got together and agreed to ask me if I would stop coaching my kid's Little League team. That was the hardest part of the whole thing.

*   *   *

Before the Bush-Gore election I'd been making maybe seven hundred thousand dollars a year. Now my total disposable income was down to something like *seven thousand* dollars a year—one-hundredth my prior level.

To bring in enough cash to eat and keep the lights on, I went into a government training office and worked from eleven at night till seven in the morning for a temp firm.

The hooker case did go to trial after all, five or six months after the whole thing blew up. By this time there were some fifteen defendants from seven different states involved. I went into court on Victims' Day to testify in front of the Montgomery County judge, the one I'd talked to back when the whole sting operation was first being set up.

"Your Honor," I said. "I came out to do my duty as a citizen and help the police here. I did everything they asked me to do. And then I got exposed, railroaded, and ruined. I need to ask you a question—and I'm going to borrow a line from a Republican, which I don't normally do."

The judge had to chuckle at that one. He knew who I was.

"Your Honor, I want to know, which office in this building do I go to, to get my reputation back?" It was Ray Donovan's famous line, from when he was indicted for fraud in the eighties and later exonerated. (Ray was Reagan's secretary of labor.)

The judge knew the line, and he was visibly moved. "Mr. Beckel," he said, "I'm afraid there is no such place."

At that point my lawyer jumped up and said, "Your Honor, my client was given a promise by the police to be identified in this matter only as Victim X. That was clearly spelled out as an a priori condition of his participation in the whole operation, which we remind the court was entirely voluntary on his part."

Victim X? This was news to the judge. He hadn't heard about that particular detail. He called up all the parties involved and brought us all into his chambers. Once we were all assembled, he said to my lawyer, "All right, tell me the story here, exactly." My lawyer explained what had happened with the search warrant. The judge turned to the Montgomery County cop and said, "Did you promise Mr. Beckel he'd be listed only as Victim X?"

"Yeah, Your Honor," the Montgomery cop replied. "But we had to send it to Virginia for the warrant, and they changed it."

The judge shook his head and said, "That's not acceptable. You guys deal with them every day." He turned to me and said, "How much money did you lose, Mr. Beckel, over this period of time?"

"Probably close to one point five million dollars," I said.

The judge went back out into court and fined the defendants $1.5 million in retribution, specifying that the full amount be turned over to me. Which was great—except that they had no money and were all going to prison. So while it was a nice gesture on the judge's part, it didn't really mean anything.

And I couldn't sue the Alexandria police, because they were what's technically called "sovereign under the law," which meant the maximum I could have sued them for would have been twenty thousand dollars, which would barely be worth the grief. The Virginia cop who'd put my name on that report got fired. That was some small bit of satisfaction, I suppose, but it didn't do anything to rebuild my life.

The hooker scandal continues to have an impact on my reputation even today. As Bert Lance (and Ray Donovan, and many others) had learned only too well, once a story like that is out there, it's out there. The fact that it was all a setup, a sting operation that the police asked me to do, and that the original story had the facts all wrong...none of that shows up on the Internet. I hired an international reputation management firm to get it knocked off the first page of Google results for my name, which they did—but it comes back up again at every election cycle.

Please, if you bump into the story online, don't click on it. You'll just move it further toward the front of the line.

*   *   *

That Gore-Bush electors scandal back in late 2000 had decimated my income by taking away practically all the speaking. The hooker scandal finished the job. I was now on the verge of complete destitution.

I called Alan Blinken and asked him if he could pay my consulting bill. He said he would pay the current bill, but that I was gone from the campaign. I completely understood, and didn't hold it against him for a moment. I wouldn't have wanted me there, either. I'd become too toxic to touch. I knew it better than anyone.

Although I actually did continue work on one aspect of the race for Alan, albeit in secret.

A little earlier in the campaign I had brought in my old oppo guy, Ron, who'd done the background check work for me in the Panama Canal Treaty business, to do some background checking on our opponent, the incumbent senator. Ron dug around a while, then came back and said, "Bob, the only thing I've got on this guy is, I think he's gay."

Gay—in Idaho? Man, if that was true, that sure wasn't going to fly too well with the good people of the potato state. This was 2002. Nobody was talking about gay marriage in those days. This was years before *Brokeback Mountain*, and nobody was even out of the closet up there in the rugged Northwest.

I told Ron we had to find someone who could substantiate this rumor. We had to out this guy somehow—but we couldn't go accusing a United States senator of being gay without some evidence. Ron tried everything. He went around to the few gay bars there were in that state, and he asked around at every place you could ask, but he couldn't sell it. The rumor persisted, but we were never able to use it.

Our opponent beat us easily, two to one. Alan returned to New York in defeat, and the senator returned to his Senate seat.

And you want to know the real bitch of it all? Our opponent's name was Larry Craig.

Yes, *that* Larry Craig.

Five years later Craig was arrested in a stall of an airport men's room coming on to the guy next to him. It blew up into a huge scandal, and Craig was forced out of the Senate. When the news broke in 2007 Blinken called me up and said, "Why the hell didn't we go with that gay story?" But there was no way we could have. We had no proof.

Earlier I said I would give you examples of the three kinds of campaigns: the good, the bad, and the ugly. This was one of the ugly ones. It was ugly all around. We played every ugly trick we could, they played every ugly trick they could, and they out-uglied us. The only possible way we could have won would have been if we could have outted Craig on being gay. We just never found the right bathroom stall.

So there it was: Larry Craig won his election over rumors that were true, but we couldn't print. And my reputation was shattered over a scandal that *wasn't* true, but was all over the papers anyway.

My grip on sobriety was now hanging on by a thread, and that thread was unraveling.

*   *   *

And then there was my father.

My father always said he wanted to get past the year 2000. That was his goal. "After that," he'd say, "I'm going to head west." He was born on Christmas Day, 1913, on the eve of World War I, which meant if he was going to ring in the new millennium he had to make it to a week past his eighty-sixth birthday. His brothers made it to barely half that age, and his sister even less. But his enforced sobriety, under the threat of losing Teenie (and her money), was evidently good for him. He made it to 2000, with some room to spare.

In the spring of 2002, just as the Blinken campaign was getting under way, the old man had a stroke.

It was severe enough to keep him in bed, but he could still speak a little, though his voice was slurred. He loved Charlottesville and he wanted to come back home for a weekend. He wanted to look out his window at the Rivanna River. He loved to go to the university, to visit Mr. Jefferson's library. He was a teacher to the end.

Teenie convinced the hospital that she could handle him if they brought him back in a hospital bed. On March 3 she brought him home, got him in a bedroom where he could look out the window—and then *she* dropped dead, right there next to his bed. He couldn't move and couldn't reach a phone. He was in the room there with her for two days, until people came looking for them. It was horrible for him.

When I got down to Charlottesville to see him, he was back in the hospital. He could still talk a little, but it was easier for him to write things out on a paper pad.

"What should I do with Teenie?" I asked him. "The funeral parlor wants to know what to do." He wrote out:

Have her cremated and buried in the old Beckel family plot in Ohio.

I said, "Does she have a will?" He wrote:

I don't think so. You should go back into the house and see if you can find one in her office there.

When they were taking Teenie's body out of the condo apparently somebody had broken off the key to the front door, so I had to get a locksmith. The guy couldn't get through the door, so we had to go around back. It was on a second story, and we had to climb up onto a second-floor veranda and break in through some sliding glass doors.

I told the locksmith, "If you've never smelled death before, you better put something over your nose, because she was in there for two days." The moment we got inside, that locksmith took one whiff and took off down the hall, unlocked the door from the inside, and split. I aired the place out as best I could, but the smell of death, one I've smelled often in my life, is one you never forget.

I went through the whole place and couldn't find anything. No will, nothing. So I went ahead and had her cremated.

It turned out she had a surviving daughter, whom none of us knew about, and that there was a will after all. And that it specified that she be buried in *her* family plot in Pennsylvania.

Her lawyer, an ancient man who referred to himself as the Barrister (and who we also didn't know existed until it was too late) harassed me for months. He even tried to sue me. He would start every phone call the same way:

"Is this Bob Beckel?"

"Speaking."

"*You burned my client!*"

Finally, after we'd had this dialogue five or six times, I couldn't help it: I started to laugh.

"Are you *laughing*?" he demanded, incredulous. "You think this is *funny*?"

"I'm sorry, Barrister," I said, "but we've had this conversation now five or six times and at this point, yes, it's getting to be a little funny." When he audibly fumed but didn't say anything, I continued. "Look, Barrister. Did I burn your client? Yes, I did. Did I know she didn't want to be burned? No, I did not. So yes, she's burned, and I'm sorry, but we're not going to put Humpty Dumpty back together again. It is what it is."

He stopped calling, and the suit never went anywhere.

Meanwhile, my father had moved back into the condo he and Teenie had shared. Before long, he had another stroke. He had loved Teenie very much, and I knew that people who are close tend to die quickly after their spouse is gone.

That August, just before the hooker scandal broke, I went to see him in the hospital. The second stroke had left him barely able to talk, but he could still write things out on his pad.

As I sat next to his bed, he wrote me a note that said:

Anything you want to say to me?

I looked at him, not knowing what to say.

He shakily set the pad aside and mumbled out loud, "Go ahead, Bob, tell me what you think."

I said, "Yeah, Pop, there is."

He took up the pad again and wrote:

Take your time but get it all out.

So I did. I unburdened myself of all of it, every bit I could think of. Every beating I took, all the anger I had, everything that had happened and everything I'd felt, crying as I talked. He sat and listened. He was quietly crying, too.

Then he took up the pad again and wrote for a minute, then handed it to me. It said:

> Bob I can't tell you how sorry I was for all of that. I've thought
> about it all my life. But I was a sick man.

Being an alcoholic myself, and just then in my first days of genuine recovery, I understood what he was saying. I'd love to say that it absolved everything, but that wouldn't be the truth. It didn't absolve it. It didn't make the pain go away. But it did feel like it completed something for me, a circle that had been broken up till then.

"To be honest, Pop, I don't think I can ever forgive all that," I said. "But I understand it a lot better. And I thank you for talking to me about it."

Then I hugged him, tight.

That was the last time I ever saw him.

I miss him still.

*   *   *

I tried to do the same thing with my mother—but she wouldn't go there. I wrote her a long letter about our painful childhood, her drinking, and all the rest of it, and gave it to her. She wouldn't read it, or if she did, she wouldn't talk about it. "Oh, poo," was her only comment when I tried to bring it up. It was heartbreaking and infuriating. But at least I closed the circle there, too.

The redemption that my old man found in his new life with Teenie—or if redemption is too grandiose a term, then at least sobriety and some level of happiness—did not come to my mother. And while I took care of her in her final years, and went to see her regularly at her little one-bedroom place in Lyme, not far from where we grew up, I never was able to get close with her, and she never did escape the tidal pull of addiction.

Some people make it out. Some don't. It's something I've wrestled with for years, and simply had to accept.

*   *   *

In 1993, not long after Alex was born, Leland and I took the baby and his nanny with us and went down to Charlottesville to see my father and Teenie. He was wonderful with Alex. While we were there we had a picture taken that is now one of my favorite photos: the three of us together. Three generations of Beckel boys.

Since my father's passing I've gone through all his letters, some writings he'd published, thoughts about the civil rights movement and other big issues. I never fully realized, when he was alive, just how far left his politics really were.

I've also had a growing admiration for his service in World War II. He was with General Mark W. Clark as an intelligence officer in Operation Torch, the North African campaign, and Operation Avalanche, the invasion of Italy. He was awarded the Italian Medal for Valor and the American Legion of Merit, the latter an award given "for exceptionally meritorious conduct in the performance of outstanding services and achievements."

I still have that medal.

CHAPTER TEN

Grace

After the hooker scandal I felt beaten into a corner. My career had been in a death spiral for nearly three years, ever since the 2000 election, and now I wasn't working at all. I was hundreds of thousands of dollars in debt. I had no idea what to do or what came next, like a pro football player who finally butts up against the hard reality that he just can't go out on that gridiron and play the game anymore. I wanted to get out of the public limelight, get away from death threats, get away from all of it. If this was what hitting bottom was all about, I'd had enough. I didn't see how much more bottom there could be to hit.

More than anything, I felt utterly alone.

Of course, I had nobody but myself to blame for that. I *could* pin it on my old man... but no. This was a choice that I had made. Survivors *want* to be alone in the world. We don't *want* anyone coming to help us, because we can't afford (or don't believe we can afford) to trust anyone but ourselves. This was the world I had created for myself. I'd always seen self-sufficiency as a great strength. It was how I made it through my childhood. Like that day in 1972 when Duffy drove away and I was finally on my own in D.C., everything always felt safer when I was solely in control of my own fate.

Of course, that was an illusion. I was *never* in control of my own fate. But I still wasn't ready to admit that. In AA they say, "Let go, let God." I had let go of booze, but I was not about to let go of anything else.

As 2002 wound to a close I retreated to my little rented farmhouse in Maryland, lonely, afraid, and by myself.

I could hardly have found a more isolated place. The people I rented it from said it was built in 1678, the oldest stone house in Maryland, sitting on some sixteen hundred acres. This wasn't just one of those places that claimed, "George Washington slept here." George Washington had *owned* part of this property. But it was out in the middle of nowhere, so despite its historic value I was able to rent it for a ridiculously low sum. Which was a good thing, because at that point that's all I had.

I spent long weeks out there, sometimes not talking to another soul for days at a time.

My favorite pastime during those solitary weeks was to climb up on a small tractor and ride around the property, cutting the lawns. Most of that sixteen hundred acres was wooded, but there was still a lot of open space, and I spent long hours driving that tractor back and forth, back and forth, just cutting the grass. Sometimes thoughts would go bouncing around in my head, trying to sort out the events of my life. Most of the time I just cut, my brain too tired to think.

In the middle of one field there was a big old rock, sitting out there by itself. Once in a while I would park the tractor and get out, clamber up on top of that rock and just sit, unplugged from everything, and let the thoughts come. Sometimes I would reflect on my life in politics. I'd been out of the campaign business for a long time now (not counting Alan Blinken's Idaho bid). I'd also been sober for nearly two years. I wondered if the distance would help me see it all with fresh eyes.

One afternoon, sitting on that rock, I thought back on a conversation I'd had with Jerry Ford.

*   *   *

In October 2000, just weeks before the Bush-Gore election contest that would send me off the rails and into the nuthouse, I attended a reception for the President's Cup professional golf tournament, at the beautiful Robert Trent Jones golf course in Gainesville, Virginia. President Bill Clinton was presiding over the tournament. Also attending was former president Gerald Ford.

I'd always wanted the chance to talk to Ford about the infamous moment in his otherwise spotless career when he announced, just thirty days into his presidency, that he was granting Richard Nixon a full pardon. This unexpected and shocking move had huge and far-reaching consequences. It effectively gutted Ford's chances of winning reelection two years later. It dealt a major blow to the Republican Party and helped fuel a wave of Democratic victories, ushering in a whole new generation of liberal leaders in Congress. It also happened to cement the career prospects for an aspiring young political consultant from Lyme, Connecticut.

Ford's move effectively made my career, and destroyed his own.

For years afterward I viewed Ford's act as a political mistake of epic proportions. Now, more than a quarter of a century later, perhaps I would finally have the opportunity to ask him why he did it.

His presence at the reception was impossible to miss. Jerry Ford was a tall, athletic man with steel blue eyes who cut an imposing figure even at eighty-seven years of age. I went up to him and introduced myself. We talked for a few minutes about the old days, about mutual friends, the kinds of things you talk about at events like this. And then I asked him about the pardon. What had made him do it, despite the huge political consequences to himself and to his party?

He looked me in the eye and said, without a trace of regret or bitterness, "Bob, the country needed to heal after Watergate."

I knew instantly that he meant exactly what he said.

And it rocked my world.

It wasn't as if this was an especially radical or original thing to say. President Ford himself had spoken words to much the same effect while he was in office. So did Jimmy Carter, in the opening words of his inauguration address in January 1977, when he took the torch being passed to him by Ford: "For myself and our nation, I want to thank my predecessor for all he has done to heal our land."

But I'd always thought this was all just politics as usual—politicians doing their best to put a positive spin on a fatal miscalculation. I had never quite grasped that Ford simply meant what he said.

In that moment I realized just how cynical I'd been about what I viewed as Ford's massive blunder. Maybe it wasn't a blunder at all. Jerry Ford had always impressed me as a fair and upright man. Despite our political differences, I admired him. Maybe the man I was talking to was simply a truly decent American who loved his country so much he was willing to risk not only his own political career, but also the prospects for his political party at the polls, for what he believed was the right thing to do for his country.

In fact, no *maybe* about it. I knew that this was true. I knew it right then, in October 2000, when we had the conversation. Maybe that was part of what pushed me off the cliff when that ugly election-tampering business happened just a few weeks later in Florida.

For days after that conversation, Ford's words echoed. I tried to think back objectively on my years in politics. But objective self-reflection was still an impossibly tall order, for the me of 2000. For years I had been dealing with the world through a chemical haze, and that had affected my judgment in ways far more profound and damaging than I realized.

Longtime alcoholics who are successful on the surface, but who just below that thin veneer of respectability are completely falling apart, easily fool most people. Having money and a successful career, wearing nice clothes and mingling with powerful people, makes it that much easier to "hide in public." Successful alcoholics and addicts are constantly amazed that they are able to travel through high-profile social events with an amount of booze and drugs in them that would kill an average person, and get away with it. The longer an addict uses, the more he learns to adjust his addicted persona to make it appear that the stoned, distorted mask people see is the sane, actual person underneath the mask, the person they *think* they're seeing.

In short, I learned how to appear normal.

There's a phrase for this state of being: *living in denial.*

The problem is that while you are busy becoming an expert at fooling everyone else, you are also learning to fool yourself. Over time you convince yourself that you *are* normal. You convince yourself that your thinking is normal and your view of history and the events around you is normal.

By the time President Ford and I were having this conversation, I had convinced myself that my political career was a righteous one and that what I had accomplished was, for the most part, for the good of the country and the democratic process. Ford's reply, and the simple sincerity with which he gave it, didn't break open that shell of denial—but it made a hairline crack in it, and that crack kept spiderwebbing out over the next two years as I pinballed from disaster to disaster.

*   *   *

Now, sitting on my rock in my field in the middle of nowhere, that shell started cracking wide open.

Alcoholics and addicts rarely attempt to think honestly about their past. Honest self-reflection could shatter the illusion. And we cannot let the mask we wear become threatened by anyone, not even by ourselves—*especially* not by ourselves.

I had always held politics as a noble calling. I had grown up in a family that, as dysfunctional as it was in itself, had always been dedicated to working on behalf of civil rights. Ever since volunteering for Bobby Kennedy in 1968, I'd worked as hard as I could to help accomplish political victories that I was convinced were good for the nation. I'd seen myself as a dedicated champion of democracy. Over time we can convince ourselves of damn near anything, especially what good and successful people we are.

Now I was forced to admit that the truth wasn't that simple.

In the pursuit of that "noble" career I'd lied, cheated, stolen, broken the law, hurt people, and done all manner of things that were wrong and that I was now deeply ashamed of. Everything I'd done, every dirty trick, every manipulation, every clever maneuver, I had justified as being in service of my noble calling. But it was really in service of my own survival. I could tell myself that political life was all about public service, about statesmanship, about civic calling, about social conscience—but for me, first and foremost, it had always been a survivor's game. *Everything in my life* had been first and foremost a survivor's game.

For a while I sat there, looking at my past with a sober eye and feeling aghast at everything I'd done.

And then that crack in my shell of denial opened yet a little further, and something else hit me.

I'd never really let myself see the harm that I'd done—but I'd also never really let myself see the good that I'd done, either. It would be easy to say that my whole life had been a waste of oxygen. But the truth wasn't *that* simple, either.

This is one of the most self-destructive things about being a survivor: Even when you do good things, you think it's bullshit. You think it's *all* just a game that you manufactured. That was why I could never accept a compliment or positive feedback. Every day I worked at the White House I expected Secret Service agents to come busting through my door with guns drawn shouting, "You fraudulent sonofabitch, get out of here!" Which was probably why it was not such a big surprise when that angry guy in that crappy bar on the eve of George Bush's inaugural stuck his .45 in my face.

I'd been expecting that gun for years.

It's the other side of an alcoholic's denial. When you wall yourself off from the terrible things you've done, you also wall yourself off from the good things, and even the noble things, that you've done.

It wasn't just my candidates who showed up as the good, the bad, and the ugly. My candidates were just reflections of me. *I* was the good, the bad, the ugly. And if I was going to cop to being the bad and the ugly, well, I was going to have to cop to the good, too, wasn't I.

The truth was, a lot of good people got elected, a lot of good people got helped, and a lot of good things got done, that might not have happened if I hadn't been there.

I wasn't better than everybody. But I also wasn't worse than everybody. I was just a human being, like everyone else.

It was time to get clean.

Yes, I had cleaned myself out of alcohol and drugs. But I hadn't yet cleaned out my mind. I had gotten the poison out of my system. Now I needed to get the poison out of my thinking.

*　　　*　　　*

One day, while I was out on the farm in my self-imposed rural exile, I got a call from the Fox News Channel. They wanted to invite me to come on one of their shows and debate Cal Thomas, the conservative columnist. I knew Cal slightly from having been on a few television panels with him. And I certainly knew about Fox News.

Fox News Channel, in case you are one of the two or three people on the planet not already aware of this, is widely viewed (at least by liberals) as the media arm of the political right wing. FNC's slogan, "Fair and Balanced," is something they passionately believe in. It also touches off howls of disbelief among those on the left whenever they hear it. Pairing me up with Fox News Channel, in other words, would be something like an elephant and a donkey going out on a date.

Besides, I wasn't doing any television. I was a pariah in the TV business. I missed it terribly, but I was far too embarrassed by the whole hooker scandal, following on the heels of the electoral scandal, to show my face. I would periodically get calls like this, inviting me to come and do a CBS News spot as a guest or be interviewed on some other network about some political issue. And I kept saying, "No, no, no, no, no." So when they called about doing an interview with Cal, there was no way I was going to say yes.

I said yes.

To this day I don't know why. I must have gone three or four times to pick up that phone, call Fox back, and say no, I was sorry, but I couldn't do the interview. But for some reason, I just couldn't seem to pick up the phone and make that call. Instead, I got in my car, drove into Washington and parked by the Fox News bureau, walked in, and there was Cal.

"Hi, Bob," he said. "How are you doing?"

What I was supposed to say was, "Fine, Cal." In Washington everybody always says, "Fine, fine, fine." You never tell the truth. Everyone says, "How are you doing?" and everyone always answers, "Fine." But I wasn't fine. I wasn't fine at all. I was broke, I was ruined, I badly wanted a drink and knew that if I took one it would absolutely, positively kill me. I didn't think I'd ever been less fine.

For possibly the first time in my life, I answered honestly.

"Not too good, Cal," I said.

He looked at me and said, "You want to talk after the show?"

I said, "Yeah, sure."

I don't remember much about the show, at least not in any detail, but it felt good to be back on television. I really had missed it.

After the show Cal got up out of his chair and said, "Bob, let's go somewhere we can talk." As I followed him out of the studio and into the hall, I felt two emotions fighting with each other. On the one hand I thought, "What a decent thing to do." I didn't know this guy very well, but he could obviously see that I was suffering. I was touched that he would go out of his way to offer a hand of friendship.

At the same time, I felt pissed off. Not at Cal, exactly, but at everything he represented. I knew where this "Let's talk" was leading. This guy was going to try to tell me all about something that I was already thoroughly aware of. As a recovering drunk, I'd been involved in AA for years. When you join AA, the first thing you get is a copy of *The Big Book*—and a Bible. I knew all about the Bible. I knew all about people who said they were "born again" and that kind of thing. And it all just seemed so hypocritical to me.

I followed Cal through the hallways in the Fox suite until we came to an empty office. It was an interior office, no windows, just some bare bookshelves along the wall, a few chairs, and a table. We sat, and started talking.

I told him about the experiences that had brought me to the low place I was in. He listened. And then he asked me if I believed in God.

"You know, Cal," I said, "if I can't see it or touch it, it doesn't exist for me."

He started to talk about faith.

Almost immediately, I started firing questions at him, challenging him. The conversation was not one I'm proud of. I was defiant as hell.

"Cal," I said, "I've got to tell you, I've always thought of people like you as Bible thumpers—people who go around door to door, trying to convince people to believe in something they don't believe in. That you've somehow found something the rest of us idiots haven't found."

He didn't get defensive at all, just nodded and kept talking. There was something about him that kept me from getting up out of my seat, something that made me want to listen despite myself. He struck me as a very honest guy, and I lived in a world of dishonest people. There was something about him that was sincere, even noble. He made it quite clear that he attributed every success in his life to his faith. Yet somehow he didn't come off as preachy.

I kept challenging him, and every time I did, he responded thoughtfully. He never got reactive or angry. There were moments when he had to know I was upset, because I was getting pretty emotional about it all. Yet he stayed calm throughout.

"Cal," I said at one point, "do you really think some guy could take a few loaves of bread and a couple of fish and feed five thousand people? How does *that* work?"

I don't recall exactly what Cal said in answer to that, but I got pretty strident. I slammed my fist down on the table and shouted, "You're telling me you believe that some sonofabitch walked on water? C'mon, Cal, that's not *possible!*"

"Well," he said, completely unruffled, "I believe it is, but I can understand how you don't believe it is. Because it does require faith. I don't have all the answers. But God does, and ultimately that's all I need to know."

We must have gone back and forth like this for a good four hours.

Finally, as we both got up to leave, he said, "Bob, would you be willing to read a few things? I'm not going to push this on you, but if I sent you something, would you read it?"

"Sure, Cal," I replied. "Send me whatever you want."

A few days later I received a book in the mail, an eight-hundred-plus-page monster of a thing entitled *Evidence That Demands a Verdict*, by a man named Josh McDowell whose personal history was almost as interesting as his book.

McDowell had started out as an agnostic law student. While in college he decided to write a research paper examining the Christian faith, his purpose being to apply the cold eye of science to the historical record and prove that the tenets of Christianity were, basically, bunk. Much to his surprise, the more research he did, the more the evidence confirmed the faith instead of refuting it. He ended up giving up his pursuit of law and instead becoming a writer, minister, and Christian apologist.

One more thing about McDowell: He was brought up in a violent, abusive, alcoholic family. Well, what do you know.

As I started reading, I kept thinking how much this guy reminded me of me. As the words came pouring off those pages, talking about all the things he didn't believe in, I sat there nodding and saying, "Exactly! I'm with you, brother. So what happened to you, man—did they drug you?"

I read the whole damn book.

Cal was smart. That was the perfect thing to send me, because this wasn't some starry-eyed armchair philosopher, some pastor who'd never experienced the realities of life outside his church walls, spouting bromides and smarmy platitudes. It was a book by a hard-nosed survivor, just like me, who walked through hard evidence with all his logic and intellect intact and in play.

When I finished the last page and set that book back down on my coffee table, I took a big breath and sat back in my chair. McDowell's arguments hadn't exactly given me a burning bush experience, but they sure as hell were making me think.

It wasn't the first time I'd taken on the question of faith. When I was at Hazelden, the counselor on my ward was a guy who was very strongly into faith and God. He didn't push it, he just encouraged me to think about it. Which, to my surprise, I did. I didn't come to any conclusions about it all, not back then, but I'd surprised myself by at least being open to thinking about it.

They had a little place at Hazelden called a reflection cottage, where you could sit by yourself, looking out over the lake, and be alone with your thoughts and the calm beauty of nature. Sitting by myself at the reflection cottage, I began thinking back on my conversations with Ron Ziegler about the whole "higher power" business. Evoking a "higher power" was just vague and abstract enough to be palatable.

Hazelden also had a set of beautiful walking trails, with a series of stations along the way where you would stop to do specific exercises. During my time there I would walk these trails with one of the other guys. One day as we walked I told him about how lucky I'd been to make it to that point—about the car wrecks where I should have been dead, the guy who pulled the .45 on me, the machete guy and his buddy in Mexico, all the barroom brawls, all the close calls. I said to him, "Can you imagine being that lucky?"

He said, "Bob, you better ask yourself whether that was luck or grace."

Hadn't someone else said something just like that to me before?

*   *   *

Cal and I kept talking. He sent me more books, and I started calling him on the phone, peppering him with questions about what I was reading. Before long I was visiting him at his home, and he was coming out occasionally to see me at the farm.

As the conversations continued and our friendship grew, Cal kept urging me to come to his church and hear his minister speak. "His name's Rob Norris," he said. "You're going to love him." I tried to tell Cal I wasn't so sure church and I were a good fit. Cal's place of worship, the Fourth Presbyterian in Bethesda, is a huge church that generates a lot of money, and the congregation is made up basically of Republicans. Oh, boy: the perfect church for me. But he kept urging.

I'll let you in on a secret about Cal. In addition to being one of the finest men on the earth and one of the best friends I've ever had, he can also be one persistent pain in the ass when he wants to be. And in my case, he wanted to be.

Finally I agreed to go.

Cal always sits in the third row, and he'd told me he'd save me a seat. When I got there, I walked in at the back and took a look around. The place was packed, a quiet buzz of conversation happening everywhere. I proceeded up the aisle toward the front, and as I got partway up the aisle a sudden hush fell over the place. All the conversation in the entire church stopped, like a sound system with its plug suddenly yanked out of the wall. It felt like a scene in an old western when the bad guy walks into the saloon and all the poker games stop in their tracks, the piano cuts out, and the bar chatter grinds to an immediate halt.

I slipped into the empty seat next to Cal as unobtrusively as I could, which was about as unobtrusive as a pit bull crashing a poodle party.

"Cal," I whispered, "is it me, or is there something going on here?"

"Bob," he said, "I don't think they've ever seen anyone quite like you here."

Then we sang a hymn or two, and Norris started talking. Cal was right. I loved him.

I'd been to church before, but I'd never listened. In fact, I typically didn't listen well, period. Survivors are not very good listeners, except when they want compassion out of you—then they'll drill their eyes on you and pay an enormous amount of attention to you, Bill Clinton style. But even then, we're probably not really listening, because we're working out our next move or the next thing we're going to say. Or more likely, the thing we're going to do or say seven steps later. It takes a lot of constant calculation to be a survivor.

When this big Welshman started talking, though, I started listening. Rob Norris is a magnificent speaker. With that lyrical Welshman's baritone, it's like listening to Dylan Thomas. Only without the booze and self-destructiveness.

The following week, I went back again. I started going every week. And then I did something that the Bob Beckel of the eighties and nineties would not have been caught dead doing: I started going to Bible study.

When I first started going to Bible study class, my view was that I'd joined a book club discussing a piece of science fiction. But the group I landed in happened to be composed entirely of men who were very smart, very accomplished, and very successful. These were not a bunch of uneducated guys crowding into a tent and falling under the spell of some charismatic joker's bullshit. These were serious, solid people. It was impossible *not* to respect these men.

I had always thought that people of faith were people who were weak. These men in my Bible group were anything but. As I began to get to know them, I started asking them some of the same tough questions I'd asked Cal. They were quick to say "I don't know," which at first baffled me. I would *never* say that! I didn't care what the subject was. Brain surgery? Fine. Rocket science? No problem. I could go on and on about anything, and even if most of it was bullshit, it usually sounded good. But these guys didn't bullshit me. Sometimes they had answers, albeit ones that were hard for me to accept, and sometimes they didn't.

After a while I started asking myself, "If these guys believe this stuff, if these guys really have faith, what am I missing here? What do they know that I don't know?"

Being with these men also made me think about Jimmy Carter.

President Carter was a man of supreme faith, though I never once heard him get preachy or weird about it. Here was a guy who was president of the United States, a strong, principled leader (one of our most underrated presidents, in my opinion) who did the best he possibly could under very difficult circumstances, and had an unbelievable record of achievements since leaving the White House. You couldn't ask for a smarter or more accomplished individual. And Jimmy Carter didn't just believe this stuff, he *taught* Bible study.

Something else I noticed.

As part of the AA program, one of the steps is that you put together this list of people you've harmed, and you get in touch with them to make amends. My list read like the New York City phone directory. Huge numbers of people. I couldn't possibly get to them all. But I got to as many as I could, and what I learned in that process was fascinating. Almost all of those who forgave me, who responded with kindness and understanding, were people of faith. Those who yelled at me or simply hung up on me when they realized who was calling were, by and large, people who did not have faith.

After a while, I couldn't deny the pattern. Was there a lesson in it?

I fought it all the way. I fought it and fought it and fought it, challenging God, and even the idea of God, every day. But I couldn't get it out of my head. And I started praying. As silly as it seemed to me—and it did—I kept doing it. Prayed morning and night. There was just no place else to go.

God knows there were an awful lot of things I did wrong, but if there was one thing I did right, it was this: I stuck with this idea, this wrestling match with the question of God and faith. I kept talking with Cal; I kept reading all the books he sent me, even though I questioned everything in them; and I kept praying.

*   *   *

One weekend Leland brought the kids out to visit at the farm. We had a great time together, and I started thinking that maybe, just maybe, Leland and I might get back together again.

Then, after they'd been there for about two hours, she said, "Okay, we've got to go now."

"What do you mean, you have to go now?" I said. "You just got here!"

Within minutes we were having a screaming argument right there in the farmhouse, while the kids waited outside in the car. I was eaten up by anger, jealousy over her leaving me for this other guy, remorse about our kids having to go through our breakup, and a lot more besides. My carefully controlled life had fallen to pieces, and I was furious at the world. As I watched Leland's car disappear down the mile-long driveway, taking my kids with it, there was just one thing I wanted to do, and I wanted to do that one thing as soon as humanly possible.

I needed a drink.

"Screw this," I said out loud. "I can't feel like this. I just can't take this anymore." I didn't *want* to go get a drink. I *had* to go get a drink. The urge was impossible to resist.

I climbed into the pickup truck I was using out there and started it up. There was a specific bar I knew, a blue-collar dive about five miles from the farm. That would be perfect. I could get there in no time at all. I nosed the truck out onto the driveway and began the trek out to the main road.

As the pickup ate up the distance from the house to the country road, I looked out at my surroundings. It was a beautiful spring day. A panoramic western Maryland valley, fields full of nothing but grass and cows. That was one of the reasons I liked it out there: It wasn't a city full of complicated people. I could see the Blue Ridge Mountains in the distance. And I found myself asking a question I'd asked before: "How the hell did this get here, this beautiful world we keep screwing up? Was this all really created by God?"

While I was gazing out at the pastoral scenery, the pickup did its job. Within minutes we'd reached the main road.

I stopped, put the truck in PARK.

As a recovering drunk in AA, when you're on the verge of having a drink, you're supposed to call someone—your sponsor, another AA buddy, a friend, *someone*. I was out in the middle of nowhere. No cell phone signal, even if I had my phone on me, which I didn't. I was all alone.

I couldn't call a soul.

I remembered something I'd heard people say in meetings, over and over again: "There'll come a point when the only thing standing between you and a drink is God." I wondered if this was that point.

"God," I said, "if you're there, and you really are the only thing between me and a drink, then you better get busy here. 'Cause I'm on my way out there right now."

I sat and waited, for what I didn't know. No sounds but the *tick tick tick* of the pickup's engine cooling. I felt foolish and embarrassed. Here I was, once again, about to screw everything up even worse. I could almost see it happening.

I remembered something else I'd heard people say in AA: "If you feel yourself about to go get a drink, stop and think it through. Think through the sequence of what will happen if you go get this drink."

I'd never really done that before.

I started to think it through.

And then I saw it all unfold, as clearly as if it were happening right there in front of my windshield. I could see the number of drinks it would take before I started to get a real buzz on. I saw how I would start shooting my mouth off and getting loud. I saw that over the first hour or so, the booze would start taking the sting out of everything I was feeling, making me feel better. I saw how things would then start going south, and fast.

And the cost of that brief shot of feeling better? In the hours and days afterward, if I lived that long? I started seeing that, too—and it was too much to bear.

I put the truck in gear, spun it around, and drove back up the driveway.

When I reached the farmhouse I parked and shut off the truck, got out, walked out into the field, climbed up onto that big rock, and sat there. I felt really good about what had just happened. "You did it," I said out loud to myself. "You actually did it!" And the moment I said the words, I knew they weren't true.

Did I really think I had survived all those years because of my own quick wits and hardy constitution? Staring at an undetonated hand grenade at my feet in the Philippines; slumped asleep in my car, stalled out dead center on the Jersey Turnpike without a scratch; sitting blind drunk on a bar stool staring at a .45 being fired point-blank in my face?

Did I really think it was *me* that had stopped me back there at the end of my driveway from heading out to that bar and ending my life?

No.

That wasn't me.

That was grace.

As I sat there on that rock, the tears began to flow. In that moment I knew, without a shred of doubt, that if I had gone out to that bar, that day would have been the last time my children would have seen my face, because that next drink—the one I'd so clearly visualized while sitting in my pickup truck—would have been the signature on my death warrant. And I knew there was a force that had wanted me not to do that, a force that loved me enough to stop me in my tracks and redirect my steps.

That loved me? *Me?*

If there is one moment I can point to, a moment when the idea of God's grace shifted from being some kind of abstract concept to being something flesh and blood, something meaty and rich, something *real*, that was it. I had a tangible experience of the words to what has since become my favorite hymn:

> *Amazing grace! How sweet the sound*
> *That saved a wretch like me!*
> *I once was lost, but now am found;*
> *Was blind, but now I see.*
>
> *'Twas grace that taught my heart to fear,*
> *And grace my fears relieved;*
> *How precious did that grace appear*
> *The hour I first believed.*

*   *   *

And God's grace, once I accepted the truth that this was what it was, felt so powerful and loving that embracing faith and turning my will and my life over to Him was the greatest relief of my life.

God saved my life, saved my soul, even saved a lot of my friendships. And this, above all, became as clear as crystal: He gave me a second chance to live.

*   *   *

Of course, I was still broke.

One day soon after that experience in my pickup truck I realized I had no cash on me. I called the bank to see what my balance was. They told me it was $9.95. I had less than ten bucks to my name.

"Lord," I heard myself say out loud, "if you really do exist, I hate to ask you this, but if you could help me out, I really need some money."

Great. My first conversation with God in my fragile new state of faith, and I was asking for a loan. I knew I should probably be praying for kids who were dying from war or disease someplace. But the truth was, I couldn't find any work. Nobody would hire me. I was barely making grocery money at the temp agency.

The next morning I walked out to the mailbox, out of boredom more than anything else, to go fish out the junk mail. The mailbox didn't have my name on it, just the farm's rural delivery number. I never got anything addressed to anyone other than Occupant.

Except today.

On this day, there was an envelope sitting in there, addressed to "Bob Beckel." Bob Beckel—I knew that guy. That was me. I pulled out the envelope, opened it, and inside there was a check, made out to me, for twenty thousand dollars.

I said aloud: "You have *got* to be shitting me."

I looked again, just in case I was having residual hallucinations. I wasn't. There it was. Twenty grand. Made out to Bob Beckel. That was me.

Now I looked at the envelope. No return address, just a name. I knew that name, too: It was a guy I'd loaned money to maybe fifteen years earlier, to help him start a business. I had asked him to pay me back a few times, but to no avail, and eventually I quit asking. He later got into AA himself, though I didn't know this at the time. Evidently, he'd decided he needed to make restitution. And evidently now was the time he'd picked to do it.

Evidently.

For a minute or so I just stood there, stunned. Then I trudged back up to the farmhouse and called Cal Thomas.

"Cal," I said, "you're not going to believe this." And I explained what had happened.

"Oh, I believe it," he said. "That's the way the Lord works."

"Yeah?" I said. "Well it's freaking me out."

I drove down to the bank, which was about thirty minutes away, and showed them the check. "Is this thing any good?" I asked. "Is there money behind this check?"

They said, "Yeah, it's fine. Put it in the account; we'll clear it today."

So I did. And they did.

I still haven't seen anyone walk on water, or raise the dead, or turn water into wine. But I'll tell you what: As miracles go, that twenty grand showing up in my rural Maryland mailbox was pretty damn good.

*   *   *

I would love to say that everything went smoothly uphill from there. But that isn't quite what happened. I thought I'd hit bottom, that all that self-important ego and illusion of total control had been pretty much wrung out of me, that I'd been brought as low as I could be brought. Evidently, though, the bottoming out process was *still* not quite finished with me yet.

In the spring of 2003 I woke up in a hospital once again, only this time not in the psychiatric ward. This time I was in the Intensive Care Unit, and I had never been in so much pain in my life.

It started the fall before, as the hooker scandal was coming into full bloom. I was out on the farm cutting down some trees and clearing brush, when I noticed a terrible ache in my right shoulder. Just what I needed: an old football injury acting up. I played a lot of ball during school and my shoulder had taken a beating. All the bar fights hadn't helped it any. Now my decades of abusing my own body were coming back to haunt me.

Which was a particular nuisance, because I'd come to love being out on the land, chopping down trees, sawing them into manageable pieces, and being out in the silence of nature. No bad press out here, no waves of vandalism, nobody trying to kill me. Just me and my thoughts.

A few doctors took a look at it and did an MRI, but nothing showed up. I figured I was just going to have to live with it. I kept chopping trees and clearing brush.

The ache didn't go away.

Finally I went to see my old doctor, Frank Chucker, whom I hadn't been to see in some time. Frank had known me for years and was a guy I trusted a lot. He was on the verge of retiring, and at that point he was taking patients only one day a week.

Frank poked around my shoulder for a minute, then said, "Bob, do me a favor, get on our treadmill here." They had a treadmill right there in the office. I got on it and started walking, and after about thirty seconds the pain came back.

Frank nodded and said, "I think it's angina."

Angina? I thought angina was something that showed up in your chest, and I hadn't been having any chest pain.

"No," he said, "it can be in your jaw, in your shoulder, lots of places. I want you to go to Georgetown Hospital for an angiogram. They'll inject a radioactive dye in your system that will let them take pictures of your heart and its associated major vessels."

"Frank," I said, "there's no way I can afford that." I was already on financial rock bottom, and I no longer had any health insurance. I could see Frank wasn't very happy with that answer, but what was he going to do?

Over the next few weeks Frank kept after me, urging me to do the test. (This was one reason I loved having Frank as a doctor. How many doctors would do that?) He kept calling and saying, "You've got to go, Bob. You've just got to do it." I kept giving him the same answer: I really couldn't. Finally he said, "Listen, if it turns out it's nothing, *I'll* pay for it." (How many doctors would do *that*?)

Finally I relented and agreed to do the angiogram. I checked into Georgetown University Hospital, where they prepped me for the test. I was still laughing and making jokes as they put me out.

When I woke up Frank was there by my bed. "Here's the good news," he said. "Your heart is in remarkably good shape for a guy your age, who's been through what you've been through. The bad news is that all four major arteries that supply it with blood are blocked up to 90 percent, and your heart *won't* be in good shape if you don't deal with it right away. We need to do quadruple bypass surgery on you tomorrow."

"*Tomorrow*? Frank, I can't possibly do that. I've got stuff to take care of, things I've got to resolve here."

"We'll give you three or four days," Frank said firmly. "But that's it. Then we've got to get you in here and open you up."

None of this seemed real. It had to be happening to somebody else. But it wasn't. It was happening to me. If it wasn't clear before that I was not in control, it sure was clear now.

The day of the surgery, three people from my prayer group at church picked me up at five in the morning and brought me in to the hospital. On the way to Pre-Op we stopped in at the hospital chapel, where we recited the Serenity Prayer together:

God grant us the serenity to accept the things we cannot change, the courage to change the things we can, and the wisdom to know the difference.

Then one of my friends led the rest of us in a prayer for my recovery. It was brief, but very moving.

The surgery lasted six hours. Quadruple bypass surgery is one of the most radical operations you can undergo. They put you on a lung machine, saw open your chest and vise it open, then stop your heart and take it out, sew in the vessel grafts, and put you all back together.

When I woke up I was in intensive care and, as I said, had never felt such pain in my life.

The ICU at Georgetown consisted not of individual rooms but of one big room with ten of us, our beds in a circle, each with his own doctor and staff. We weren't allowed to drink anything at first, not even water, because they'd packed our open chests with ice while each of us was on the heart/ lung machine, and it takes a while for the body to thaw and be ready to accept fluids again. I was thirsty as hell. They swabbed my lips with these tiny swabs, which was just not cutting it. This big drill sergeant of a nurse in charge of the unit was on the floor, and I told her, "I need water."

She said, "You can't have water."

I said, "I'm twenty-one years old, I'm white, I'm free. I want a cup of water."

She said, "No!"

I may have accepted Jesus into my life, embraced my faith in God, and turned my life over to Him. But I was still me. Having faith doesn't mean your personality goes away. I was still Bob Beckel.

I organized a protest.

Within a minute or two we had a chant going around the room, all ten of us in unison, "We want water! We want water!" This poor bastard next to me had come up to D.C. from North Carolina just to play some golf and had dropped like a sack of potatoes on the golf course. There was an old lady across from me who was obviously on her last legs. Everyone had a different story and was in a different condition—but all of us, even the old lady, were going, "We want water! We want water! *We want water!*"

About that time the heart surgeon, Garcia, walked into the ICU to see how his patients were doing. The nurse said, "Doctor, one of your patients is giving me a lot of trouble about water."

Without even looking around the room he said, "Huh. I bet it was Beckel, right?"

She told him it was Beckel, all right.

He looked over at me and said, "No surprise there. Okay, give him water." The nurse threw him a look that said *Are you kidding?* and he said, "Look, just give him water. You'll have a terrible time here if you don't."

She was not happy about that, but she gave me a cup. "I can go to the bathroom," I said. I had all these things hooked up to me, IV drips and all the rest of it, but I got them to unhook it all so I could be mobile for a minute. Once I was free and clear I headed toward the bathroom. The nurse started to follow me in, and I said, "No, no, no. Nobody comes in the bathroom with me."

I got in there, closed the door behind me, and started slurping down cups of water, one after another after another. When I was finished I slipped the cup into the trash can, where it would be easy to retrieve. I had told the guy next to me that I would leave the cup there so he could get at it, if he could work his way into the bathroom.

Once I was out and on my way back to bed to get hooked up to all my gizmos again, my neighbor got up to head into the bathroom after me. Two nurses started in after him, and he said, "Excuse me, ladies. I'm a gentleman from North Carolina. We do not allow ladies in our boudoir." He went in, locked the door, and after a minute we could all hear him going *slurp, slurp, slurp, slurp*.

I've been beaten by ax handles and tire irons, kicked and punched. I've been in a lot of bar fights, some of them so vicious and violent I haven't dared to describe them in these pages. But that surgery was the toughest physical thing I'd ever been through. Recovering from it took months, and it was horrible.

When I first came out from under, my right hand, which is my writing hand, was crabbed up and wouldn't open. Nobody could figure out why. Finally someone realized what had happened: I'm a fairly big guy, and the operating table they'd used was a little too small for me. As a result my hand had gotten badly jammed during the surgery. So for the moment I couldn't write; I couldn't cook for myself or take care of myself; I couldn't do anything. I was at the mercy of people bringing me food. This is something a survivor is not used to doing and doesn't do well: being taken care of.

By this time I'd left the farm and rented a house in Bethesda overlooking the river, where I still live today. I didn't know anyone in the neighborhood and had nobody to take care of me, except one neighbor who was a nurse and came over once a day to look at my stitches, and the people who brought me food, plus periodic visits from Cal and my friends from church. Most of the time I was alone and more or less immobile.

If I thought I'd hit bottom, I now discovered that there was still more bottom to go, a sub-basement down there underneath the basement, and the elevator was still going down, down, down. The doctors had told me that after going through a heart bypass operation there's a heightened chance of feeling depressed for a while. Apparently there's a good deal of research on this. It's a common side effect. But in no way was I prepared for what hit me after that surgery.

For the first time in my life, I became deeply depressed. Not doleful, not melancholy, not a little blue. I mean, full-blown *depressed*. I'd never experienced such a thing before. It was like trying to walk through Jell-O. You don't want to get up. You don't want to eat. You don't want to do anything. It was like being on another planet—a really horrifying, nightmarish planet.

My brother used to be depressed, and I confess that I was never very sympathetic about it. I suppose it's similar to the way people can't understand why an alcoholic keeps drinking. "I don't get it," they'll say. "If you know you're killing yourself, why don't you just stop?" I'd never said the words, but I'd probably thought something much like that: *Just cheer up! If you're depressed, why don't you just do something to take your mind off it?* I'd never really understood it before, but it doesn't work that way. You *can't* cheer up.

My depression did not last long, two weeks at most. But for people who go through that every day? "Dear God!" I remember saying. "No wonder people blow their brains out." Which was another thing I could never understand: how anybody could kill themselves, or even think about doing so. Now that I was deep in my very own depression I thought, "You know, if I had to live like this all the time, the top of the George Washington Bridge would not look so bad."

My doctors' warnings notwithstanding, I knew it wasn't just the heart operation. It was also the fact that I was still coming to grips with what a mess I'd made of my life. I prayed almost continuously, and kept telling myself that this, too, would pass. The Twenty-Third Psalm came to have new meaning to me during these weeks: If I'd ever felt like I was walking through the valley of the shadow of death, this was it. I especially focused on the last part of that psalm: *Surely goodness and mercy will follow me all the days of my life, and I will dwell in the house of the Lord for ever.*

Man, I sure hoped so.

And here, strangely enough, was something I had to credit to my own earthly father.

Despite all the shit he put us through, and all the shit he put himself through, the old man always was an optimist, and it seemed that, beyond the predilection for booze, optimism was something I had inherited from him. Somehow even in the midst of that terrible black depression, I retained an optimist's view that this was going to be okay.

And bit by bit, it was.

*   *   *

But I was *still* broke. At this point I still had no television work. Yet that changed, too, in 2004, when I got a call from just about the last person on the planet that I expected to hear from.

Back in the fall of 1984, in the days before the election that turned my first and only presidential campaign into a crushing forty-nine-state defeat, I had done my best to coach my candidate, Mondale, before that critical last debate. There was an even more experienced pol coaching Reagan on *his* side of the debate—the one where he ended up delivering that classic line about not using Fritz's youth and inexperience against him. The one that won him the debate and the presidency.

The guy who had coached Reagan was the guy on the phone. His name was Roger Ailes, and he was now CEO of Fox News, the bastion of conservative media pundits—and he was calling to offer me a job.

"Bob, Roger Ailes," he said. "How would you like to come up here to New York and come into the belly of the beast?"

"I don't know, Roger," I said. "I'm not sure that's such a good idea, me being a liberal on your channel."

He said, "Why don't we just talk about it."

So I went up to New York and met with him.

At this point I was still under a gag order on the prostitution sting case and wasn't able to say a thing about what had really happened—but the judge wasn't, and he had told me that whenever I got a job offer, I should have my prospective employer call him directly and he'd explain what happened. I told Ailes about what the judge said. Ailes picked up the phone and called the judge, told him he was talking to me about working there and wanted to know what had happened.

The judge said, "He got screwed, simple as that. It was a bad deal, the cops messed it up for him, but there was nothing I could do about it, I had to keep everybody under a gag order. The guy's a good guy. None of it was his fault."

Ailes said, "That's all I need to hear." And he gave me a job on the spot.

In case you're wondering how Roger Ailes came to put a call in to me, the answer is simple: through the power of friendship. Cal Thomas, a longtime Fox contributor, made a pitch to Roger on my behalf. So did my old friend Fred Barnes, from the CBS days.

My guess is, there were two reasons Ailes decided to take me on. First, he thought that what happened to me was unfair and it shouldn't have happened, and he wanted to correct a wrong. Also, I think he saw in me a chance to have a liberal voice on his channel who was pretty well-known and tough enough to stand up to the conservatives he had there. Whatever the reasons,

Ailes gave me a shot when nobody else would, and I'll always be grateful to him for that.

Grace, I have learned, can take many forms. It can be a gun that jams; an old debt unexpectedly repaid; or a political opponent who suddenly shows up as an ally. You know the expression, the one about God and His mysterious ways. I didn't see how it could get much more mysterious than this: when I, Bob Beckel, lifelong liberal, started working for Fox News. God's ways may be mysterious, but I can tell you this for sure: He has a hell of a sense of humor.

I started out as what they call a contributor. (This is part of the genius of the network: They don't have as many full-time employees as other networks, but they have a lot of on-air people who have expertise in their particular areas, whom they retain as contributors.) I would go down to the Fox studio in Washington, where Cal and I had shot that show together, and they would pipe me into their New York studio by satellite to debate with one of Fox's conservatives, of whom there was no short supply.

They started out paying me five hundred bucks a spot, which at that point was the lifeline I needed to begin putting my life back on its feet.

Over the next several years I did a lot of political commentary with Fox, and they steadily upped my pay. One year I did over a thousand spots there. And once I was on Fox regularly, my speaking opportunities began to pick up again. As I began the painfully slow task of rebuilding my reputation, I also began to dig myself out of the financial hole.

*   *   *

If I had to list the things that matter most to me, there would be three: my faith, my family, and my friends. My advice to people who ask how I survived the darkest time in my life is this: Keep your friends as close as you possibly can, and hug them that much closer. They are the people who will be there when you need them.

Friendship, too, is a vehicle for the unfathomable working of God's grace.

You may have noticed at the front of this book that I've dedicated it to Cal. I did this for a number of reasons. For one thing, if it weren't for Cal this book would not exist. Cal was the one, week after week, year after year, who kept urging me to put my experiences down on paper and share my story. But beyond that, without Cal I'm not sure *I* would be here, either.

As I said, when it came time for my quadruple bypass, three friends from our church came with me. They stayed with me right up until I was wheeled into surgery.

When I woke up six hours later, there was Cal. And he's been there ever since.

During those early years, when I was picking myself up after hitting bottom and putting my new life back together, Cal was there every step of the way, always gracious, always helpful, never judging. During many long hours over those years we talked about everything. About our lives, about faith, about God—and also about politics.

The conversations about God were the most important for me personally. The ones about politics turned out to be the most important professionally.

Here we were, two strong-minded and highly opinionated people on opposite sides of the political fence—yet we kept finding ourselves bumping into points and perspectives and paths of possible solution that we actually agreed on. Not in every particular; far from it. But in important areas, and more of them than either of us expected.

The more we found these areas of common ground between the two of us, the more we talked about how it was too bad Washington didn't have the climate it used to have. These days, as Cal puts it, when you hear people being interviewed on a news show, one guy says, "You're a Bible-thumping bigot!" and the other guy says, "You're a pinko commie radical!" and then the host says, "We'll be right back, folks, for more civil discussion after a word from our sponsor."

We both remembered a time when you could have a sane conversation with someone of the other party. Tip O'Neill and Ronald Reagan would rail at each other during the day; then in the evening Tip would go over to the White House and the two would sit down for a glass of booze and work things out. We wished there was more of that kind of across-the-aisle colloquy (though not necessarily the booze part).

Over the next few years that conversation evolved into the idea of our writing a column together. In 2005, we decided to give it a shot. We thought we could call it Common Ground.

Cal is one of the most popular and widely read columnists in the country. The year 2014 marked the thirtieth anniversary of his syndicated column. *Thirty years.* Cal started writing that thing back when I was running Mondale's campaign! His column had been running in *USA Today* since 1999.

He said, "I think we should go to *USA Today*."

So we did. We met with Ken Paulson, *USA Today*'s editor, and Brian Gallagher, the director of the paper's editorial page, outlined our idea, and asked if they were interested in giving it a try.

"Are you kidding?" said Ken. "This is our DNA. This is perfect for *USA Today*."

It's been running ever since.

*   *   *

In 2011 there was one show on Fox News that drew especially large audiences and especially vocal controversy.

Glenn Beck had been in the radio business for several years and then at CNN before coming to Fox News, where he'd had his own show since the beginning of 2009, weekdays, 5:00 to 6:00 p.m. That the Beck show got such extremely large audiences was especially impressive given his time slot.

When I was in the campaign business, we considered five to six in the afternoon the Death Hour in television. The reasons were obvious. Many people were driving home from work or going to their kids' after-school events. Campaigns avoided advertising during the Death Hour. Before Beck, all the Fox shows in the 5:00 p.m. time slot had gotten dismal ratings. Beck broke that long streak, his audience increasing so much his ratings surpassed many of the Fox News prime-time programs.

The problem was that Beck was a controversial figure, to put it mildly. He drew an exceedingly conservative audience, many of whom were young and libertarian-minded. They did not like big government and hated liberals. I know this, because for several years before this I had polled Fox programs at Roger Ailes's request, so I had a pretty good fix on Beck's audience.

Privately, I called them the Visigoths.

Beck was given to elaborate conspiracy theories, which he often drew on blackboards. Most of these conspiracies focused on the federal government, international financiers, and liberals. On a few shows he labeled the targets of his critique with the Nazi symbol. This got to be too much for the companies that advertised on his show, and they quit their sponsorship in droves.

It soon became clear that Fox had to break its relationship with Beck, and they did so in June 2011. That left the five-to-six-o'clock hour, Monday through Friday, with no programming.

There were dozens of television personalities and show formats that begged for the hour. But Roger Ailes, one of the most brilliant television minds since the birth of the industry, had something else in mind

With only weeks to make a decision, Ailes wrote a show concept that would be a talk show format, but different from normal cable news talk shows, which generally featured one or two hosts and lots of guests. Ailes envisioned the show with five equal hosts who would cover not only the day's news but also various social and cultural topics, and would have guests only very rarely. He wasn't interested in using well-known established TV personalities, but instead wanted to cast the show with lower-profile people who had some background in television, but who also brought other credentials to the show. He wanted the cast to represent the kinds of archetypal characters you'd find in a medieval or Renaissance play: a king, a queen, a court jester, a femme fatale, and a Falstaff—that is, a swaggering, vain-but-vulnerable raconteur, a crazy-uncle sort of character.

Guess who he had in mind for his Falstaff?

He also decided, given the Fox News audience, that four of the hosts would be conservative, to varying degrees, with a single liberal.

The Falstaff character.

He decided to call his new show *The Five*.

CHAPTER ELEVEN

The Five

I almost didn't do *The Five*. When Fox News first asked me to be part of this new show, which they billed as a summer replacement for the freshly departed Glenn Beck show, the programming guy said I'd need to be up in New York Monday through Friday. I told him, "I can't do five days a week. I live in Maryland. I've got two kids." Alex was seventeen, MacKenzie about to turn fifteen. Leland and John Keyser, now married, lived not far from me, and the kids went back and forth on a very fluid schedule, spending a lot of time in both places.

John had turned out to be an excellent stepfather. I couldn't have asked for better. He was great with the kids, and they both seemed to like him a lot. He never tried to say he was their father, or usurp my place in their lives, or do anything that would have made them feel torn loyalties or unnecessary awkwardness. He and I also got along very well; in fact, we are good friends to this day.

The Fox guy said they had to have me five days a week. End of discussion. No five-day commitment, no me on the show.

"I'll do three days," I said. "But I've got to talk to my kids about it first."

He insisted it had to be five days. I told him I'd get back to him.

I went to talk with Alex and MacKenzie. "Look," I said, "Dad's been to all your games. I've never missed anything. You know you two come first. So I really need to know what you think here. I would really like to do this show. They say they want me five days a week, but I'd only agree to do it three days a week."

Kenzie gave me a look and said, "Why three? Why don't you do all five days?"

"Hey," I said, "where's the love? Where's the pushback here?"

She laughed, and said, "No, really, Dad. This could be a great thing for you. And it's obvious that you really want to do it. I think it would be awesome. And we'll be fine."

With my kids' blessing, I went back to the programming guy and said okay, I would be willing to do five days a week. Starting in early July 2011, I became a commuter, taking the train up to New York every Sunday night, shooting the show Monday through Friday, then taking the train back down to Maryland on Friday evening to be with my kids for the weekend.

I wasn't too worried about this arrangement. I didn't expect the show to last long, anyway.

Neither did anyone else.

While nobody at Fox came out and said this, everyone knew that *The Five* had no more than a slim chance of establishing an audience and was likely to pull in the same anemic numbers as all the other shows that had aired in that dismal 5:00 to 6:00 p.m. slot before Glenn Beck. Beck's success, in fact, only made the situation worse for us. Any show that replaced him was more than likely to suffer from unflattering audience-number comparisons by television critics and advertisers.

Several Fox executives saw *The Five* as nothing more than a quick fill-in replacement to buy them time to create another show, with a well-established TV personality as host, to launch when the new season began that September. In the meantime, no advertising was created to promote *The Five* and there was none of the usual fanfare typically accorded a new show. Producers were borrowed from existing Fox News shows and little funding was allocated to it. Privately, people gave it two months.

Ahh: low expectations. An underdog with no chance of surviving. My kind of story.

On July 11, 2011, *The Five* launched quietly, with the following cast: Eric Bolling, a successful commodities broker and business analyst formerly on CNBC; Dana Perino, George W. Bush's former press secretary; Greg Gutfeld, a former magazine editor, writer, and comic who had a late-night show on Fox called *Red Eye*; Andrea Tantaros, Fox contributor and Republican political operative, who would be alternating with Kimberly Guilfoyle, a former California prosecutor and Fox News contributor; and, in the show's sole liberal seat, me.

We took two practice runs before we went live, but still, it felt an awful lot like a blind date on a summer day. We were all just starting to get to know each other. The first show was passable: a few hits, not many errors, not many runs, and certainly no grand slam.

We went into the Green Room afterward and asked the producers what they thought. "Magnificent," they said. "A home run." "Couldn't be better." Yeah, sure. The bullshit was so deep in that room that Greg Gutfeld (who stands a little under five foot one) almost drowned. We knew these producers' jobs were riding on coming up with a good show, so we cut them some slack. But their feedback was worthless.

Next to weigh in were our families and friends. They sounded just like the producers. What did we expect? If your family and friends tell you that you really suck, then you *know* you're in trouble. But when they all said they loved it, what did that really tell us?

I knew a guy in Montana named Fitz who was probably the world's greatest cynic. Fitz watched Fox News all day long, so he'd have to have seen the show. I called him and said, "So, Fitz what do you think of the new show?"

He said, "It didn't completely suck, and the girls were beautiful, but you guys are all ugly. I might watch it on occasion, if I'm not fishing. Or if I'm in bed with the hemorrhoids."

Pretty high praise, coming from Fitz.

For the first two weeks, the audience numbers were mediocre at best. We couldn't help noticing that there was no advertising for *The Five*—not even on Fox News Channel itself, let alone on any other channels. But we were in no position to complain. *The Five* was, after all, seen inside Fox as a temporary show.

The TV critics were not as kind as Fitz. The *Huffington Post* panned us. TVNewser, which tracks the number of viewers, declared that we were doomed to trail behind Glenn Beck's audience. One TV critic singled me out as "an overweight bully who is hopelessly out of touch with the issues of the day and, despite a superficial attempt at humor, was about as funny as Lyme disease." That was my favorite. (I wonder if he knew I was actually *from* Lyme.) There's a common belief among television people that all publicity is good publicity, as long as they spell your name right. This guy called me "Bill Beckley." I wasn't sure if that counted as good publicity.

Every day, as my cohosts and I milled around in and out of the Green Room preparing for the show, some of us making calls, some looking over the lineup of topics, me having my ceremonial preshow cigar just outside the studio door, an interesting ritual developed. Starting about four-fifteen, everyone would start looking at their phones, checking them for new messages every thirty seconds or so. The reason? Every day at 4:18 p.m. the ratings come in from the day before.

For those first few weeks, we all had to tap into whatever inner optimism we had at four-eighteen every day—because the numbers on our phones were not very cheery.

The shows in those first few weeks were rough; topics were all over the place. We hadn't yet caught our stride. As we started getting to know one another better, though, the chemistry started to click. We found that we genuinely liked each other, both on and off the set.

Then, about the end of July, something strange started happening. The audience for *The Five* started growing.

By the end of August the numbers were increasing almost daily. With each increase in numbers came more and more confidence among the players. We began to see it was a challenge to the rest of the people at Fox News, several of whom wanted *The Five* to fail, either because they wanted the time slot themselves or because the idea of a nontraditional cable news show was somehow threatening to them.

This attitude surprised and amazed me. In the world of campaign politics, if another Democratic consultant won a race, I was happy for that person. A win for one of the team was a win for the whole team. In the world of TV, it seemed one person's success was viewed as a threat to everyone else's success. One day, as I walked past an office on the executive floor of Fox News, I heard a group of people trash-talking *The Five*. One of them referred to it as a comedy. The thing was a flash in the pan, they said, and there was no way it would last. And that would not necessarily be a bad thing.

Not being one to let shit like that go in one ear and out the other, I circled back around to that office and walked straight in—and was greeted with, "Hey, Bob, congratulations!" "Historic!" "A game-changer in cable news!"

Blah, blah, blah.

Despite the naysaying assholes there were several people, both on-air and in management, who rooted for *The Five*'s success. On-air talent like Sean Hannity, Greta Van Susteren, and Shep Smith were especially gracious. A few key executives, including Bill Shine and Suzanne Scott, gave *The Five* their enthusiastic support, for which we were all grateful.

But the only voice that mattered in all this noise was that of Roger Ailes.

What would the Boss do? Take down the temporary show to make way for a new program with more star power and better prospects? Or let the thing keep going and see where it went? We were given not a single clue.

As the summer's end approached, we tried everything we could to glean hints about which way the Boss was leaning. But Ailes was keeping his own counsel. We grilled his brother, Bob, and Bob's wife, two wonderful people and committed fans of the show. "He's thinking about it" was all I got from Bob. Andrea Tantaros, who is 100 percent Greek (Greeks are notorious for their ability to ferret out gossip), wielded all the feminine wiles at her disposal, which is saying a lot: Andrea is a stunning-looking woman. But she got bubkes. I believe bubkes is Greek for "nothing."

We knew there were a few factors in our favor. *The Five* was Ailes's own creation, and he liked all the talent on the show. And of course, there were those solid numbers. Still, those last few weeks of the summer were nerve-racking.

Decision time. Right after Labor Day, when *The Five* had been scheduled to be replaced by another show with a "big-name" host, Ailes announced that *The Five* had earned a permanent slot in the Fox News lineup.

We were in—not just as a temporary fill-in, but as a real, honest-to-God Fox News regular.

*   *   *

On Thursday, October 13, we all met with Roger for a celebratory lunch at Del Frisco's Steakhouse, next door to the Fox building—very expensive, very popular—where they had set aside a room for us. In addition to Ailes and six of the seven players on *The Five* (Juan Williams, the liberal columnist who subbed for me occasionally, joined us; Andrea couldn't make it), we were also joined by Bill Shine, the executive vice president of programming, and vice president of programming Suzanne Scott.

I was seated next to Ailes, wearing suspenders, as usual, and a big red tie. The mood was ebullient as we all talked about the show. We placed our orders and Ailes started going through his thinking about the show, why he thought it could be very successful, the things we needed to be careful about, and so forth. Our appetizers began to arrive. I had ordered a shrimp cocktail. At Del Frisco's the shrimp are about a foot and a half long.

As we talked, I took a shrimp, chewed, swallowed—and it got stuck fast in my throat.

I've been a scuba diver all my life. I know how long I can last without breathing. I didn't want to disrupt the lunch, so I kept trying to drink water to get it to go down, but it wouldn't. That thing had lodged hard in my esophagus, and it wasn't going anywhere.

After about ninety seconds I had no air left.

You've probably heard stories about people seeing white lights and a long tunnel before they go. When those ninety seconds were up, sure enough, here came that looming white light and that tunnel.

At that moment Ailes happened to turn to look at me. My face had turned the same color as my tie. He said, "Are you okay?"

I managed to shake my head and point to my throat.

Ailes jumped up and got behind me in an attempt to do the Heimlich— but he couldn't get his arms all the way around me. I'm six foot one and a big guy. He was just able to get enough leverage to push hard enough that I managed to get a swift gulp of air—just enough to get something in my lungs and stay alive another few seconds.

At that point Eric Bolling, who is a former pro baseball player, jumped across the table, put me in the Heimlich, squeezed hard—and the shrimp came out.

That certainly took the mood of the lunch down. Surprisingly, though, not for long. We recovered fairly quickly and I made a few jokes about this being a hell of a way to start the season. I turned to Juan Williams and said, "Have you signed a lease on your new house? You may have to move up here."

We finished out our lunch, then went back to the studio to get ready for that day's show. Eric was leading the show that day. He started talking about unemployment, which was the lead topic of the day, and turned to Greg to pass the baton to him. "Hey, Greg, that's a lot of jobs. Five million jobs."

And Greg Gutfeld—the comedian, the caustic satirist, of all people— said, "I can't...I can't discuss this story until we acknowledge what happened this afternoon." He looked over at me. "Bob?"

"I guess you can't make these things up," I said, and I briefly told the story of what had happened. I put my hand on Eric's shoulder and said, "And then my brother here saved my existence. It's been a long and rough day, and I want to thank everybody for doing what you did."

It seems I'm always having my life saved, one way or another.

The next day the *New York Post* ran a story on page six headlined AILES

SAVES A LIBERAL, and the story got on newscasts and went around the country. Of course, Ailes got all the credit. It makes a better story that way. And he deserved credit, too. I can't say for sure I'd still be here if he hadn't gotten me that brief chance to take a breath. But it was Eric who kept me from dying.

After I told the story on-air that day, my four cohosts declared that day "Bob Day," and applauded for me. Kim said, "We're happy you're okay."

"Not everybody in the audience might be as happy," I said, in an effort to lighten things up a little.

It was no surprise to me that this comment proved accurate.

As time went on, I would become popular with many of Fox's conservative viewers and we would get lots of emails addressed to me saying things like, "I don't agree with you on anything—but I like you," or people saying I was their "favorite liberal" (meaning, the only one they could stand for some reason). But not now. This was still early in the history of the show, and the emails I was getting then typically started out much like the letters I used to get in the *Crossfire* days: "You fat commie sonofabitch . . ." and then went on to rant about how stupid and wrong I was on whatever the issue was. I would always reply politely with something like, "Thank you for your kind words. And by the way, was it your mother who married her brother, or your father who married his sister?" I wrote that to an angry guy from Kentucky once, and he came right back at me with this email reply: "You lying commie bastard, it was my father who married his cousin!"

After "Bob Day," Fox News got lots of emails on the general theme, "Why didn't you let the sonofabitch choke?" You can't please everyone.

But here was the really interesting thing about it: The event seemed to bring the whole group together. It was the first time we had a genuine sense of family there, a real sense of concern that triggered a sharing of other serious life events that had happened to each of the others. In its own way, the shrimp incident helped *make The Five.*

*   *   *

In my travels around the country in the years after *The Five* became popular, I would always ask people, "What is it about *The Five* that you like so much?" I used to conduct focus groups when I was in politics, and I'd learned that if you hear the same thing consistently, over and over again, there comes a certain point where you can be fairly certain you're getting accurate information. And if there was one word I kept hearing over and over again, it was *chemistry*. That was far and away the most common answer I heard: "It's the chemistry between the people on the show."

People also said the show had a "family feeling" to it. In many parts of the country I heard people say the show felt like a family getting together at Thanksgiving, discussing politics and current events, including bringing the crazy uncle up from the basement, which of course was me. Another common comment: "I always feel like I could pull a seat up around that table and feel comfortable."

I figured Walter Cronkite would have approved.

Part of the show's concept was that there would be no one host, no guests (or only very rarely), and no studio audience. Having an audience in the room with you can break up the feeling of intimacy and personal conversation that develops on the set. If you're always thinking there are a bunch of people over there getting ready to laugh, or applaud, then you start playing to their reaction. But we didn't do that. We really were what we appeared to be: five friends sitting around talking with each other, sometimes arguing, often disagreeing, but always having a good time.

Despite our disagreements—which were very real and vehement—in the end people knew that we all loved each other, even when we argued.

I think people want that quality in their own families. They probably wouldn't mind seeing more of it in Congress, too.

One day in the Dallas airport a guy came up to me and introduced himself. He was a professor of communications at a college, and he told me that every week, for one of his three weekly classes, he would edit an episode of *The Five* down to about five minutes and show that to the class, using it as an example of the role of chemistry in communication.

The thing is, that kind of chemistry is not something you can create out of whole cloth. It has to be real. And it *was* real for us, to the point where if one of us was arguing with another, and were winning the argument, and suddenly sensed that he or she had put the other guy in a corner—me particularly, since I was the likeliest target—that person would find a way to give the guy an escape hatch. Which I can promise you never happened on *Crossfire*.

There were a lot of factors that went into the show's success. Our producers were brilliant in the topics they chose, the material they prepared, and the various aspects of how they designed the show. But to me, the bottom line of it, the core thing that people responded to, was how the five of us felt about each other.

*   *   *

Of all the other cast members, Dana Perino was the one to whom I was probably closest, in part because we both came out of politics, and in part because we had some concentrated time right at the beginning to get to know each other well.

When we first signed up for the show we were both living in Washington. For the first three months, while the show's future was still in question, we would ride the Acela train to New York together every Sunday, stay at the Muse Hotel on Forty-Sixth Street, a few blocks from Fox News, then take the train back to Washington every Friday, and come back every Sunday.

The ride from Union Station in Washington to Penn Station in New York is about three hours. When you spend three hours alone with someone, twice a week, for months on end, you cover a lot of ground. In the course of those trips, we talked about everything—life, politics, the ups and downs of the show, our own relationship, her feelings about George Bush, all sorts of things.

Dana grew up in rural Colorado. She always got straight A's, never smoked and very rarely drank, and then only once she became an adult. She has always been just as straight as an arrow. Which means she was just about the complete antithesis of me.

Dana was fascinated by my past. She said she'd read books about people like me (mostly fiction), and asked me all kinds of questions about my various tawdry and bizarre experiences.

At first I was a little worried to really go into it. I said, "Look, I'll try to keep this G-rated."

"No, no, no," she said. "I want the X-rated version."

"All right," I said. "You asked for it." And I told it to her the way it all really happened.

This got to be sort of a running joke with us. On Friday night, going down to Washington, I'd tell her all sorts of hair-raising stories about my past. Two days later, on the way back up to New York on Sunday, I'd ask her about her life and what it was like to live in a peaceful, supportive environment. It was as impossible for me to imagine a childhood like the one she had as it was for her to imagine mine.

Once the show was made a permanent fixture Dana and her husband, Peter, bought a place up in New York. I continued living in Maryland, but Fox gave me an apartment in Hell's Kitchen—not far from where my aunt Barbara drank herself to death—to use during the week. On those rare weekends I didn't go home, Dana would always reach out to include me in whatever she and Peter happened to be doing that weekend. I can't tell you how important that was to me. She's a good friend.

Dana invited me to Peter's sixtieth birthday, along with about a hundred people from all around the world, which they held at the 21 Club in New York. She asked three people to give toasts. The first two were Peter's oldest buddies from Britain (Peter is British), and the third was me.

The two Brits went first. When it was my turn I got up, took the mike, and said as I walked to the front of the room, "Are you ready to hear from an American now?"

The other guys had made some jokes about the age difference between Peter and Dana, so I said, "Peter, I'm not going to make a joke out of the whole age difference thing. I think that's obvious, and I'm happy to let these other guys do it. Frankly, it was kind of a weak effort on their part. But I do have to tell you something. In the months that we've lived at the Muse Hotel, you were on the road a lot." (Peter sells medical equipment all over the world.)

"Dana and I have talked this over and decided we need to tell you, we have been having an affair for the last two years, whenever you were gone."

By this time everyone in the room was cracking up, because this was so *not* who Dana is. (And also, perhaps, because to those who knew my past reputation it *did* sound a lot like me.)

I said, "Now, I used to have a rule, when I had an affair with a married woman, that the husband had to be at least fifty miles away before I would do it. In your case, Peter, you travel to *Australia*, for God's sake, so it was easy pickin's."

Now the room was in hysterics. Time for the punch line.

"So, Peter, I'm sorry, we've had this affair for two years running now— but don't feel bad about it. Here's the good news: At your age, you'll have forgotten about it by tomorrow."

*   *   *

Eric Bolling, who sat on my left on *The Five*, grew up dirt poor in a Chicago neighborhood. Early on it became clear that Eric was an excellent baseball player. He got a full scholarship to Rollins College, in Florida, to play ball, and he was so good that he got drafted right out of school into the Pittsburgh Pirates as a shortstop, but he threw his arm out and had to quit playing.

He decided to move to New York to work in the commodities business. I could not imagine anything more stressful, getting down in that pit and yelling those numbers back and forth all day at lightning speeds. But he did very well at it. I imagine it was a little like being on a pro baseball field.

One day he was down on the trading floor and somebody from CNBC interviewed him. Eric is a very handsome guy, and it was obvious he had good presence in front of the camera. He decided he would go into television. He sold his commodities business for a lot of money and went to work for CNBC, then eventually came over to Fox.

Eric would love to have his own prime-time show. I hope that happens for him. Eric was probably the most emphatically right-wing cast member on the show, and he would stand his position very strongly. He and I established a relationship on-camera as the two bully adversaries. Yet offstage we were very close.

At one point, I got into some tax trouble with the IRS. They decided I was a New York resident, not a Maryland resident, which meant they suddenly wanted another two hundred thousand dollars from me. I am a big believer in the government's ability to serve the people, but that is one government agency I wouldn't mourn if it disappeared tomorrow. In any event, they started taking my paycheck without warning, so I would suddenly be out of money, and Eric would always give me cash to cover it. I'll always be grateful for that.

Eric wanted me to find a woman, settle down, and get married. Exactly what I *didn't* want to do after going through my divorce. But Eric thought it would be good for me. He and his wife met somebody in New Jersey who loved *The Five* and especially me, and who said, "Gee, if he's single, I'd love to go out with him." They set us up for a date. So they could help break the ice, they arranged for all four of us to meet at a place near Fox News.

I walked in and the place was packed. I said, "You have a reservation for Beckel, for dinner for two." (Eric and his wife were meeting us there but not staying for dinner.)

The guy there said, "No, sir, we don't. We have no reservations available."

Oh, shit. I called Eric. He was walking over from the Fox News building to meet me. "Eric, there's no reservation," I said. "And they say they've got nothing available tonight. This is going to be a disaster when this woman shows up."

"Don't worry about it," he said. "I'll be there."

When he showed up, he immediately asked to see the manager. The guy came out, Eric took him back in the corner, and a moment later the manager walked over to me and said, "Mr. Beckel, your table's ready any time you want it." It was the best table in the place.

Did I mention that Eric has a reputation in Midtown Manhattan as the biggest spender and biggest tipper there is?

The woman and I had a nice dinner, but I really didn't want to settle down with anybody. It was not to be, but it was a nice effort on their part and I appreciated it.

It was rare that genuine anger flared on the show, but it happened now and then, and often it was when Eric and I had a clash over political philosophy. One day he said something to me and tried to whack me in the stomach, and I said "You fuckhead!" Not generally viewed as ideal language for live TV. That was the second time I'd used the word "fuck" on television, the first time being on Hannity's show about a year before, and it got me into all kinds of trouble. Our emotions were running high.

Be that as it may, the two of us have a very strong friendship.

*   *   *

For the first three years of the show Andrea Tantaros sat in the end chair stage left, on the other side of me from Eric. (She alternated in that seat with Kimberly Guilfoyle.)

When *The Five* began Andrea was the one cast member I already knew well. When I started working for Fox News as a contributor, they would set me up in the Washington studio and her in the New York studio, hook us up by satellite, and we'd debate. By this point we'd been doing this for seven years, and had established a longtime relationship. Andrea knew me so well that when I started on one of my rants, she had developed the ability to turn her earpiece off and look like she was paying attention to me while hearing absolutely nothing at all.

Andrea's father came from Greece over to the U.S. on a boat in the thirties, penniless, and worked in a restaurant while living outside on the streets of Allentown. He eventually made enough money to buy his own diner, and went on to open up several more diners and a bank. Andrea was very close to her father and would work for him after school, often unbelievably brutal hours. She went to Lehigh University and the Sorbonne. Talk about smart. Andrea wanted to be in television all of her life. Television is a tough business, but she's both pretty enough and smart enough to do it.

Andrea would often come to me for advice on her life and career. When *The Five* first started she was part-time at Fox and working a regular job at a public relations firm. Fox asked her if she would leave her PR firm, and she didn't know what to do. The two of us spent hours talking this over. I encouraged her to give up the PR business and do it, which she finally did. Over the course of the 2013–14 year, her father died, her autistic brother died, and she had gone through a breakup. It was a rough year for her. She and I spent many hours talking things through. But things turned the corner for her.

From 2011 to 2014, Andrea and Kimberly had switched back and forth in that end chair. Then, in the summer of 2014, the executives at Fox News decided it was time to put Andrea on her own show full-time, a news show called *Outnumbered*, on at noon every day. She has a brilliant career ahead of her.

From that point on, Kimberly took that seat on *The Five* full-time.

*   *   *

Kimberly Guilfoyle was already very experienced on television by the time we started *The Five*. She had been an anchor on Court TV, a commentator on ABC and legal analyst for Anderson Cooper on CNN, and worked as an on-air host at Fox News for years. Kimberly used to be First Lady of San Francisco, when she was married to Gavin Newsom, now the lieutenant governor of California, who was then mayor of San Francisco. You can only imagine those dynamics: a very liberal guy in a very liberal city, married to Kimberly, who's very conservative. I used to poke fun at her about it; I'd ask her if she used to go to the gay pride parade with her husband, things like that. She married again a few years later, briefly, and had a child. Now she was a single mom, and absolutely devoted to that kid. But I knew she wanted to get married again. I would joke about this on the air, saying things like, "How many times have you been married, again? Four? Five? Is that right?"

Kimberly was very sensitive about how she looked, so she would bring her cosmetics and eyeliner and all that stuff on the set with her, and I was forever ribbing her about this. I would pick up her eyeliner and use it to make notes; she would scream at me; that sort of thing. She and I had this back-and-forth banter that was a lot of fun. We laughed a lot. When things got a little tense, she had the ability to crack a joke or create some distraction to draw down the tension.

The chemistry between Kimberly and me was so good that at the end of 2013, Fox decided she and I would host the first two hours of their four-hour New Year's Eve special, and then stay on as roving reporters in the crowd.

I'd never been to Times Square on New Year's Eve. It's a complete madhouse out there. And it was freezing, maybe ten degrees Fahrenheit, just brutal. Bill Hemmer and Elisabeth Hasselbeck, who anchored the last two hours, were placed up on a riser, but our set was right down on the street, right next to the largest amplifier for all the bands that played. While we were doing our part of the broadcast, our teleprompter broke, so basically everything just went to hell, and we had a blast making it all up as we went along.

The joke that developed and ran through the two hours was that Kimberly was looking for a date for me in the crowd, and I was looking for a husband for her. The problem was, every time I asked somebody, they'd just go all giggly on us.

At ten o'clock we handed off the coverage to Hemmer and Hasselbeck for the two hours leading up to midnight. Kimberly and I stayed there on the street, and they would come back to us every now and then for comments.

At midnight, the confetti started pouring and the music played "Auld Lang Syne," and then Frank Sinatra doing "New York, New York." Hemmer and Hasselbeck came back to us, freezing our asses off down on the street. By this time we'd been there for four hours, in the freezing cold, our ears being blasted out, completely ad-libbing all our dialogue, going through the crowd trying to find each other mates, and getting seriously slap-happy. Here's how our closing back-and-forth went:

Me: I thought I wasn't going to like it down here, but this is unbelievable, isn't it?
Kimberly: Unbelievable. And I'm so happy to be spending it with you, Bob. Happy New Year, happy 2014. Now, you found a lot of husbands for me tonight, but none of them stand up to the fine man that you are, Bob Beckel.
Me: Hey, you know what I'm glad I'm not tonight? I'm glad I'm not the sanitation department of New York...

Kimberly: It's incredible—the confetti falling, the music, the crowd, it's electric, an incredible way to start 2014, that is for sure, and I'm so happy I'm doing it with you. Happy New Year, Bob, I choose you over all of 'em—

And then, to the great surprise of both of us, she planted this big fat kiss on me, right smack on the lips. It became known as "the kiss heard around the world." Afterward I said she must have confused me with one of those navy SEALs she's always falling for. Though I would have to guess that was the first time I could ever claim to be confused with a navy SEAL. I wonder if Sergeant Johnson was watching.

Kimberly is a consummate professional. There's nobody better at handling breaking news. With her background as a California prosecutor, she would take the lead on any legal issues that cropped up, and she was very good at it. She also does a great job as a mother; her boy is a good kid, and her whole life is dedicated to him along with her career. I'm still keeping my eye out for a good husband for her. Although, as she says, "Bob, anybody you would recommend to me for a husband would be somebody I would not want to marry."

And she's probably right.

*   *   *

Finally, there was Greg Gutfeld.

Greg was the Woody Allen of *The Five*. He's riddled with anxieties, doesn't like to fly, is a passionately committed New Yorker (although he was actually California-born and -bred) who doesn't like to leave his neighborhood. Greg was the editor for *Maxim* in the U.K. for a few years, where he met his wife, who is Russian, and she then emigrated here and became a New Yorker right alongside him.

Greg is an accomplished satirist and a dyed-in-the-wool comedian who hangs around with comedians. Comedians tend to have a very dark side; there's a very real layer of anger in there, and Greg is no exception, by his own admission. If there was ever a time when we had out-and-out anger on the set, it was usually Greg directing it at either Eric or me. He always apologized afterward. It's just part of his makeup. He's very conservative, the committed libertarian of the five of us, and believes in the legalization of marijuana and that sort of thing.

Greg was probably the most difficult guy to get close to on the show. He didn't even pretend that he wanted to get close. He had a second show for Fox called *Red Eye*, that aired at 3:00 a.m., almost the opposite side of the twenty-four-hour cycle from *The Five*, and he would spend a lot of time on that.

Greg is an absolutely brilliant writer. I've never seen better. He put out a monologue every day, which was his signature contribution to the show. They were superbly written, and he would dash one of those things off in about ten minutes. I saw him do it. It was amazing.

Greg is a short guy, five-one or five-two, and Dana's about the same, and they were seated next to each other, so the two of them had a sort of running shtick together on the show, much like Kimberly and me.

Once we held a barbecue on the street outside the studio with some big-name New York chef. While this guy was talking and grilling on his huge grill, with me sitting on one side and Greg on the other, I said, "You know, that grill's big enough you could grill Greg on that."

Greg shot back, "That's the best meat you'll ever taste."

And as usual, I said the first thought that popped into my mind: "Yeah, that's what Dana tells me."

When that clip came out online Dana said something sweet to me, like, "You rot in hell, Bob."

The show had a kind of soap-opera quality, with all sorts of little subplots and running interplay between the various players. As I went around the country speaking, people would often ask me, "Have you ever had an affair with Kimberly? Why are Kimberly and you always so close? And what about Greg and Dana? What's going on with those two?"

This is as good a place as any to put the rumors to rest.

Sorry to disappoint anyone hoping for some juicy inside dirt here, but the truth is: no affairs. There was nothing romantic or sexual between any of the cast members of *The Five*. Honestly, none of us even dreamed of it. Why risk screwing up a good thing?

*   *   *

As much as I loved them all, they still could be a pain in my ass.

Juan Williams, the liberal columnist and NPR commentator who subbed for me, once asked me, "Bob, how do you stand it? How can you sit there and not have your head explode?"

My answer: "You have to have a sense of humor." And I did. But it wasn't always easy.

Greg and Eric both hated Obama with a passion. They really couldn't stand him. They were ruthless, just refused to give him an inch. And they would jump on me about it all the time. There were days when I felt like the only fireplug at the Westminster Dog Show.

Being the only liberal on the set, I was often asked, "How do you handle four on one?" Some days, when I was cornered by the others, I would just change the subject. I developed one of my favorite tactics in the early days of the show.

During commercial breaks, the conversation among us could best be described as equal parts locker room profanities, bitching about the producers (who were the best and brightest in the business, but we would still bitch about them), our next topic, and what each of us was doing in the coming weekend. If the next topic coming up was, for example, Barack Obama, where I was constantly under siege, then while we were still on break I'd say something like, "So Kimberly, what are you doing this weekend?"

Kimberly replied, "I've got a date with a hot navy SEAL."

Then the countdown: "Five, four..." the last three seconds were not spoken out loud but simply counted down on the producer's fingers, held up in front where we could see them, and silently in our heads. Then the red light popped on.

We were live.

After the next topic introduction I would immediately cut in and say, "Hey did you all know that Kimberly's got a date this weekend with a navy SEAL?" The others couldn't resist chiming in. There went the topic. It drove Kimberly nuts. But they all got a taste of it.

Or we'd be about to go back on the air, and someone would ask Eric what he was doing that weekend. "Nothing much, just taking the weekend off at my beach house," he would say.

In a few minutes we'd get the countdown, and then the red light went on.

Kimberly would announce the topic for the next segment, some controversial statement or action or development that was about to give them all fuel for a frontal attack on me, and then she would hand the baton over with an "Eric?"

I would butt in.

"Before we get to that, Eric, how come you never invite any of us to your beach house?"

The others would take the bait and pile on. There went the time—and

Obama was relatively safe for another day, at least from the slings and arrows of this TV show.

They even coined a term for it; they called it being "Beckeled." Worked nearly every time.

*   *   *

We had a lot of fun together, but there was a method to the madness, and a larger message, too. As I've said, the affection you saw on the set, that was real; the five of us genuinely loved each other. But the disagreements you saw on the set? Those were real, too. And that was kind of the point. Is it possible to love someone you totally disagree with? Is it possible to have civil discourse and an honest, mutually respectful conversation with someone whose viewpoints you think are dead wrong? Of course it is. And it's something people in this country need to remember and relearn how to do.

This is most obvious in Congress, of course. To say Congress has become gridlocked and polarized to the point of dysfunction is a hopeless cliché. But the reason it's a cliché is that it's so true. When I first entered the political business, people disagreed, but they worked together and got things done. These days, as I said before, you'd be hard put to get sixty-seven votes in the Senate for Mother's Day.

But it isn't just politicians. Politicians, after all, are only our representatives. It's us, too, all of us. People have become too quick to see each other as labels first, and human beings second, or third, or not at all.

Here's an interesting thing: A lot of liberals and Democrats take pot shots at me now, saying I've betrayed the cause, sold out, call me a "so-called liberal" and "phony liberal," because I have friends who are conservatives and I worked for Fox News.

To those critics, I have just two things to say:

First, I don't need to defend or justify my liberal credentials to anybody. I was getting kicked in the face (and I mean that literally) by angry bigots with murder in their eyes while registering black voters in the South when most of these critics were still in their Pampers.

And second, when it comes to friendship, I go for the person, not the politics. When I was at my lowest point it was mostly conservatives who stuck by me and extended a hand. Over the years, my best friends in the world have been conservatives, from Ed Rollins and Tony Snow to Haley Barbour and Cal Thomas.

During those years I spent in New York, the person who became my best friend there was one most people wouldn't expect. You want to talk about two guys who are complete opposites: That would be me and Sean Hannity.

Hannity grew up as straitlaced as they come. He went to Sacred Heart Seminary and St. Pius Seminary and was planning to be a priest when the radio bug hit him. Hannity and I hit it off famously. We agreed to not talk politics. I would spend weekends at his house on Long Island. As we got to know each other, he got a kick out of being able to live vicariously through my stories. (Much like Dana Perino.) One day I was with Sean and a friend of his, Keith, telling them about some of the crazy things that had happened to me, including the hooker extortion scandal. The next day Hannity called me and said, "Hey, Keith went and checked out everything you told us—and it's all true!"

I said, "Yeah, it's true, Sean, it's true."

Over the years Hannity asked me to help friends of his who were alcoholics, which I did. He finally gave me a key to his house. I'm sort of a member of the family there now, and we remain very close.

My brother, Graham, is as conservative as I am liberal, and we've been guests together a few times on Sean's show. You can find those clips online; they're worth watching. The two Beckel boys, loving each other like the brothers we are, and disagreeing as completely as two people can.

One time Fox held a book party for Dick Cheney and told the cast of *The Five* that they wanted us all to go up there and join the party.

Oh, boy, I thought. *What's this going to be like?*

I went up into this fancy room at Fox headquarters and kept to myself until somebody came over to me and said, "My friend wants to talk to you." His friend, of course, was Cheney.

We walked over there, Cheney stood up, the two of us shook hands like old buddies, sat down, and talked together for the next hour and a half or so. A crowd gathered around, expecting a big explosion. But no explosion. He and I went back and covered the politics he and I both remembered, when he was in the House, and it turned out to be a delightful discussion.

Among the very few guests we ever had on the show was former Alaska governor and former vice-presidential candidate Sarah Palin. As you can imagine, Palin and I did not get along. When she appeared on the show, in the middle of 2012, she handed me my head when I tried to criticize something she was saying about Obamacare. It was hot times. The following spring, on Valentine's Day, I got a call from the number-two guy at Fox News, Bill Shine, saying, "Please come up to my office." When I walked into his office, there was Sarah Palin. She gave me a box of chocolates in a heart-shaped box, and we had a long and very pleasant conversation.

People are people.

At *Crossfire* they wanted you to shout. That was the whole idea of the genre. As time went along, that started to wear thin with audiences. Civilized debate was the new idea, and that was fine with me because I was tired of us all screaming at each other. I could do it; I could debate loudly as well as anybody could. But, for me, *The Five* format was a wonderful change. We disagreed with each other, but we didn't scream and yell.

*   *   *

Which isn't to say the show was without controversy. I was constantly putting my foot in my mouth. It wasn't intentional. It would just happen.

One day Eric did a brief spot about an episode of a reality show, *The Bachelorette*, where this poor bastard who came in second was devastated because he learned the girl had slept both with him and also with the guy she eventually picked. The others took turns commenting on this, and when it came around to me I said, "She's a slut. What can you say?"

The comment drew fire immediately. I was denounced on *The View*, on E Entertainment, by all the women's groups, by all my crowd—that is, the left—by everyone. I took a real beating on that one.

That happened on a Tuesday. That week I'd planned to take off the last two days, Thursday and Friday, to do some writing. The following Monday I got called up to Bill Shine's office to meet with Shine and Suzanne Scott. *Okay*, I thought, *here it comes.*

I got up there to Shine's office, fully expecting to get the shit kicked out of me. Shine said, "Bob, we want to thank you for that magnificent tweet you sent out." Over the weekend I had sent out a tweet saying that I'd said some inappropriate things on the show, and that the bosses weren't happy with me, and they had every right not to be happy with me, and that I shouldn't have said these things. Shine continued, "It was very thoughtful on your part, and we appreciate it. But you know what I did this weekend?"

I said, "I don't know, Bill. Go golfing?" Bill usually played golf on Sundays.

"No," he said. "I didn't get to play golf on Sunday. And I didn't get to take my wife shopping on Saturday, like I'd promised her. You know why?

Because I spent my weekend responding to thousands of emails from people saying, 'Why are you being so mean to Bob Beckel?'"

Apparently when I didn't show up on Thursday or Friday, some of our viewers thought I'd gotten in trouble. All of a sudden a huge wave of email and phone calls came in to Fox News saying, "Don't you dare think about taking Bob off *The Five*! We don't agree with anything he says, but if you take him off, we'll stop watching the show!"

They had no intention of taking me off. They weren't punishing me. Those two days off had nothing to do with any of it. But the viewers didn't know that.

"Please," said Shine, "do us a favor. You're hot, right now. People love you. And that's great. But can you just try to stay out of controversy?"

I wished I could say yes...but I couldn't. Most people have a filter in their heads, positioned between the moment when they have a thought and the moment when that thought comes out their mouth. That filter says, "Is this an appropriate thing to say right now?" In my case, that filter was burned out by drinking a long time ago.

And they knew that.

"I'll do my best," I replied. "But you guys have to remember all the times when the show is dragging and I get your voices in my ear saying, 'Pick it up. The thing's slow, Bob, get it rolling.' Now you're saying, 'Pull back.' But you can't have it both ways. I don't have that many gears. I'm either full-speed-ahead or take-it-easy. I'll try the best I can. But you have to remember who you hired here."

And of course, they did remember. How could they forget?

You should have seen the control room at Studio D when the show was on. There must have been twenty-five people in there, all managing different aspects of the technology and production at a breakneck pace. It was like watching the control room at Cape Canaveral for a moon shot. Sometimes it looked like that control room when the oxygen tank exploded on *Apollo 13*.

While the show was live, it actually was not *quite* live; it was on a six-second delay, with a button that bleeped the sound out for a second if someone happened to say something that went way beyond the bounds of what was permissible to say on television.

That someone, of course, was always me.

I pitied the poor bastard who was in charge of that button then. He had to keep his eyes glued on me the entire hour. It must have been nerve-racking.

*　　*　　*

There is one more person I want to talk about, and he was the key reason the show worked so well: our executive producer, Porter Berry.

Porter grew up in Oklahoma, then moved to LA to work in the movies, so he had these two sides: a worldly kind of guy, but with salt-of-the-earth Ozark roots and common sense. Porter is a man of sterling character. And he and I disagree on just about everything under the sun, at least when it comes to politics.

His choices of topics were always brilliant. They made the show work. It was his decision to lead with news stories, but then move on to other things, cultural topics and other issues of interest. Porter came up with a little feature that many viewers said was their favorite part of the show, a segment called "One More Thing," where a single cast member would take a minute or two to talk about whatever mattered to him or her. It told a lot about the personalities of the individual people.

Porter knew perfectly well from the start that our audience did not like my politics at all (neither did he)—but he wanted to be sure they liked *me*. So for two years he put me out at the Summer Solstice Yoga Event in Times Square, doing yoga. (How could you not like me when I was willing to show up in Times Square on a blisteringly hot day and do yoga with a few thousand hot women?)

During the lead-up to the Sochi Olympics in 2014, he put me out in Times Square and had me do a slalom run. I played a curling match against the coach of the curling team and actually beat him. I interviewed a former U.S. figure-skating champion from Long Island. She said our prospects were good, we had some good skaters going, and I said, "Is Tonya Harding coming back to take care of the number-one girl?" at which point the PR person for the Olympics jumped in and said, "This interview is over."

I have to give Porter credit: He took chances with me.

He also came up with topics for the show that were genuinely meaningful. For several weeks he had us concentrate on bullying, which is a subject dear to my heart, and one that struck a chord with a lot of viewers.

And it was Porter who encouraged me to talk more about my alcoholism on the air.

In fact, this was something I had begun to do anyway. I figured if I didn't, I'd be outed by the right sooner or later. And besides, if hearing my story could help any of our viewers, then I would be using our platform for a good cause.

Porter would feed me news items about binge drinking, college students dying from too much drinking, that sort of thing, that would provide me the opening to give people a little bit of an education on alcoholism. Invariably I would get hundreds of emails or texts a week, most of them messages from people who were in trouble and needed some guidance, and I would be able to connect them with AA groups in their areas.

Here's how I saw it. If my work on the show could entertain millions of people, I counted that as a good thing. If it could offer people a modest example of cordial disagreement and civil exchange of differing viewpoints in an increasingly hostile and polarized world, even better.

But if I could use that platform to help even one person climb out of the hell of alcoholism and addiction and start to rebuild his or her life? Or ten? Or a hundred?

That was worth all the hate mail you could throw at me.

*　　　*　　　*

By 2013 *The Five* had blown by Beck's numbers and become the second-most-watched show in all of cable news, surpassed only by Bill O'Reilly's *The O'Reilly Factor*, Fox News' perennial number-one show. On several days, and even at one point for a few weeks at a time, *The Five* actually beat O'Reilly and his heavily advertised show.

What was even more remarkable was that, on average, only 40 percent of the television sets in the country were turned on between 5:00 and 6:00 p.m., while during O'Reilly and other Fox News prime-time shows an average of 65 percent of sets were in use. Which meant a full 50 percent *more* sets in use were available to Fox News prime-time shows than were available to *The Five*.

And yet our numbers held.

Did I enjoy the show's popularity? Of course. But I didn't let the success push me around. I knew the time would come when we would no longer be the hot thing. Sooner or later, I figured, some other show would come along and push our show to the side. Like politics, television is a fickle business. I thought, *Who knows?* Maybe within another year or two *The Five* would exist only in the archives and in YouTube clips. Or maybe it would still be going strong, every day from 5:00 to 6:00 p.m.

Either way, it had been a hell of a good run.

CHAPTER TWELVE

Beyond Surviving

One day in the fall of 2013 I approached Porter Berry, our senior producer, and told him I needed a particular Wednesday that October off from *The Five*. He asked why. I told him I had to go to D.C. to accept the 2013 Caron Alumni Award for my work with fellow alcoholics, which was going to be presented at Caron's second annual Recovery for Life Gala. The gala is sponsored by the Caron Foundation to raise money for scholarships to Caron, for alcoholics who are committed to sobriety but cannot afford to pay for rehab themselves. The event was being held in Washington on Wednesday, October 9, at 6:00 p.m. Since *The Five* ran from five to six, this meant I would need the day off that day, so I could get down to D.C.

A few days later, he came back and told me, no, I wasn't getting the day off.

"Why the hell not?" I demanded. I rarely missed an episode of *The Five* while I was on the show, and this award was very important to me.

Because, Porter said, the entire show was being moved to Washington for the day—so they could all be there to support me.

The presentation was an emotional moment for me. Cal Thomas was there and introduced me. When I accepted the award I gave a short speech, portions of which I include below.

*　　*　　*

My son, Alex, and my daughter, MacKenzie, are with me here tonight, with their mother, Leland Keyser, for which I am both grateful and proud. Also here tonight are my cohosts from my show on

Fox, *The Five*, which was brought down here today to be broadcast out of Washington so that I could be here with you tonight. I want to thank my cohosts on *The Five* for being with me here, and our senior producer, Porter Berry, who brought the show to Washington. I also want to give a special thanks to Roger Ailes, the CEO of Fox News, whose personal resources played a role in our being here.

I want to say to my fellow alcoholics here tonight, in four hours [by this time it was 8:00 p.m.] we will pass the threshold into another day of sobriety. We'll have put another day under our belt. Some of us have a lot of those days, some have very few. But if there's someone here tonight who just quit drinking yesterday, you're no different from those of us who've been around for years. We're all one drink away from disaster.

Alcoholism is a cunning and baffling disease. You never get over alcoholism, you simply retard it by not drinking, one day at a time. For those of you who have been out there, you understand what I mean by one day at a time. There was a time, for many of us, when it was one minute at a time.

Most of us began our journey into alcoholism in the light world, where most of you here tonight reside. But in time, the light world for an alcoholic begins to change.

As an alcoholic, you wake up in the morning sick and tired and look out the window at your car, hoping that there's not a dent on the front, or worse, blood on it. Your friends begin to mention that you're drinking a lot. You get invited to fewer and fewer events, which is understandable, since by now you've knocked down four or five Christmas trees at parties. Your family begins to drift away. If you have relationships they begin to falter, if you have hobbies you begin to ignore them, and you find yourself drifting over into the only place you can, which is the dark world.

The dark world is full of alcoholics, just like you. They're all convinced that they could stop drinking if they wanted to. But in their hearts they know they're lying to themselves. They are all con artists. They tried to con me, but I was the biggest con in the joint.

In the dark world you find yourself doing things and saying things and going places you could never have imagined doing or going when you were sober. And it doesn't bother you when you do it.

Then comes a day when you're finally sick and tired of being sick and tired. You decide to seek help. In my case, I was fortunate enough to have the resources to go to a place like Caron.

The day I left for Caron was the saddest day of my life. My two children were very young then, and when they asked me where I was going, I told them, "Daddy's going away for thirty days to the North Pole to help Santa make Christmas toys."

Alex and MacKenzie, I can finally tell you the truth tonight. Kenz, I did not make your Barbie doll, and Al, I did not paint your Thomas trains.

The day I arrived at Caron I was scared and alone. I began to look around and saw lots of other people who were scared and alone. Then we began to talk to each other, alcoholic to alcoholic, and suddenly you realized you were not alone and your story was not much different from the other patients' stories. Most knew that they could not control their drinking, and for most of them, they wanted to find their way back to the light world. After talking to other alcoholics and the Caron counselors, most of whom were alcoholics and addicts in recovery themselves, you began to see, day by day, little by little, the road back to the light.

I could not have gotten here tonight if it wasn't for Caron and Alcoholics Anonymous. There are thousands of alcoholics out there tonight who are trying desperately to find their way to the light. To find their way out of the dark world.

The alternative, which is the reality for many of them, is to die.

Because this is a progressive disease. It doesn't go away. As I said: You simply retard it by not drinking, one day, a day at a time.

At Caron you find you get very close to people. When I went there, there was a fellow there by the name of Ron Ziegler, a name many of you will remember as press secretary to Richard Nixon. Ron and I had been in different White Houses and came from different political parties, but we spent hours talking—about life, about drinking, about God, and about our families. When he and I left Caron we stayed in touch, because I loved Ron very much. Then I lost track of him.

A few years ago I found out that Ron had died from complications from alcohol. I still love Ron and I miss him very much.

So I accept this alumni award in Ron's honor. If he were here tonight, like me, fortunate enough to have found his way back to the light world again, he would ask each of you to provide a beacon to lead a struggling alcoholic out of the dark world and back to the light.

*   *   *

I spent the first eighteen years of my life surviving childhood, and the next thirty-five fighting to survive the life I spun around myself as a result. I almost didn't live to see my sixties. It's a miracle that I did, and I use the word "miracle" advisedly.

Now I've begun to experience that there is more to life than surviving.

In one sense, my life these days echoes my life in the 1990s. By day, I talk about politics. By night, I head out into the streets and enter the sleazy bars and seedy joints of the dark world. Only there's one big difference. Now I don't go into the dark world as a citizen of that place. I go in there to help pull other people out.

There's a saying in AA, "Whenever an alcoholic is suffering, anywhere, the hand of AA is there to help you." We take that creed seriously. If I get called, I go.

The other night I got a phone call. It was late at night, and it was a guy I knew who was still fairly new in AA. He told me who it was, and I asked him where he was.

"I'm sitting at a bar, and there's a shot of Scotch sitting in front of me."

"Don't move," I told him. "Stay there. I'm on my way."

I knew the place. I'd been there before.

Within minutes I was walking into the joint. I walked up to him, sat on the stool next to him, and said, "Tell you what let's do. Let's you and me walk out of here, right now."

The bartender came over to me and said, "Listen, friend, this is a place of business. I'm trying to make a living here. You got no right interfering and taking my customers out of here."

I said, "Listen, *friend*, this isn't about business, it's about saving someone's life. If you don't like what I'm doing, I have a fist that would be more than willing to rearrange your facial features."

Dr. King would not have approved of my tactics, and it wasn't the most elegant way of stating my case. But when a man's life is on the line, I'll do what I have to do.

We left the bar together and I brought the guy home to his place, got him packed, and drove him to Caron. It meant I'd be up all night, but that's what my nights are for.

One day at a time.

Looking back through the pages of my life it is abundantly clear to me that the phrase "I should be dead" isn't just a catchy idea for a book title. It's the plain truth. How is it possible that I came through all that? It wasn't luck; luck just doesn't cut through odds like that. And it sure as hell wasn't me. There were some days, frankly, when I was so screwed up that I really didn't care if I died or not. But here I am.

I can only conclude that God took me through it all and kept me here. And if He did, then He must have done so for a reason. And I think the reason is for me to work with other alcoholics, as much as I can't stand it. I hate alcoholics, even though I am one. They drive me crazy. But there you go.

It's what I do. It's why I'm still here.

*   *   *

Having been through an intervention that saved my life, I decided to become an interventionist myself. There are people who are supposedly trained interventionists and charge something like five grand a whack. Among AA people, there's some resentment for that crowd. You can also learn to be an interventionist by working with people who have done them before, people who are in AA. That's what I did. I spent four or five months doing meetings a couple days a week to train, and then volunteered to do two interventions a month in Washington, when I was there. When I moved to New York to work for Fox News full-time, I agreed with AA there that I would do one a month.

The first one I did was with "John," a businessman on Staten Island.

I went out there the night before. He wasn't home. The idea is that when an intervention happens, the person's supposed to be surprised when he walks in. He's not supposed to know there's something going on. Like a surprise birthday party.

I met with the kids and his wife, his minister, his boss, and his accountant. There were twelve or thirteen people there in all. I walked them through what would happen, what my role would be, and that I was going to try to do as little as possible other than keep it moving along. I had the kids, who were very young, write out their feelings for their father; otherwise, if they just tried to say it when the time came, they'd start to cry and wouldn't be able to get it out.

The next day found me up early and taking the Staten Island Ferry. It was like déjà vu, going back to Wagner College. I got to this guy's house about an hour before he did; everybody else was gathered there. We formed a circle of chairs.

Then in walked the businessman. About fifty years old, I guessed, white, successful—the most difficult crowd to get sober. Demographically, professional white guys are very tough to get through to because they're so fucking arrogant. They think they know all the answers. I know that bracket quite well.

His brother brought him in, and the very first thing this guy said to me was, "Beckel! Why are you here and not on television?"

"Because I'm not here as a TV guy," I said. "I'm here as a drunk, just like you."

"I'm not a drunk," he said.

I said, "Why don't you sit down and listen to what these people have to say to you."

John agreed not to say anything, and to just sit and listen while everyone else spoke. It was one of the most heart-rending few hours I ever spent. They all went around the room, taking turns telling him how they felt about him and what it was like watching what he was doing to himself, and there was not a dry eye in the room—except for his. He was completely unmoved. Yeah, I'd seen his type before.

I said to him, "Where's the booze in this house?"

He said, "There is no booze in the house. Only one bottle of vodka, and it's right over there on the bar."

I turned to "Mary," his wife. "Mary, do you mind if I walk through the house and take a look around?" She said that was fine, I could go ahead. I got up and started walking around the place. I went into the guest bathroom, looked inside the toilet tank, and there was a bottle. Into the bedroom, under the mattress: there was a bottle. In the air-conditioning. Hidden away on a high shelf in the closet. And so on. I walked back into the living room with six or seven bottles full of booze.

"Where did you find those?" the guy said.

"Places like your toilet tank," I said. "And your air conditioner."

"How the hell did you know where to find them?"

"Because when I was drinking, that's exactly where I hid them."

Even with all those bottles sitting there on that table, the guy still insisted that he had no idea how any of them had gotten there. That's how much denial you can be in when you're in the grip of this disease.

At that point I kind of lost it on him, although not in front of the rest of the group. I said, "John, can I talk to you for a second, in your home office?"

He got up and went out with me into another room, just the two of us.

Once we were inside and the door was closed, I said, "Let me tell you something, you sonofabitch. There are a lot of people out there who need my help. I don't have to sit here with your sorry ass. You listened to everything these people said and you didn't have a shred of emotion on your face. I know, because I watched you the whole time. You're a sick man. Now, let me tell you something. If you don't go to rehab right now, your wife and your kids are going to leave you. And believe me, my experience is that when they go, they never come back."

He said, "They'd never leave me. That's my *family*."

I said, "Is that right? Let's go see."

We went back out into the living room and I asked the wife, "Mary, are you prepared to take the kids and leave here if he doesn't go to rehab and get sober?"

She said, "Our bags are packed, and we're ready to walk out the door."

That did it.

"All right, all right," he said. "If you guys all think. It's ridiculous, but I'll do it."

All the way from his house to the Staten Island Ferry he cursed me up one side and down the other. He argued about drinking, about whether he was an alcoholic or not, about politics, about anything he could think of to argue about. And he got loud. It was embarrassing.

At one point he said, "Can I drink?"

I knew the answer to that one. I'd asked it myself. I said, "Sure, you can drink all you want—until you get to Hazelden. There I guarantee you're not going to drink. But go ahead. I'll buy it for you."

"Really?" he said.

I said, "Yeah, sure. No problem."

So I bought him some of those little bottles of booze, like they have in hotel room minibars, and he sat on that ferry, drinking one little bottle after another, yelling at me the whole way across, until I finally got him to Presbyterian Hospital where there was someone waiting to fly with him out to Minnesota.

I hope he made it home, I mean all the way home, clean and sober.

I hope his family was still there when he did.

*   *   *

I have witnessed some terrible things in the realm of alcoholism.

There was a girl, Becky, who lived in my neighborhood. Becky had been coming to AA for about six months. Sometimes I would drive her to meetings on Saturday or Sunday, just to be sure she got to at least two meetings each weekend. One Friday I bumped into her at a store and her shopping cart was loaded up with all this food. I said, "What are you doing, Beck?"

She said, "I'm getting food for the whole weekend."

I said, "That's great."

The next day she didn't show up at the meeting, and on Sunday she didn't show up at that meeting, either. Her AA sponsor and I went over to her place, and it was locked. We asked the super to let us into her apartment. We walked into her place, went into her bedroom, and found her lifeless body hanging from an exposed water pipe.

I've seen a lot of dead bodies in my life. This one particularly got to me. Here was a sweet girl who I'd thought was on the mend, who I thought had found her way into the clearing, who got too far lost and finally gave up.

About forty thousand people kill themselves in the United States every year; 25 percent of them have in their systems drugs and/or alcohol well over the legal limit.

I spent a lot of time with George McGovern and his wife, talking with them about their daughter, Terry, who was an alcoholic, trying to explain it to them. In 1994, after stumbling out of a bar somewhere in Wisconsin, Terry fell into a snowbank and froze to death. People who have alcoholic kids but are not alcoholics themselves have a very difficult time understanding why their children can't stop drinking. I try to explain to them that these are forces beyond their control, unless they get to AA, get some people around them who are clean, and get enough sober days in them to realize that there is another life possible.

Alcoholism is a progressive disease—a wretchedly destructive one that forces you to be alone in your own world where you don't trust anybody else. You get to a point where there appears to be no way out. You come to believe that you are now a citizen of the dark world and you are never going to get back to the light.

But you can.

*   *   *

My kids are survivors, too, in their own way. Not like me; thank God, they didn't go through a childhood like mine. I was determined to raise them exactly the opposite from the way my father raised me. I figured I knew as much about bad parenting as anyone, so I was prepared. Or at least, so I thought.

I spent a ton of time with them when they were young. I took them to school every day and brought them home again, and you learn a lot about your kids on those little everyday car trips. With rare exceptions, I never missed any of their events—sports, plays, band practice, parent/teacher meetings, you name it, I was there. We established a very close relationship.

But then again, for the first six or so years of their lives, I was an active alcoholic. Although I made sure they never saw me drunk, I walked around every day with a constant blood alcohol level to keep from going into tremors. At night, I would disappear and slip into the dark world, but I was careful never to bring that world home with me.

Or so I thought.

Of course, even though I wasn't drunk in front of them, I was still a drunk, and for an alcoholic there is always a preoccupation with drinking. That's what you're really thinking about: where your next one's coming from, what you need to do to get to that place. So even if you're with someone, you're not really with them. Although I was there, and had prided myself on that, I *wasn't* really there. I was present, but not present. I wasn't paying the kind of attention I should have paid, and didn't involve myself in the details of their lives the way I should have. And I always wondered, and always will, if that made a difference, if that hurt them.

So far I haven't seen any evidence of that. But it's hard to imagine that my drinking did not affect them in some way. They insist that's not the case. But I know better. I know it's been a rough ride for them.

In the years since, I have done my best to compensate for that, and I maintain a very strong and close relationship with them today. I work at that.

I feel I owe it to them, for the years that I was absent despite being present. There's still damage from the divorce and from my drinking, but it could have been a lot worse. They're good kids, and I feel incredibly fortunate about that. I praise God for that.

I remember taking MacKenzie to a dance when she was eight years old. All the twelve- and thirteen-year-old girls were in the back of the room, snickering and paying zero attention to the dads. Then there was a group of us with our eight-year-old girls, dancing a slow dance, and Kenzie was standing on my shoes, just like you see in the movies. At one point, while we were all dancing, I turned to a few of the other dads and said, "Boys, freeze this moment, because it ain't going to happen many more times."

I was right, too. In no time at all my daughter went from being very attached to Daddy to saying, "Hey Dad, can you drop me off a block away from the party?"

"Why a block away?" I'd say. "I can drive you right to the door."

"No, no, I could use the exercise."

Uh-huh. Got it.

I've gone in now and then to speak in front of class as an expert on politics and government, in both my kids' classes. The first time I spoke to Alex's class, I thought about that terrible day in 1965 when my old man showed up drunk, intending to speak to my tenth-grade history class, and had to be escorted out by the teacher. I was so grateful that I was able to appear there sober, and not repeat for them the horror and humiliation that I'd suffered in the same situation. I praise God for that one, too.

Both the kids are keenly interested in public affairs, both domestic and foreign. Whenever I'm with them, they ask endless questions about politics. They used to come sit in on my classes in politics when I taught graduate school at George Washington University. On some of the questions I'd ask, they could beat some of those graduate students hands-down. I was proud of that.

They're very good in public, these kids. They look adults right in the eye, give a firm handshake. Either one of them would be a good politician. I tell them that, and they say, "Well, Pop, we've watched you."

*　　*　　*

If you cut down a tree and look at all the rings, you see some rings are thicker than others, because it was a better year for rain and sun, and some are thin because it was a tough year. For me, the rings for those early years were all pretty thin. But how could I complain? I've had some good thick-ring years, too. I certainly have them now. All those thin rings, they're just part of what's gone into growing the tree I am today, and I accept that. I accept myself, finally.

I've stopped trying to be the driver, and am content being the passenger.

For me, every day is a free one, a day I shouldn't have had, given the path I was on. Each day is a reprieve from God. And I'm grateful as hell for it—for all of it. Even the ugly parts. If I hadn't gotten drunk, if I hadn't gotten so addicted to alcohol, I would not have found faith. I would not have come to where I am today, which is battered and bruised but at peace.

My brother says, "Do you really want to write about how you cheated to get votes for the Panama Canal Treaty? You really want to talk about all these whorehouses you went to? Do you have to go into all this ugly stuff?"

And I say, "Yeah, Buddy, I do. It's all part and parcel of who I am."

Unrepentant survivors will do some of the worst addictive things, until they get it dealt with. To not make that clear, or to gloss over the worst stuff, would not do it all justice, and not do *you* justice, you who are reading these words. I haven't gone into all the gory details, dragged you through all the fistfights and violence. There were car crashes, other beatings, other heartbreaks. I've spared you some of the worst of it. But I think it's important to point out that for a long time, I was a thug, and that that came from the experience of a childhood where chaos reigned and peace didn't dare to tread.

I'm not really concerned about what people are going to say or think about all this. I have a principle for living that I've come to, something I've been telling my kids lately: "I care very much what you think. I just don't care what you think about *me*." I've found this to be a liberating thing.

One thing I am certain of: You can't find peace until you've found faith. I know some people say they find peace through meditation, some through communing with nature. For me, peace comes through surrendering, turning my will and my life over to God. When I can do that, accept that He's in charge and I'm not, then peace follows.

But hey, who am I to judge. Disagree with me, and I'll disagree right back—and we can still be friends.

Epilogue

I had intended to end this account here, perhaps returning to my seat outside Studio D and the last few puffs on my cigar, with just a few minutes before heading inside to go on the air, musing for a moment about what it all means. Wrapping up where I began. After surviving the many minefields in my life, it would have made a good ending.

But life doesn't always follow the story you're trying to tell or unfold in a neat narrative that winds to an orderly conclusion. Life is messy; it thrives on the unexpected.

In the spring of 2015, soon after this manuscript was completed, the long-standing pain in my back dating all the way back to my high school football days forced me to go in for an extremely difficult—and, as it turned out, somewhat risky—surgical procedure. The team of doctors who performed the surgery were amazing, and it was successful. For the first time in a *long* time, my back was completely pain-free.

There were, however, complications. Some 75 percent of people who have this kind of radical back surgery may suffer temporary (often mildly) diminished use of one or both legs, a setback from which they generally recover quickly. The other 25 percent take a hit to the leg (or legs) for longer, or even for an indefinite period of time. Turns out I am in that latter category. Probably, the docs told me, I waited too long to have this surgery, and the nerves that serve my left leg were compressed for a dangerously long time. Having a solid shot at recovering even partial use of that leg, I was told, would require a strict routine of extensive physical therapy and rehabilitation for at least a year, maybe more, together with severe limitations on travel and mobility.

This would mean I would have to give up, at least for the time being, my current television career.

I thought about that, long and hard. Actually, I take that back. I thought about it *hard*, but not for long. The conclusion came quickly.

I want to be here to see my grandkids; I'd like to bounce them on my knee. And when I do, it would be good to have a working knee to do the bouncing. Placed on the scale of life priorities, television and politics and the public life, love them as much as I do—and I do love them with a passion—do not carry near the same freight as do health and my ability to take an unimpeded walk in the park with my family.

"Who knows," I had written at the end of chapter 11. "Maybe within another year or two *The Five* would exist only in the archives and in YouTube clips. Or maybe it would still be going strong, every day from 5:00 to 6:00 p.m." To which I can now add: Either way, I am no longer a part of it. After four wonderful, amazing years together, *The Five* and I have had to go our separate ways. My leg, my health, my life mean too much to me to gamble them again, as I have done so flagrantly in the past. I have been through the rehabilitation of my soul and the rehabilitation of my career. Evidently the next item on the agenda is the rehabilitation of my leg. And I have two things on my side now I did not have in younger days: my faith and my sobriety. Both, I'm happy to report, are intact.

Though the second of these was sorely tested, and from an unexpected quarter.

As bad as the back pain was for years beforehand, the agony following surgery—much like that following my heart bypass surgery in 2003—was no picnic. The medications my doctors prescribed for the pain were amazingly effective. They are also horribly addictive. I elected to check in to the Betty Ford Pain Management Center to help me manage the meds. I am, after all, an addict.

While I was at Betty Ford I soon realized that, ironically, I was one of the lucky ones. My long history of addiction notwithstanding, these pills didn't particularly get their hooks in me. I'd been exposed to drugs with effects quite similar to Percocet and OxyContin back in the sixties, and never cared for them much. They were not my drug of choice. Now, in 2015, I found I didn't have a hard time getting off them as my post-op recovery progressed, and never felt the kind of irresistible gravitational pull that I did when using alcohol and cocaine.

I saw a lot of people who were not so fortunate. It was appalling. One after another, I met a steady procession of people coming through the clinic who (unlike me) had never in their lives been addicts or alcoholics, good people who had done nothing but follow their doctors' orders and taken the meds they were prescribed to take—and as a result had plunged off the cliff of addiction. The problem of prescription-induced addiction, as I've since come to learn, is at epidemic levels. It's a national tragedy. It's something we need to change.

In any case, once again, I survived. My leg is not entirely intact (at least not yet), but my sobriety still is, and so is my brain, much to the chagrin of some. I'll miss the back-and-forth of *The Five*, but I expect that before long I'll be back at the table in one forum or another, fighting the good fight and helping to move forward the dialogue on how we can make this great nation an even better place than it already is. (Note to conservatives: I would not applaud my exit from the stage just yet.)

"You look like you're enjoying life," my passing friend commented on that sunny day outside Studio D where this narrative began. Today I'm no longer sitting outside Studio D in New York City; instead I'm plunked down in my favorite armchair in my Maryland home, left leg resting on an ottoman (doctor's orders), as I think about what my friend said.

He was exactly right. There was a time when life was a constant struggle, when I would often find myself consumed by anger, or indignation, or fear, or anxiety.

These days, I mostly just find myself at peace.

It drives some of my friends crazy when I say that. Others just laugh. I can understand why. Most people who know me from television, or from politics, probably see me as combative and argumentative, the last person they'd describe as "peaceful." Yes, I disagree with my colleagues, sometimes vociferously. But I don't get too caught up in any of it. Life is too precious. I say what I think. And then watch the world go by.

So what comes next, once my leg is healed? At least one more chapter, I think, perhaps several more. As to what's in those chapters, I'll have to wait and see.

No hurry.

I've got all the time in the world.

Acknowledgments

Writing a book is a humbling experience: You find out (if you didn't already know) just how much you depend on the generosity, encouragement, expertise, and patient participation of a lot of people who know what the hell they're doing and believe in you enough to do it with you. My thanks go out to all those whose paths have crossed mine and who have helped make my life something worth saving—and especially:

To my brother, Graham ("Buddy") Beckel, the family historian, and my sister, Peggy Proto, who have both been gracious in allowing me to air the family laundry, although we three don't always agree on the events of our childhood, and to report the truth as I experienced it.

To my fraternity brothers from Theta Chi: Fred Fachner, Joe Feliccia, Whalen Lou, Dr. Mark Nemiroff, and Chuck Scranton, who helped me remember our college years—the good, the bad, and the ugly.

To Jim Cando, my old friend, ace cameraman, and producer, who has stuck with me through thick and thin, and his wife, Laura, a partner with the heart of a saint.

To Stanley Brock, my attorney and dear friend who has encouraged me to keep working at this thing until it turned into a book.

To Dr. Steve Wolin, who with his wife Dr. Sybil Wolin has been a pioneer in the survivor movement and a great help to me personally in the process.

To the people at Fox News, who have cheered me on tremendously in the process of writing this book, including my family on *The Five*: Eric Bolling, Kimberly Guilfoyle, Greg Gutfeld, Dana Perino, and Andrea Tantaros; executives Bill Shine and Suzanne Scott, Fox News counsel Dianne Brandi, and my producer and good friend Porter Berry.

To the Boss, Roger Ailes, chairman of the Fox News Channel, for his support, encouragement, and never-ending patience with me.

To Sean Hannity, who has shown me great friendship and steadfast encouragement along the way.

To Margret McBride, my literary agent, who has been patiently after me for many, many years to take this project on and has helped it along at every stage; and to her stalwart assistant Faye Atchison, for keeping the i's dotted and the t's crossed.

To Paul Whitlatch, our editor, and Mauro DiPreta, our publisher, Michelle Aielli, Betsy Hulsebosch, Lauren Hummel, and the rest of the team at Hachette Books, for believing in this project and helping us make it into reality.

To John David Mann, my partner in crime and alter ego of the page, who took our long and sometimes rambling conversations and somehow turned them into a coherent narrative in my voice, an act I consider just this side of magic.

To Betty Ford, whose courage in acknowledging her addictions publicly opened the door for millions to come out of the shadows and seek help in confronting the disease of addiction; and to the caring and highly professional staff at the Betty Ford Clinic, especially Dr. Peter Przekop, director of the Pain Management program at Betty Ford, and Tania McCormick, my extraordinary counselor there, who helped me understand aspects of addiction that I never fully grasped in all my previous fourteen years of sobriety.

To Cal Thomas, who extended the hand of friendship when I was at about the lowest point in life I've ever been, and has kept on extending it ever since; you want to talk about someone who exemplifies what they call "the heart of Jesus," I'll show you Cal.

And finally, to my two children, Alex Beckel and MacKenzie Beckel, who constantly pushed me to get this book out so they could show it to their friends and who, whether or not they were even aware of it, gave me the best of all reasons to keep living.